SS-DAS REICH

SS-DAS REICH

THE HISTORY OF THE SECOND SS DIVISION 1939–45

Gregory L. Mattson

SPELLMOUNT
Staplehurst

British Library Cataloguing in Publication Data:
A catalogue record for this book is available
from the British Library

ISBN 1-86227-144-5

First published in the UK in 2002 by
Spellmount Limited
The Old Rectory
Staplehurst
Kent TN12 0AZ

Tel: 01580 893730
Fax: 01580 893731
Email: enquiries@spellmount.com
Website: www.spellmount.com

Editorial and design by
Amber Books Ltd
Bradley's Close
74-77 White Lion Street
London N1 9PF

Project Editor: Charles Catton
Editor: Vanessa Unwin
Design: Mike Rose
Picture Research: Lisa Wren

Printed and bound in Italy by: Eurolitho S.p.A., Cesano Boscone (MI)

Picture credits
Ian Baxter/History in the Making: 19, 56, 112, 118, 121, 122, 126, 127, 141, 155, 182.
POPPERFOTO: 38, 42, 58/59.
Süddeutscher Verlag: 6, 10, 11, 14/15, 22, 158, 164, 176, 181.
TRH Pictures: 1, 8/9, 12, 17, 18 (US National Archives), 21, 25, 26, 28, 30, 31, 33, 34, 35, 36/37, 40, 41,
45, 46, 47, 48, 50/51, 52/53, 55, 60, 63, 64, 67, 68, 69, 70, 72/73, 74, 75, 76, 78, 80, 81, 83, 85, 86,
88, 91, 93, 94, 96/97, 99, 100, 101, 102, 104, 105, 106, 108, 110, 115, 116, 117, 123, 125, 128, 130,
132, 133, 134, 136, 137, 138, 143, 144/145, 146/147, 148, 150, 151, 152 (US National Archives), 155,
157, 160, 162, 165, 167, 168, 169, 171, 172, 175, 178/179, 184, 185.

Contents

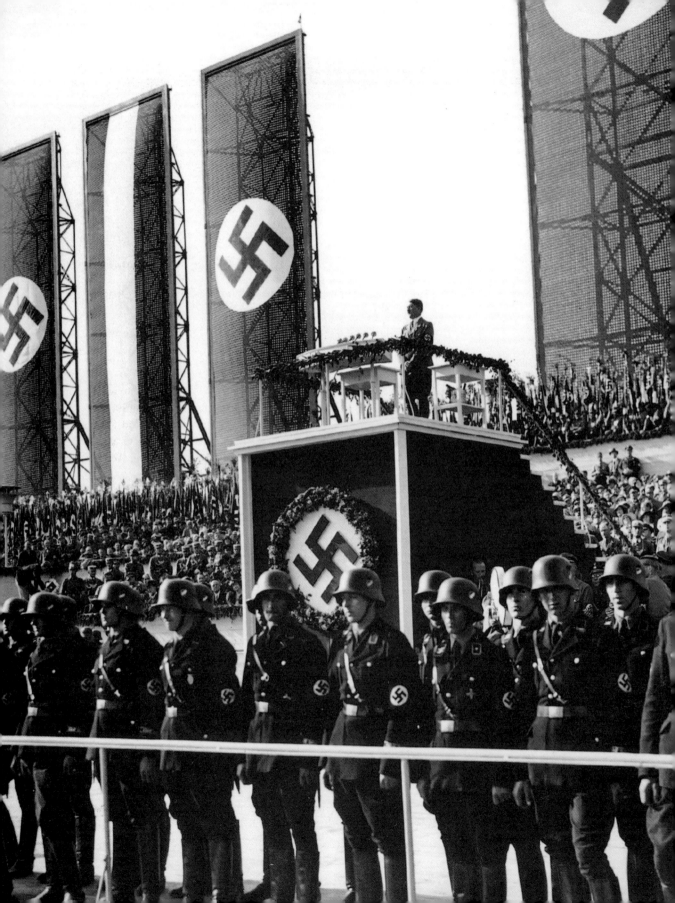

CHAPTER ONE

FOUNDATION

Like Nazi Germany itself, the roots of the 2nd SS-Panzer-Division *Das Reich* lay in World War I. Nazi ideology was fuelled by Germany's defeat, but the combat success of the *Waffen-SS* division drew on the lessons learned by the crack *Stosstruppen* in the last year of the war.

On the morning of 21 March 1918, soldiers in the British 5th Army received an unpleasant surprise when an artillery bombardment began and pummelled their forward positions in an area near the Somme River. While German gunners hurled shells onto this section, small groups of élite, light infantry commandos crept past the British Army's front line, hidden by the morning fog and clouds of gas remnants. Armed with light machine-guns, portable mortars, flame-throwers, grenades and other weapons, these company and battalion-size units were known as the *Sturmtruppen* (storm troops) or *Stosstruppen* (shock troops).

When the artillery barrage ended, the storm battalions struck, using their weapons to disrupt communication and supply lines within the 5th Army and open wide gaps within the forward zone of the British defence network. This surprise action enabled General Oskar von Hutier and his 18th Army to advance 11.2km (7 miles) by the end of the day. Less than a week later, his forces seized the French rail centre of Montdidier and opened a gap 16km

Left: Adolf Hitler, Chancellor of Germany, addresses a rally at Templehof in Berlin in the mid-1930s. The SS men in the immediate foreground are members of his personal bodyguard, the Leibstandarte-SS Adolf Hitler.

(10 miles) wide between the British and French armies. Thanks in part to the *Stosstruppen*, the German Spring Offensive of 1918 had a promising beginning, and seemed as if it might break the long stalemate that had prevailed along the Western Front during World War I.

FURTHER SUCCESS

On 9 April, another group of shock troops under the command of General Ferdinand von Quast routed a division of Portuguese soldiers during an assault on the Belgian rail centre of Hazebrouck. This operation enabled Quast and his 6th Army to advance 4.8km (3 miles) into enemy territory before being checked by the British 1st Army. Later in the month, the Germans occupied Passchendale Ridge, and it seemed possible that they might achieve a breakthrough in Flanders.

On many earlier occasions, military commanders had used infiltration tactics to achieve decisive victory in the war. In September 1917, Hutier seemed to have perfected the effective deployment of storm troopers when he used them to capture the port of Riga from the Russians. A month later, General Otto von Below crushed the Italians at Caporetto using similar units. Late in November, a successful counterattack by *Stosstruppen* commandos enabled the

Germans to recapture Bourlon Wood near Cambrai. Suitably impressed with the results of these actions, General Erich von Ludendorff ordered Hutier and Below to use storm battalions on a large scale to inaugurate Operation 'Michael', the great spring offensive of 1918.

Ultimately, the spring offensive failed due to miscalculations made by Ludendorff, its chief architect, and the insufficient number of German forces available that were needed to exploit the initial successes achieved by the storm battalions and other units. In effect, it was the last bolt fired from the German war machine aimed at achieving a victory in World War I. Its failure ensured that the growing numerical superiority of the Allied armies would eventually force Germany into suing for an armistice and accepting the terms imposed by its enemies.

FELIX STEINER

Despite this unfavourable outcome, the effective deployment of the storm battalions gave some of the younger and more innovative members of the German officer corps the inspiration to construct a new military organization that would employ similar methods of mobility and infiltration against enemy forces. If this feat could be accomplished, they might be able to prevail when future conflicts engulfed Europe. One such officer was Second Lieutenant Felix Steiner, a decorated soldier who was disillusioned by the futility and waste of the static trench warfare he had experienced on the Western Front. In the aftermath of the war, he and other young reformers would develop an organization that would eventually be known as the *Waffen-SS*, the personal army of Adolf Hitler and his *Nationalsozialistishe Deutsche Arbeiterpartei* (National Socialist German Workers Party, or NSDAP).

During the interwar period, Nazi protection squads known as the *Schutzstaffel* (SS) attracted volunteers from all over Germany, eventually enabling the SS organization to establish an armed paramilitary force with regimental-size units. By the outbreak of World War II, the Third Reich was able to organize these regiments into divisions. One such

division would eventually be known as the *Das Reich* Division, or the 2nd SS-Panzer-Division *Das Reich*, a formidable collection of crack troops equipped with modern tanks, weapons and other equipment. As a military appendage of the NSDAP, it was the first, and one of the most effective, *Waffen-SS* divisions to develop from what was originally just a small cadre of bodyguards charged with the task of protecting Hitler and other Nazi political leaders.

If the élite storm battalions of World War I served as a model for a new German army for Steiner and other reform-minded officers, the divisive political

atmosphere of post-war Germany created the environment that would draw zealous young men to the Nazi party and its uniformed, activist organizations. Unable to find satisfying explanations for their defeat in the conflict, many Germans found scapegoats to blame for the 'stab in the back' that had led to the humiliating and (in their view) vindictive Versailles Peace Treaty imposed by the Allies. Such scapegoats included liberals, socialists, Jews and other elements in society that seemed unpatriotic. The fragile Weimar government was also an object of vilification and was widely perceived as weak and corrupt.

Amid this post-war malaise, extremist political groups flourished. While some sought to restore Germany to its pre-war glory, others – such as the Communists and the NSDAP – wanted the creation of a completely new social order. In addition, paramilitary groups proliferated throughout the country and engaged in organized violence against

Below: *Stosstruppen* **undergoing training with flame-throwers near Sedan in France in May 1917. These elite troops acted as the spearhead of the German spring offensive of March 1918.**

their political opponents. On the left, the Communist Spartacists waged their battles on behalf of the proletariat. On the right, nationalist war veterans, still wearing their uniforms, joined such militarist groups as the *Freikorps* and the *Stahlhelm*, which were determined to restore Germany to its pre-war greatness.

In the early 1920s, the NSDAP was one of many obscure, extremist political parties competing for power in post-war Germany. However, their most noticeable spokesman, Adolf Hitler, was emerging as an effective and charismatic leader who was attracting attention and growing support for the party. During this time, he and other National Socialist politicians provoked strong reactions as they delivered fiery speeches throughout the country. In this climate of strife, discontent and deep ideological divisions, such activities led to violent clashes with Communists and other left-wingers. To protect Nazi leaders from possible assassination attempts, the party formed a security organization in 1923.

Above: Members of the *Freikorps* on the streets of Berlin during the General Strike of 1919. Ex-soldiers, they had been radicalised by Germany's defeat, and many had sympathies with the views of the early Nazi Party.

A new uniformed political force emerged at the same time and began to compete in this violent arena. Called the *Sturmabteilung* (SA, or Storm Detachment), they were the paramilitary wing of the Nazi party. Dressed in distinct, brown uniforms and adorned with armbands bearing the swastika, the infamous emblem of the NSDAP, its volunteers were referred to as 'Storm Troopers' or 'Brown Shirts'. During Nazi political rallies, these men kept order by beating up any hecklers who attempted to disrupt speeches.

The *Sturmabteilung* consisted mostly of rowdy street thugs and hooligans whose loyalty rested primarily with their leader, Ernst Röhm. Hitler was not yet the undisputed ruler of his party, and he needed an organization with members that were loyal to him personally. Accordingly, he and his supporters recruited the more disciplined members of the SA into the *Stabswache* (Headquarters Guard), a new security unit that filled such a role.

NEW BODYGUARD

Within a few months, Hitler had dissolved the Headquarters Guard and replaced it with a new outfit known as the *Stosstruppen* (Shock Troop) *Adolf Hitler*. On 9 November 1923, members of this unit distinguished themselves during the Beer Hall Putsch, a notorious fiasco in which Hitler led a small force of SA 'Brown Shirts' in a feeble attempt to overthrow the government of Bavaria. While the SA fought with government forces, his shock troops placed themselves in harm's way to prevent any injury from befalling their leader. By the time the attempted putsch was over, at least 10 *Stosstruppen* had sacrificed themselves so that Hitler might live.

Impressed with the dedication shown by his bodyguards, Hitler ordered his faithful chauffeur, Julius

Schreck, to form a larger and more formidable security service after the two men served a brief prison sentence for their attempt to overthrow the Bavarian government. Accordingly, in April 1925, Schreck and a small group of other party activists established a detachment known as the *Schutzkommando*, which would be the nucleus of a new organization, the *Schutzstaffel*, or SS. Eventually, the SS would fall under the control of the *Reichsführer-SS*, Heinrich Himmler, one of Hitler's most loyal lieutenants.

Nominally attached to the much-larger SA, the SS grew quickly, establishing local units throughout Germany. Although Hitler did not wish to see his new organization deluged with masses of low-quality volunteers, he allowed it to increase its membership so that it would serve as a counterweight to Röhm and

Below: Hitler supporters during the abortive Munich Putsch of 1923, when Hitler attempted to seize power in a coup. Although worn by several men here, the swastika was not yet exclusively a symbol of the Nazi Party.

his unruly, autonomous, brown-shirted organization. To create more of a visual distinction between the two organizations Himmler (not a friend of Röhm) issued black uniforms to the SS in 1932.

Shortly after becoming the Chancellor of Germany in 1933, Hitler used the burning of the Reichstag as a pretext for issuing a series of decrees enabling him to establish a totalitarian regime. While his party consolidated its power and eradicated the last remnants of competing political groups, the growth and organization of SS units within the districts of the country became more standardized and systematic. In each district, local officials mobilized about 100 armed SS troops into a *Stabswache*, or 'Headquarters Guard'. These units would become the building blocks of an emerging armed service within the SS. When the men in each Headquarters Guard

Above: The 120-strong *Stabswache*, Hitler's first bodyguard, formed up for a photograph on the steps of the Feldherrnhalle (the Nazi Party HQ) in Munich in 1930. Sepp Dietrich is second from the right in the front.

completed a prescribed training regimen, it became a *Sonderkommando* (Special Detachment), performing the role of an auxiliary police force. If this detachment grew larger than an army company, its commander could declare it a *Politische Bereitschaft* (Political Readiness Squad, or Political Alarm Squad) and establish a military organization, dividing his force into sections, platoons, companies and battalions. Eventually, this nationwide network of Politcal Readiness Squads would be absorbed into the *SS-Verfügungstruppen* (SS-VT, or Special Purpose Troops), which in 1940 would be called the *Waffen-SS*.

LEIBSTANDARTE-SS ADOLF HITLER

In Berlin, Hitler authorized his long-time bodyguard, *SS-Gruppenführer* (Lieutenant-General) Josef 'Sepp' Dietrich, to form a headquarters guard which would be charged specifically with the task of protecting the Führer himself. After undergoing some changes in name and assimilating other detachments into its ranks, the new outfit would be known as the *Leibstandarte-SS Adolf Hitler* (SS Bodyguard Regiment Adolf Hitler). Stationed in the Lichterfelde barracks in Berlin, the regiment quickly became a noticeable presence in the capital, with its members dressed in distinct, black uniforms while they marched through the streets and surrounded their ruler with a phalanx of protection. Although this unit was nominally an SS unit under the jurisdiction of Himmler, it was actually an autonomous force that Hitler had delegated directly to Dietrich.

Until June 1934, the SS remained a relatively small and obscure outfit compared to its parent group, the SA. At its peak, after forcing the right-wing *Stahlhelm* to merge with it, Röhm's SA boasted at least 2.5 million members. Now a cabinet official in the German Government, Röhm, an ex-Army captain, sought to reorganize the Ministry of Defence and bring his Brown Shirts into the armed forces. Not surprisingly, the very conservative, aristocratic officers of the military establishment recoiled at the idea of incorporating a large body of rowdy street brawlers into their ranks and, with some justification, suspected Röhm of attempting to usurp their authority and turn the army into his own revolutionary organization, thereby increasing his own power base.

Fortunately for them, Hitler also perceived his old comrade as a threat. Although Hitler was now the Chancellor of Germany, he was not yet the unchallenged leader of the NSDAP. As the chief of staff of the SA, Röhm remained a potential rival, representing a faction within the party that sought to initiate a genuine political and social revolution. Eventually, Himmler, Reinhard Heydrich and other SS leaders convinced Hitler to see the SA commander in this light. By this time, these SS officials wanted the decimation of the SA in order that their own network

could monopolize the control of state terror. Suddenly Röhm had become a common enemy to Hitler, the German Armed Forces high command and the SS.

To remove this threat, and to gain the support of the senior officers of the armed forces, Hitler authorized the SS to move against the SA. In June 1934, the Führer personally led a raiding party that arrested Röhm and other Storm Troopers near Munich. With these men confined in the Stadelheim prison in Munich, Hitler dispatched two companies of the *Leibstandarte* under the command of Sepp Dietrich to the area. Scrupulously following Hitler's orders, Dietrich and his killing squad shot Röhm and several other inmates in the facility. Throughout Germany, SS firing squads liquidated at least 150 SA activists and other imagined enemies during a period that would be known as 'The Night of the Long Knives'. In the wake of this purge, the SA faded into obscurity, while the SS continued to grow and gain greater power in the Nazi regime.

Later in the year, Himmler sought to develop his *Politische Bereitschaften* into a larger and more cohesive fighting force that would resemble a true army. At first, Hitler endorsed this initiative without any apparent reservation and allowed the *Reichsführer* to issue confiscated SA weaponry to the SS units. However, senior officers in the military establishment was just as wary of this action as they had been of those taken by Röhm and thus pressured the Führer into curtailing Himmler's efforts. As a result, Hitler initially allowed the SS commander to raise only three armed infantry regiments and rebuked a request to form them into a division with pioneer and artillery detachments. In addition, Hitler further placated the generals of the German Army by decreeing that the new organization, the *SS-Verfügungstruppen*, was merely a party organization and would not be used for any military purposes unless war broke out.

Despite these restrictions, Himmler remained determined to construct a formidable paramilitary organization, and he recruited seasoned army veterans to train and organize SS-VT volunteers. One such veteran was Lieutenant-General Paul Hausser, a tall

Prussian who had won several medals in the Great War and continued to serve in the army before retiring in 1932. After leaving the army, Hausser had served briefly as a member of the *Stahlelm* World War I veterans' organization and the SA before electing to join the SS at the rank of *Standartenführer* (Colonel). He would ultimately achieve the rank of *SS-Oberstgruppenführer und Generaloberst der Waffen-SS* (Colonel-General).

HAUSSER'S TRAINING REGIME

The following year, in his new role as the official responsible for overseeing the training of SS personnel, Hausser established an officer's training academy, the *SS-Junkerschule* Braunschweig, in a castle that had once belonged to the Duke of Brunswick. Even before the creation of this institution, the SS had another facility, the *SS-Junkerschule* Bad Tölz (Bad Tölz SS Cadet School), which another of its officers, Paul Lettow, had founded in October 1934. Within these establishments, Hausser sought to emulate many of the training methods of the old army.

In a short time, these efforts proved to be very successful. The SS quickly attracted a large number of ex-police officers, army veterans and youthful zealots that formed the nucleus of a commissioned and non-commissioned officer corps for an emerging NSDAP army. When these volunteers graduated from their training schools, Hausser dispersed them to the various SS-VT battalions in order to build these units up into full-size regiments. Impressed with the results, Himmler promoted Hausser to the rank of *Brigadeführer* (Major-General) and appointed him Inspector of the SS-VT.

Although he now possessed an impressive-sounding title, Hausser was not the absolute leader of the *SS-Verfügungstruppen*. Instead, his appointment merely authorized him to oversee the training of the organization's volunteers. To keep the district

Left: An SA lorry on the night of Hitler's accession to power in January 1933. Little more than a year later he would break the organization utterly. The banners on the truck carry propaganda messages.

commanders content with their own local power, Himmler permitted them to retain their autonomy. He also avoided any conflict with Sepp Dietrich, his nominal subordinate, by allowing Hausser to attend *Leibstandarte* parades only as a passive observer while Dietrich retained total control over that unit. Despite this concession, friction between the *Leibstandarte* and other SS outfits continued.

COOPERATION

Gradually, Dietrich became less hostile to outsiders influencing his regiment. Although wearing handsome uniforms, the men in the *Leibstandarte* received little training in combat skills and thus found themselves the object of ridicule among both the troops of the *Wehrmacht* and the SS-VT. Dietrich allowed Hausser and other SS-VT commanders to oversee the training of the regiment in an attempt to gain more respect for his organization by developing it into a more serious military force. In 1938, Dietrich also consented to a rotation scheme in which his regiment would exchange a battalion and a group of company commanders with the SS-VT. These policies eventually helped turn the *Leibstandarte,* or 'asphalt soldiers' as they were known, into a viable combat formation.

Despite his growing prestige and influence within the SS hierarchy, neither Hausser, nor other officers schooled in the traditional Prussian method of training and deploying soldiers, enjoyed total control over the SS-VT. Within this organization, younger and innovation-minded leaders such as Felix Steiner openly repudiated the idea of emulating the old army, which they saw as an anachronistic institution run by the sort of unimaginative strategists that had sacrificed so many young men in fruitless trench battles during the Great War. Instead, these reformists looked to the storm battalions of that conflict as the key to achieving victory in future wars.

Many of the conservative generals in the *Wehrmacht* (the German armed forces) conceded the usefulness of the *Stosstruppen* in many campaigns during the last war. However, most of them dismissed the use of small-unit infiltration tactics as an emer-

gency expedient that the Imperial German Army had enacted when the tide of the war was turning against the Central Powers. In their view, storm battalions were at best a very peripheral part of a military organization. For them, large formations remained the cornerstone of strategic planning and battlefield victories. This conservatism led many SS-VT officers and volunteers to see the army as a fossilized institution controlled by senile reactionaries.

In contrast, Steiner and other reformers envisioned a military organization dominated by small, élite, light infantry units that would strike enemy positions like bolts of lightning, cracking open defensive lines and scattering opposing armies into disorganized fragments that could be easily destroyed. Within this strategic framework, large formations existed only for purely defensive purposes. Promoted to the rank of *SS-Standartenführer* (Colonel), Steiner assumed command of the 4th SS-Regiment *Deutschland* in June 1936 and immediately set out to implement the reforms that he advocated. By this time, he had become one of Himmler's favourite officers. This appointment indicated that the SS-VT was becoming a professional military organization and that it was fertile ground for new ideas about warfare.

Another characteristic of the SS-VT that made it seem more innovative than the *Wehrmacht* was the emphasis it placed upon merit rather than social status as a criteria for recruitment and promotion. In fact, the SS-VT was an ideal source of employment for young farmers, tradesmen and other commoners who aspired to become professional soldiers but lacked the connections to obtain a commission in the regular armed forces. Not surprisingly, this opportunity to achieve distinction and upward mobility caused many SS recruits to become devoted followers of Hitler. While the old Army existed as the protector of the German nation, the SS-VT served as the loyal defence force of the Nazi party.

Predictably, mutual feelings of contempt between the Army and the SS-VT led to open conflict among members of the two organizations. Within the lower ranks, soldiers and SS volunteers often brawled in the streets and inside taverns. At higher levels within the

military hierarchy, SS officers engaged in malicious slander and gossip about General Freiherr von Fritsch, the Commander in Chief of the *Wehrmacht*. During practice manoeuvres, army and SS-VT units vied for areas within the fields of operations.

This friction finally reached a flashpoint when Fritsch and other army generals pressured Hitler into issuing decrees that restricted further expansion of the *SS-Verfügungstruppen*. In an effort to placate the regular armed forces further, he also prohibited the SS-VT from forming into a division and from obtaining any artillery detachments. Finally, the Führer endorsed the policy of allowing *Wehrmacht* officers to inspect and review SS-VT units, as if to show that the Army had jurisdiction over them and thus prevailed as the nation's supreme military organization. Declaring these orders to be in effect until the outbreak of a war, he even hinted that in such an event, he might disband the SS-VT and transfer its members into regular army units.

Above: A group of cadets marching at the SS *Junkerschule* at Bad Tölz, founded by Paul Lettow in October 1934, The training facilities at Bad Tölz and Braunschweig dramatically improved the quality of the SS-VT.

Although the SS-VT now seemed as if it were decisively checked – and possibly destined for dissolution or absorption into the *Wehrmacht* – subsequent events revived the prospects of the Nazi army. Early in 1938, Fritsch and the Reich Minister of War, Field Marshal Werner von Blomberg, fell out with Hitler and lost their jobs because of their opposition to the annexation of Austria. After dismissing them, the Führer appointed himself supreme commander of the armed forces and abolished the War Department. In August he issued a decree declaring the SS-VT to be a permanent standing military force available for service against both foreign and domestic threats. In addition, he usurped Himmler's hegemony over the SS-VT, and effectively assumed direct control over it.

Above: Sepp Dietrich (on the left) seen in Russia in 1941. As head of the *Leibstandarte-SS Adolf Hitler* he agreed to closer cooperation with the SS-VT to reduce rivalry and improve the quality of the former as a combat formation.

For the next several months, SS-VT regiments and battalions fulfilled their function as Hitler's personal army with great enthusiasm. In March 1938, they participated in the bloodless invasion of Austria, risking the possibility of being mobbed by crowds of hospitable residents who were welcoming the armed forces of the Third Reich with stiff-arm salutes and warm embraces. With much of the country so willing to join the Hitler regime, the *SS-Verfügungstruppen* now had another source of recruitment for its units. During the infamous *Kristallnacht* pogrom against Jewish residents still living within the growing Nazi Empire, some of its detachments destroyed several synagogues throughout Vienna.

Later in the year, the SS regiments *Deutschland, Germania* and *Leibstandarte* helped the German Army to achieve similar results when Hitler persuaded the governments of Great Britain and France to allow him to take the German-speaking Sudetenland region from Czechoslovakia. At a conference in Munich, the Führer assured these nations that this territorial concession was his last. With this diplomatic

feat accomplished, the SS units marched into the area, along with the *Wehrmacht* forces. As in Austria, most of the inhabitants in this area welcomed these troops as liberators.

In March 1939, these SS regiments also participated in the seizure of the rest of Czechoslovakia. By ordering this action, Hitler openly repudiated his promise not to occupy any more territory. Moreover, he effectively indicated that he intended to use war as an instrument of foreign policy in order to turn Germany into the dominant power of Europe. As a result, the governments of France and Great Britain resolved not to allow the Nazi jackboot to march over any more countries. Meanwhile, Hitler curried favour with other totalitarian regimes, forming the 'Pact of Steel' with Italy and concluding a non-aggression treaty with the USSR, thereby ensuring Russian acquiescence to Nazi ambitions in Poland. Once again, Europe was dividing into two alliances and drifting into war.

MOTORIZED TRANSPORT

Although the SS formations did not face any real combat in these campaigns, they gained practical experience in moving as units across national boundaries. In addition, they were some of the first military groups in history to use motorized vehicles as modes of transportation. By this time, the likelihood of war engulfing Europe meant that the SS-VT would almost exclusively serve a military role. Eventually, this reality would also cause the organization to expand into a full-size division capable of acting as an independent force with its own artillery and supply services.

Before the future *Waffen-SS* organization could achieve this coup, it still had to face more obstacles imposed by the top army commanders. Although they could not deprive the SS-VT of replacement troops for depleted outfits, the generals in the *Oberkommando der Wehrmacht* (the High Command of the Armed Forces, or OKW) had the power to determine which units in the armed forces would receive new recruits or conscripts. Thus, these officials could prohibit the SS-VT from adding more men to their ranks and, not surprisingly, senior officers in the *Wehrmacht* ruthlessly exercised this prerogative to prevent it from reaching division-size strength.

Fortunately for Hausser, Steiner and other SS officers, their organization had a champion who would liberate the *SS-Verfügungstruppen* from regular army control. A veteran of the Great War who had been wounded as a Second-Lieutenant leading troops in battle, *SS-Brigadeführer* Gottlob Berger was a long-time NSDAP activist who had served in the SA before transferring to the SS after the Night of the Long Knives. Although he was a skilled tactician and athletics instructor, SS-VT officers distrusted him, seeing him as a duplicitous sycophant who had risen through the ranks by currying favour with Himmler. In 1938, he had become one of the *Reichsführer*'s principal advisors and assumed control of the recruiting department of the *SS-Hauptamt* (Central Office of the SS).

Above: Felix Steiner, commander of the SS-VT's *Deutschland* regiment. The *Waffen-SS* departed from the standard *Wehrmacht* uniform by wearing the titles of their regiments or units on their cuffs, as seen here.

In his new job, Berger devised a recruiting strategy aimed at skirting the injunctions set up by the *Wehrmacht*. Among the organizations under Himmler's control, three groups contained men who were exempt from service in the traditional Army. One was the *Totenkopfverbände* (Death's Head Formation), the organisation responsible for providing guards for the concentration camps established by the SS. The second was the Reinforced *Totenkopf*

Standarten (Death's Head Regiments), the wartime reinforcement units of the SS. Finally, Himmler had at his disposal a section of the *Ordnungspolizei*, which was the regular uniformed police. By tapping into these sources of manpower, Berger was able to bring more troops into the SS-VT.

In order to receive recruits from these sources, Berger implemented two directives issued by Hitler. One such decree, issued in August 1938, authorized the transfer of concentration-camp guards from the *Totenkopfverbände* to the SS-VT in the event of war. The second order, proclaimed in May 1939, granted Himmler the discretion to raise up to 50,000 men from the *Allgemeine-SS* (the general or administrative branch) to serve as reinforcements in the SS-VT. With another European war becoming increasingly imminent, Berger was poised to manoeuvre around the *Wehrmacht* and turn the *SS-Verfügungstruppen* into a sizeable military organization.

In August 1939, during his preparations for the invasion of Poland, Hitler placed some *SS-Verfügungstruppen* units under the command of the Commander in Chief of the Army, who was to deploy them according to the dictates of the Führer. Meanwhile, Paul Hausser became a liaison officer to a *Wehrmacht* semi-armoured division under the command of General Werner Kempf. In addition, Felix Steiner and his *Deutschland* Regiment joined the division, as did other SS-VT units. Despite the frequent infighting between the *Wehrmacht* and the SS, the two organizations were learning how to co-exist and work together as they faced a common destiny in the coming war.

When Hitler inaugurated World War II by launching the invasion of Poland on 1 September 1939, the SS formations experienced their baptism of fire. At best, the performance of the SS-VT units received mixed reviews. During the advance on Mlava and Modlin, Steiner, his *Deutschland* Regiment and other SS-VT outfits won praise for behaving well under fire. Under the command of the 14th Army, the *Germania* Regiment achieved similar distinction at Lwow. In central Poland, the *Leibstandarte* distinguished itself at the River Bzura and other areas.

However, many *Wehrmacht* officers professed dissatisfaction with their unwanted auxiliaries. Some of them criticized the SS-VT for being too willing to suffer unnecessarily high casualties in ill-conceived actions, while others claimed that the officers of the *SS-Verfügungstruppen* were unfit to work as a part of a division or to deploy sizeable groups of men in complicated operations. In reaction, SS-VT commanders blamed these problems in the field on the unwillingness of the *Wehrmacht* to provide enough heavy weapons and adequate supplies. Privately, many of them conceded the inadequacies attributed to their units and believed that they could overcome them by forming their own divisions that could act independently and without help from the *Wehrmacht*.

SS DIVISIONS

Fortunately for them, the outbreak of war provided Gottlob Berger with the pretext he needed to accomplish this objective. He persuaded Hitler to authorize a plan in which the central office of the SS would recruit a sufficient number of recruits to fill two divisions. In addition, Berger gained permission to transfer thousands of *Ordnungspolizei* officers and *Totenkopfverbände* concentration-camp guards to the SS-VT, ensuring enough manpower to form at least three divisions within the armed organization. Ultimately, he succeeded in creating the conditions that would lead to the formal establishment of the Waffen-SS early in 1940.

Paul Hausser at last was able to form his own division. On 10 October 1939, he assembled the *Deutschland, Germania,* and *Der Führer* regiments into a cohesive, motorized organization. Originally known as the *SS-Verfügungs* Division or SS-VT Division, its name would undergo several changes before being called the 2nd SS-Panzer-Division *Das Reich*. Although it was the oldest *Waffen-SS* unit in the Third Reich, it would have to be designated 'second', behind Hitler's favourite SS formation, the *Leibstandarte*.

A month later, *SS-Gruppenführer* Theodor Eicke formed his concentration-camp guards and police officers into what would later be known as the 3rd SS-Panzer-Division *Totenkopf*. In addition,

SS-Brigadeführer and Police Major-General Karl Pfeffer-Wildenbruch created a formation that would be known as the 4th SS-Panzergrenadier-Division *Polizei*. Until 1942, the *Leibstandarte SS Adolf Hitler* was to exist as a motorized infantry regiment, before being reinforced and designated the 1st SS Panzer Division. During the course of World War II, the SS would establish a total of 38 divisions.

Although he had successfully outmanoeuvred *Wehrmacht* injunctions against expanding the size of the nascent *Waffen-SS*, Berger was already bringing an unsavoury reputation to the organization by enlisting Eicke and his concentration-camp guards. Known for being a motley crew of sadistic thugs, miscreants and malcontents, they also demonstrated a strong antipathy to military discipline and values. Eventually, the *Totenkopf* Division came into its own as a formidable armed force. However, its presence helped create an association between the *Waffen-SS* and the other branches of the *Schutzstaffel* responsible for carrying out some of the most notorious atrocities in the history of modern warfare.

Himmler and Berger were oblivious to this issue and were content to have enough manpower to create full SS divisions. Before the invasion of Poland, the SS-VT collectively possessed roughly 18,000 recruits. With Germany now in a state of war with Great Britain and France, these units grew dramatically and eventually boasted at least 100,000 men by the time of the 1940 offensives in Western Europe. In addition, Berger established a special office charged with the specific task of acquiring reinforcements for SS field formations. Ultimately, he hoped to establish more reserve units to expand the *Waffen-SS* into a larger and fully autonomous armed force.

Below: Early recruits for the *Waffen-SS* were extremely unsavoury – for example, the *Totenkopf* Division was staffed almost entirely by former concentration camp guards – and atrocities like the one shown were the result.

CHAPTER TWO

ORGANIZATION

After Hitler became Chancellor in 1933, the popularity of the SS soared, and the organization grew rapidly as a result. Although initially tests for the potential recruits were stringent, as war loomed the barriers were lowered and the *Waffen-SS* developed into a sizeable force.

While Heinrich Himmler, Gottlob Berger and other senior officials in the SS manoeuvred their way through military politics in order to develop their own armed formations into division-size units, *SS-Verfügungstruppen* (SS-VT) commanders developed recruitment standards and training regimens aimed at turning their troops into élite warriors. From the time these units were established until the latter stages of World War II, SS-VT officials were vigorously selective about who could join their regiments. Specifically, they wanted perfect physical specimens of the 'Aryan superman' archetype who had a predisposition for conversion to the ideology of the National Socialist German Workers Party (NSDAP).

Predictably, the high numbers of applicants that sought membership of the organization in the wake of the Nazi's seizure of power enabled such officials to select only first-rate candidates for enlistment. When young German men in cinemas saw newsreel images of *Leibstandarte* 'Black Guards' marching in their crisp, black uniforms in the presence of Adolf Hitler, they flocked to SS recruitment centres in

Left: New recruits being drilled in 1938. At first the *Waffen-SS* were clothed in standard *Wehrmacht* uniforms, and were indistinguishable from their army colleagues apart from the SS runes on their collars.

droves. To expedite the admission of successful applicants and the rejection of those deemed unfit, Gottlob Berger established 17 recruiting stations in each military district within Germany and enlarged the central SS recruiting office in Berlin.

SUCCESSFUL RECRUITING

Within just a few months, the SS recruitment branch received about 32,000 volunteers. Many of these applicants were already ardent Nazis indoctrinated in the *Hitler Jugend* (Hitler Youth) organization. Traditional German admiration for military institutions combined with this élite mystique to ensure abundant sources of manpower throughout the 1930s and during the early stages of World War II. Only in later years, when the conflict was going against Germany, did the *Waffen-SS* relax its recruitment standards, seeking volunteers from other service branches and among a wide variety of 'non-Aryan' nationalities throughout Europe.

To enter the SS-VT, volunteers had to be between the ages of $17\frac{1}{2}$ and 22, stand at an above-average height, and be in perfect physical health. The *Leibstandarte* was especially thorough about height requirements and quickly gained a reputation for having true giants in its ranks. In the early days of the *SS-Verfügungstruppen*, inspectors purportedly rejected applicants for having minor tooth decay. During this time, only a small percentage of applicants gained admission into the organization. This selectiveness gave successful applicants a sense of superiority over other military personnel, even before they had begun their training.

Not surprisingly, for admission into the SS, new recruits also had to prove their Germanic racial purity by producing a record of family lineage which went back to 1800. Those aspiring to officer status in the SS-VT were required to prove a pure ancestry back to 1759. At recruitment centres, inspectors verified this racial status by measuring facial features and other physical attributes, rejecting those who appeared to be Slavic, Semitic or 'Mongolian'. Such inspections began at the top of the head and proceeded to the bottom of the feet. In addition, many other perceived physical 'imperfections', such as short legs, also provided grounds for rejection. Moreover, *SS-Verfügungstruppen* volunteers had to prove the racial purity of their current or future wives.

Moral Character

In addition to these physical and racial standards, applicants for the SS-VT also needed to possess the right moral character to join the organization. Thus, criminal records, past involvement in political activities deemed repugnant to Nazi ideology, and other undesirable traits were grounds for rejection or expulsion. At first, actual membership of the NSDAP was not a prerequisite for membership in the SS-VT. However, recruits had to show a sense of idealism and enthusiasm for helping to build a stronger and better German fatherland, and it was imperative that they shared the anti-Semitic and anti-Bolshevik views held by Hitler and other high-ranking National Socialist leaders. Such a mindset would enable SS officials to mould their young volunteers into faithful Nazi warriors with careful indoctrination.

When potential recruits succeeded in joining the SS-VT, they were obliged to serve for a period of time, and this varied according to rank. A common *Grenadier* or *SS-Schütze* (Private) enlisted for a four-year term of service. A *Scharführer* (Sergeant) or other

NCO (non-commissioned officer) served for 12 years, while commissioned officers had to serve in the SS-VT for 25 years. In order to gain admission to cadet school and thus earn an officer's commission, a recruit first had to serve in the ranks as a common soldier for two years. Unlike the *Wehrmacht*, the SS-VT did not offer any preferential treatment for the educated or the affluent.

With a promising crop of healthy, loyal and enthusiastic recruits in their ranks, Paul Hausser, Felix Steiner and other SS-VT commanders were able to develop their own training programs for their units. When first established, the *SS-Verfügungstruppen* initially consisted of three *Standarten* (regiments): *Deutschland, Germania,* and the *Leibstandarte SS Adolf Hitler.* While the *Leibstandarte* remained in Berlin to serve as the bodyguard detachment for the Führer, the other two regiments served in other parts of the Third Reich as the foundation upon which the *SS-Verfügungs* Division (later re-named *Das Reich*) and other *Waffen-SS* formations would be built.

As the armed SS formations grew and formed more units, veterans from these two regiments transferred to new groups and instilled the tactics, training and values that they had learned serving in the *Deutschland* and *Germania* formations. When first formed, the two regiments collectively possessed roughly 5000 volunteers, while the *Leibstandarte* had 2600. A large percentage of these recruits came from rural areas and were thus accustomed to spending long periods of time living a rustic lifestyle while bivouacked in the countryside. Many of them also hailed from the lower classes and were all too grateful to the NSDAP for providing them with the opportunity to rise from the drudgery of their existence.

Perhaps the most important of the SS-VT formations in the history of the *Waffen-SS*, the *Deutschland* Regiment, was a horse-drawn infantry group that consisted of four battalions. First established in October 1933, the 1st Battalion of this formation included volunteers that mostly hailed from southern Germany. In 1936, it received a permanent home in the Munich Freimann barracks. Three years later, the facility became the headquarters of the regiment.

Like many standard German army infantry units, this and other battalions contained anti-tank, motorcycle and other specialized companies.

In the spring of 1935, a group of Austrian SA and SS expatriates under the command of Carl-Maria Demelhuber joined the *Deutschland* Regiment and became its 2nd Battalion. In earlier years, these men had been serving in an independent Nazi-affiliated outfit that was first known as the Austrian Legion, then the *Hilfswerk Osterreich*, and finally the *Hilfswerk Schleissheim*. Poorly funded, badly fed and ill-equipped, many of its members did not even have uniforms until March 1934.

DIPLOMATIC ROW

By the spring of 1935, the *Hilfswerk Scheissheim* became involved in a diplomatic controversy when the governments of Austria and Italy demanded the

Above: Four *Rottenführers* (corporals) of the *Waffen-SS* pose for a studio shot during leave from the front line. The man second from left wears a *Deutschland* cuff title, and they all wear Infantry Assault combat badges.

dissolution of all Austrian Nazi organizations operating in Germany. Determined to preserve the independence of Austria, the two governments were wary of the NSDAP and its known support for an *Anschlüss* (the political unification of the German-speaking peoples of Austria and the Third Reich). Because Nazi Germany was not yet a major power in Europe, and because the Italian dictator Benito Mussolini was not yet an ally of Berlin, Hitler was forced to respect this demand.

To avoid conflict with its neighbouring countries without disbanding the *Hilfswerk Schleissheim*, Nazi officials found a simple solution merely by granting

Above: Men of the SS-VT on parade. They are all armed with the KAR 98K bolt-action rifle, a development of the Mauser rifle used during World War I. Equipment was scarce for the SS-VT before 1940.

German citizenship to the members of the legion. Within the *Deutschland* Regiment, the 2nd Battalion maintained a barracks in the Ingolstadt Landstrasse, situated halfway between Nuremberg and Munich in Bavaria. After the annexation of Austria in March 1938, the battalion left this regiment to form the core of a new one that would be known as *Der Führer*.

At the Munich Freimann barracks, members of the 1st and 4th Battalions formed the nucleus of what would be designated as the 3rd Battalion of the *Deutschland* Regiment in July 1936. Thanks to an enthusiastic recruiting campaign, the unit quickly grew. In a short time, ample supplies of volunteers from Bavaria and Württemberg ensured that the battalion would achieve full strength and complete its training schedule by the following year.

Although it had joined the *Deutschland* Regiment before the 2nd and 3rd Battalions, a formation known as the *Politische Bereitschaft Württemberg* was officially designated as the 4th Battalion of the organization. A part of the regiment since October 1934, the battalion maintained a barracks in Ellwangen, a town situated roughly halfway between Stuttgart and Nuremberg. As its original name implied, most members of the battalion were from the Württemberg region in south-western Germany, a strong pro-Nazi region of the country.

In the summer of 1935, Felix Steiner served as the commander of the 4th Battalion for about a year before being promoted to the rank of *SS-Standartenführer* (Colonel) and assuming control over the entire regiment. Unlike many other SS-VT organizations, the unit had a good relationship with the German Army. Early in its existence, when it initially suffered from a shortage of non-commissioned officers, the 5th Infantry Division at Ulm sent sergeants and corporals to help train such specialists. Moreover, the infantry division allowed NCOs of the SS battalion to be attached to military formations in order to learn effective management techniques. When the battalion became a motorcycle unit in November 1938, it left the regiment.

In October 1936, the SS assembled a group of battalions into a second SS-VT regiment. Called the *Germania* Regiment, it possessed a barracks in Hamburg and contained three infantry battalions along with three specialist companies: motorcycle, anti-tank gun and infantry gun. Although *Germania* was a cohesive regiment on paper, its battalions rarely served together. In fact, only its 1st Battalion and the specialist companies occupied the regimental barracks. As a result, the regiment did not develop a standardized training regimen. On 10 October 1939, *Germania* and *Deutschland* became two of the regiments in the *SS-Verfügungs* Division, although *Germania* would leave the organization the following year to serve in the 5th SS-Division *Wiking*. Its replacement was the 11th *Totenkopf* Regiment.

The third formation that became part of the *SS-Verfügungs* Division was the *Der Führer* Regiment, a Vienna-based unit that came into being shortly after the annexation of Austria. With this country brought into the Third Reich, SS officials found a new source of manpower for their SS-VT formations. Thus, *SS-Obersturmbannführer* (Lieutenant-Colonel) Georg Keppler received orders to form a new outfit. A decorated veteran of World War I who also had experience as a police official before joining the *Deutschland* Regiment in 1935, he was well-suited for the task.

The *Der Führer* Regiment possessed three battalions. The 1st Battalion, which had been the 2nd Battalion of the *Deutschland* Regiment, was stationed in Vienna, the site of the *Der Führer* regimental headquarters. The 2nd Battalion of *Der Führer* was based in Graz, while the 3rd Battalion maintained a barracks in Klagenfurt, near Yugoslavia. These two units contained veterans from the *Germania* Regiment and the *Leibstandarte* to help the Austrian volunteers with their training. In May 1939, during war games in Pomerania, the men of the *Der Führer* Regiment had live ammunition fired over their heads, a standard practice in SS-VT training. Assigned to guard duty in Prague until the outbreak of war, they later spent time in the Black Forest before being sent to Pilsen to join the *SS-Verfügungs* Division.

In addition to these regiments, the SS-VT also possessed independent specialist battalions. Established late in 1934, the *SS-Nachrichtensturmbann* (Signals Battalion) drew its volunteers primarily from eastern Germany. At its peak strength, it possessed two horsed platoons, one motorized platoon and a band. After the seizure of the Sudetenland, the battalion became an all-motorized group. Sent to Königsburg, East Prussia, in July 1939 to serve with the *Kempf* Panzer Division, the Signals Battalion participated in the invasion of Poland. Several months later, the *SS-Pioniersturmbann* (Engineer or Pioneer Battalion) *Dresden* assembled in March 1935. Containing volunteers mostly from central Germany, Saxony and Thuringia, the unit became fully motorized within a few weeks.

CEREMONIAL DETACHMENT

Formed by officers and NCOs from the *Leibstandarte* and the *Deutschland* Regiment in the autumn of 1936, *SS-Sturmbann* 'N' (Nuremberg) was a mounted infantry battalion originally established as a ceremonial detachment for Nazi party rallies and similar occasions. Initially, the Nuremberg Battalion had difficulty finding enough recruits, until the annexation of Austria in 1938 provided it with ample enthusiastic volunteers. When the unit reached its intended strength, it contained three rifle companies, one machine-gun company, a band, a signals section and a headquarters detachment. The unit later became a

motorcycle formation and, later still, was converted into an anti-tank battalion.

Towards the end of the 1930s, the SS-VT established more units, including a Flak machine-gun battalion, a reconnaissance battalion, and an anti-tank battalion, along with an artillery regiment. Thus, a full year before the formal creation of the *SS-Verfügungs* Division, SS commanders were already putting together the requisite numbers and specialist outfits needed for such a formation. When war broke out in September 1939, these officers were able to assemble their division with little effort.

When first created, many SS-VT units received much of their training from the *Wehrmacht*. Attached to nearby Army units, the SS soldiers learned how to become proficient with standard infantry weapons and other martial skills. In these early years, when the SS-VT was a small and seemingly insignificant organization, relations between the two service branches during such activity were civil, if not exactly cordial. However, as the armed SS organization grew and rivalry with the Army became more acrimonious, *SS-Verfügungstruppen* formations eventually acquired enough experienced veterans to develop their own training facilities and thus wean themselves from their dependence on the *Wehrmacht*.

ZEALOUS IDEALISTS

During the course of this period of growth and organization, the men in the SS-VT units became tough, well-trained and disciplined soldiers that would prove themselves more than worthy to serve the German Fatherland in autonomous, full-size divisions. The officer most responsible for forging these zealous young idealists into salty warriors was Felix Steiner, whose training techniques in the *Deutschland* Regiment would provide other SS-VT units with an effective methodology for educating recruits. Unlike most other military officers, he was not willing to fight

Left: An *Untersturmführer* (second lieutenant) of the *Der Führer* Regiment of the *Reich* Division seen in the Balkans in 1941. His cuff title is just visible. As he is not in action, he is wearing a forage cap.

with the accepted tactics and strategy developed from the previous war. Instead, he combined the infiltration methods of the Storm Battalions from World War I with his own innovations.

At his barracks in Munich, Steiner de-emphasized drilling, marching in formation and other orthodox military exercises. In place of these practices, he stressed physical fitness and individual initiative, as if trying to turn his recruits into hunters and athletes who were able to move quickly, fight, adapt and endure in any terrain or condition during campaigns. As a proponent of this methodology, he coined the maxim, 'sweat saves blood'. Specifically, this assertion meant that regiments and battalions filled with men in top physical condition suffered lower casualties because of their ability to strike rapidly and neutralize enemy forces before any battle could degenerate into the type of stalemate he had seen in World War I.

Not surprisingly, the physical training implemented by Steiner and other SS commanders was as diverse as it was exhausting. Woken up at 06.00 hours, recruits started their day engaging in calisthenics, running and long-endurance marches. In 1937, Steiner gained national attention for his training methods when the 450 men in his 4th Battalion marched 25km (15.5 miles) at an average speed of 7km/h (4.3mph) with full pack and equipment. At the end of their route, they performed the gruelling goose-step in front of the saluting platform. By this time, the men in his regiment were able to march 3km (1.8 miles) in 20 minutes, creating a strong impression among senior officials in the NSDAP, including Himmler.

Steiner also stressed the value of boxing and other intense contact sports as activity that would cultivate effective hand-to-hand combat skills. Because so many of their battles in the Eastern Front were at close quarters, this training proved to be invaluable. In contrast to physical activity, SS-VT instructors placed less emphasis on intellectual or academic pursuits, seeing such activities as irrelevant to the training of good soldiers. However, they encouraged soldiers to play chess and similar games to promote logical tactical judgment.

Like other military personnel, *SS-Verfügungstruppen* recruits had to face the drudgery of cleaning the floors, sinks, toilets and other facilities in their barracks. Not surprisingly, they were also expected to keep their uniforms and equipment in immaculate condition. In fact, these soldiers even received instruction on how to wash their feet and were required to keep their handkerchiefs folded in a certain way and placed in a specific trouser pocket. However, they also lived in first-rate accommodation and enjoyed food that was both savoury and nourishing. In effect, the men of the future *Waffen-SS* were being groomed and conditioned like champion racehorses in preparation for a great contest.

During training for combat situations, Steiner stressed the importance of flexibility, in which the men in his command would be capable of manoeu-

Above: SS troops undergoing machine gun training in 1935, soon after the *Waffen-SS* had been officially formed. Again the machine gun being used is not the latest type, but dates from World War I.

vring in small assault detachments, then assembling into larger formations when situations required consolidation. To maintain order among the ranks in the field, he and other leaders also ensured that soldiers in their command learned how to fulfill the duties of superior officers if these commanders were killed in action. Thus, corporals could act as sergeants and lieutenants as captains when necessary.

IMPORTANCE OF COMRADESHIP

In addition, Steiner and many other SS-VT commanders stressed the importance of comradeship among all ranks. Unlike their *Wehrmacht* counterparts, *SS-Verfügungstruppen* officers and sergeants fraternized and bonded with their men and realized that they should be at the front of their units during combat, inspiring others with their heroic examples. In the barracks, officers ate food that was of the same quality as the troops, and in the same mess hall. Not surprisingly, the required two-year term of service in the ranks for officer candidates helped promote a relationship based upon mutual respect and empathy.

SPECIAL BOND

When the Germans invaded the Soviet Union and *Waffen-SS* units fought hordes of Soviet troops for months at a time before being relieved, this comradeship was necessary to prevent *Das Reich* and other divisions from suffering total annihilation. In the midst of this ordeal, junior and non-commissioned

officers were the first to lead assaults on enemy positions and the last to withdraw, performing rear-guard actions for their retreating forces. During the war, this admirable behaviour led to a high ratio of officer casualties within the ranks of the *Waffen-SS*.

Thus, the three distinguishing features in the training regimen prescribed by Steiner included physical fitness and aggressive battlefield tactics, combined with the development of close comradeship among the ranks within each unit. In addition to this training, SS-VT recruits became proficient with the type of weaponry and equipment befitting mobile, light infantry formations. Such hardware included submachine-guns, small portable mortars, hand-grenades and explosives. To maximize speed and stealth, these troops were to be unencumbered with unnecessary equipment.

SS-Verfügungstruppen soldiers were also the beneficiaries of cutting-edge innovations. To increase their ability to infiltrate enemy lines, they wore specially designed camouflage patterns on their helmets and uniforms. Carefully developed by experts in the art of concealment, this garb was the finest of its kind in the world at the time. Moreover, Steiner and other SS commanders were determined to provide their forces with motorized vehicles at a time when most of the armed forces in the world were still using horses for transportation. Although some SS-VT units acquired a few trucks and other vehicles, only the *Leibstandarte* became an all-motorized unit by the time of the 1939 Polish campaign.

To test their troops' learning, *Schutzstaffel* commanders also sought to ensure that practice manoeuvres and war games would be as realistic as possible. During such exercises, SS soldiers crawled across the ground while live machine-gun rounds flew over their heads and artillery shells exploded near their positions. Presumably, the experience taught them the value of keeping their composure and lying

Left: SS signallers practise their craft during a field exercise before the war. From the outset, SS training was designed to mimic reality as far as possible, and this quest for realism could lead to serious injury or death.

low. Another exercise involved forcing recruits to excavate decent foxholes within a specific time before a group of battle tanks rolled over their positions. In some instances, those who had dug incomplete or poorly-constructed foxholes were killed or injured. Himmler and other *Schutzstaffel* officers considered such mishaps to be acceptable losses for the sake of creating a well-trained, military organization.

If such training practices enabled the SS to produce crack troops, they also enhanced the organization's reputation for brutality and led to fantastic tales about cruelty in the SS-VT. One improbable legend involved the use of a hand-grenade with the safety pin pulled out of it. Supposedly, a recruit had to balance the live explosive on his helmet and wait for it to detonate. If he remained calm and kept his balance, his helmet would deflect the shrapnel from the exploding grenade and leave him with nothing more than ringing in the ears. If he panicked and flinched, the device would fall and explode on the ground next to him, inflicting serious injury or death.

INDOCTRINATION

This harsh aspect of SS-VT training was merely an indication of the grim ideological world-view that the NSDAP leadership held and obliged SS volunteers to follow. Thus, political and racial indoctrination was another important aspect of training for its volunteers. Already imbued with a sense of superiority as members of an élite formation, members of the SS-VT were encouraged to look upon outsiders with disdain, especially those without Germanic ancestry. As the shock troops of a totalitarian regime, its men learned to devalue human life and even see themselves as expendable creatures who were willing to sacrifice themselves to the state.

Because SS-VT volunteers were already enthusiastic German patriots eager to serve in a dynamic armed force that would help with the revitalization of the nation, most were inclined to embrace Nazi values. Along with the standard NSDAP views on Jews, Bolshevism, democracy and other bugbears, they learned about the 'stab in the back' theory of World War I. Convinced that their country would have won the conflict if not for the treachery of socialists, liberals and Jews, enthusiastic SS-VT men resolved not to allow such an occurrence to happen again in any future wars. To reinforce this view, SS political officers required SS-VT soldiers to read tracts written by Walter Darre, Alfred Rosenberg and other Nazi ideologues.

In addition, SS recruits were supposed to internalize the Nazi doctrine of *Lebensraum* (living space), an idea rooted in an assumption claiming that Eastern Europe belonged to the German people. Thus, the Germans had a right to conquer the Slavic 'sub-humans' living in the area, take their land and lift it out of 'barbarism'. Determined to protect the Third Reich from all enemies and ensure German hegemony throughout Europe, SS officials taught their soldiers to believe that mercy to Russians, Poles, Jews and other adversaries was a weakness that would lead to another 'stab in the back' for their nation. This grim mindset provided members of the *Waffen-SS* with a ready-made justification for committing atrocities in any future war that might engulf Europe.

Another controversial component of this indoctrination into the Nazi/SS ideology was the effort exerted upon SS-VT recruits to renounce the Christian religion. Not surprisingly, many SS officials recoiled at the doctrines of tolerance and forgiveness as unpatriotic, Jewish ideas that made men effeminate and undermined the vitality of the nation. If religious SS-VT volunteers clung to these beliefs, they might be unwilling to engage in the ruthless and violent actions that the leaders of the atheistic Nazi state considered necessary to preserve and strengthen the German nation. Thus, members of the *Verfügungstruppen* and other SS organizations faced strong pressure to repudiate past affiliations with the Catholic or Protestant church.

Ironically, Steiner himself never succumbed to such an influence from his peers, nor was he willing to marry or become the father of Aryan children,

Right: A flak gun crew supporting ground troops in Normandy in 1944. The crew wear one of the SS camouflage design patterns that were patented by the *Waffen-SS* to prevent the *Wehrmacht* from using similar designs.

Above: SS-VT hand-to-hand training using rifles and bayonets. These exercises gave the SS troops an undoubted advantage when it came to real combat, as they were fitter and better-trained than their opponents.

which was another duty expected of SS officers. However, the indispensable services that he provided to the SS-VT organization obliged Himmler to overlook these ideological deviations. In later years, when the *Waffen-SS* was becoming desperate for new recruits, this anti-Christian policy ultimately backfired. Throughout the beleaguered Nazi Empire, Catholic priests, Protestant ministers and religious parents denounced the SS as an atheistic clique and discouraged young men from joining the organization.

By the end of the 1930s, the SS-VT was coming into its own as a professional military service. During practice combat manoeuvres in the spring of 1938, Steiner's tactics impressed many high-ranking observers when his soldiers used them while capturing a fortified position. A year later, Hitler personally witnessed the *Deutschland* Regiment in action during a similar event and immediately recognized great potential in these NSDAP shock troops. As a result, he permitted the SS-VT to form an artillery regiment from the infantry gun and heavy machine-gun companies within the *Verfügungstruppen* regiments.

During the course of the decade, the SS-VT also developed a collection of specialist training schools. In addition to the two cadet academies, the *SS-Junkerschule* Bad Tölz and the *SS-Junkerschule* Braunschweig, the *Verfügungstruppen* possessed a school for NCOs, which was called the *SS-und-Waffen Unterführerschule* Laünburg. In addition, the organization established an artillery school at Glau and a Panzergrenadier school at Keinschlag. By the end of the 1930s, SS-VT were training their own specialists and developing their own military hierarchy with little aid from the Army.

Along with a distinct military hierarchy, armed SS units also acquired their own uniforms and insignia. Unlike their counterparts in the *Allgemeine-SS*, most VT – and later *Waffen-SS* – members did not generally wear the trademark black uniforms often associated with the *Schutzstaffel*. Instead, they wore greenish-grey field uniforms, single-breasted with four buttons, similar to those worn by *Wehrmacht* soldiers. For battle, SS troops also had green-and-brown camouflage patterns, with shades varying, depending on the season. In later years, when SS divisions acquired tanks, crewmen in Panzer (armoured) units would ride into battle wearing black jackets, a colour that obscured the visibility of dirt and grease.

THE TOTENKOPF

SS-Verfügungstruppen headgear was also similar to that of the Army. However, its troops wore the *Totenkopf* (Death's Head, or skull-and-crossbones) badge on the front of their caps, signifying their willingness to die for the Führer. Their helmets also resembled those used by the *Wehrmacht*, except that the SS version had the double Sig rune on the right side. Although this insignia resembled the initials 'SS', it actually symbolized victory. *Schutzstaffel* personnel also wore this emblem on their right collar.

On the left collar of the uniform, a patch indicated the rank of the soldier. Not surprisingly, the higher ranks had more ornamentation on this part of the outfit than the lower ranks. The *Schütze* (private) and the *Oberschütze* (lance-corporal) possessed a plain black left collar patch, while the *Sturmmann* (corporal) wore two vertical stripes along the left edge of the patch. The *Unterscharführer* (junior sergeant) had one diamond on his collar, while higher-ranking sergeants had two.

Among the ranks of the commissioned officers, the left collar patch was even more elaborate. The *Untersturmführer* (second lieutenant) wore three diamonds arranged in a diagonal formation. The *Obersturmführer* (first lieutenant) possessed a similar design along with a vertical stripe on the left end of the collar patch, while the *Hauptsturmführer* (captain) had two such stripes, along with the three diamonds. The *Sturmbannführer* (major) wore a collar patch with four diamonds. Meanwhile, the *Obersturmbannführer* (lieutenant-colonel) had four diamonds plus a vertical stripe along the left end of the collar patch.

Higher Ranks

Above the level of *Obersturmbannführer* (lieutenant-colonel), higher-ranking officers did not wear the double Sig rune on their right collars. Instead, both of their collar patches were adorned with their rank emblems. Thus, the *Standartenführer* (colonel) wore an oak-leaf design on his left and right collars. Those holding the rank of *Oberführer* (brigadier, or brigadier-general) and *Brigadeführer* (major-general) possessed collar patches bearing three oak leaves. The *Gruppenführer* (lieutenant-general) had three oak leaves and a diamond positioned on the end of the collar, while the *Obergruppenführer* (general) had the same number of leaves with two diamonds added. At the top of the SS military hierarchy, the *Oberstgruppenführer* (colonel-general) wore a handsome set of collar patches, consisting of three oak leaves and three diamonds arranged along the far end of the patch.

Towards the end of the 1930s, armed SS formations also adopted shoulder straps and shoulder

Above: Pre-war training was undoubtedly coloured by Germany's experiences in World War I. Here a pioneer practises wire cutting: during the *Blitzkrieg*, the enemy had little time to erect such defences.

boards (for general officers) similar to those of the Army. As in the case of the left collar patches, higher-ranking officers wore more elaborate shoulder board decorations than did the lower ranks. While the private wore plain black straps adorned only with his *Waffenfarbe* (service-branch colour, indicating his specialization) as a coloured trim, the colonel-general sported an elaborate set of shoulder boards, both of which were covered with three diamonds and gold-and-silver knot patterns. These first appeared on SS uniforms at the end of the 1930s, after the *Wehrmacht* reluctantly consented to their introduction, despite harbouring misgivings over their similarity to regular Army shoulder boards.

Up to the rank of major-general, shoulder decorations also had a colour signifying service branch, which appeared as piping lining the edges of the straps of the lower ranks and as underlay on the shoulder boards of the officers. For the most part, *SS-Waffenfarbe* corresponded to that of the Army. For the *Das Reich* Division and other armoured formations, this colour was pink. Other examples included red signifying artillery, white infantry, golden yellow cavalry, and medium blue for supply, administration and technical service branches.

In August 1942, the *Wehrmacht* introduced rank badges to be worn on the left sleeves of camouflage and other special combat clothing that were ill-suited for collar patches and shoulder straps. The *Waffen-SS* adopted these the following February. The insignia consisted of simple horizontal stripes signifying rank. Thus, the junior sergeant wore one green stripe, the sergeant two, and the colour sergeant three.

OFFICER INSIGNIA

Badges for junior SS officers included a set of crossed oak leaves (also green) stitched over the stripes. With this emblem added, the second lieutenant wore a horizontal stripe, the first lieutenant two, and the captain three. From the rank of major through to brigadier, the arm badge consisted of two sets of crossed oak leaves stitched over horizontal stripes. The major possessed one stripe, the lieutenant-colonel two, the colonel three, and the brigadier four. *Waffen-SS* officers above the rank of brigadier wore gold oak leaves and bars to signify their rank while dressed in combat uniforms. Thus, the major-general wore one bar, the lieutenant-general two, and the general three. At the top of the SS military hierarchy, the colonel-general sported three silver diamonds stitched into a thick gold bar beneath the oak leaves.

Armed SS formations had several other badges, emblems and other devices to distinguish themselves in uniform. On the upper left sleeves of their field grey tunics and overcoats, officers wore a patch showing a silver eagle clutching a wreath that encircled a swastika. Like many other branches of the German armed forces, SS units also had their own cuff-titles

worn on the lower part of the left sleeve. These items were narrow black strips of cloth with silver edgings. Between the edgings, the cuff-titles had inscriptions denoting a division, regiment, or other formation. The inscription for the *Deutschland* Regiment was stitched in standard script, while that of *Der Führer* was in a medieval Gothic style.

Yet another adornment for some members of the SS-VT and *Waffen-SS* was the *Alte Kämpfer* (Old

Left: Two *Untersturmführers* from the *Reich* Division receive their orders from a despatch rider in a rubberized coat in the Balkans in 1941. The officers are wearing the standard *Waffen-SS* camouflage smock and helmet cover.

tangible benefits and imposed a great deal of risk on the party member.

The SS version of the Old Fighter's Chevron included three, silver V-shaped stripes stitched upon a black, triangular cloth. Another version with a silver starburst design placed between the arms of the chevron appeared in 1935, to be worn by SS members who were also veterans of the German police or armed forces. In later years, the decoration was also available to Austrian SS members who had joined the organization before the *Anschlüss* of 1938, when the Austrian Government harassed and prosecuted those who supported unification with the Third Reich.

Even SS musicians had a distinctive emblem. Like other branches of the armed forces, some SS-VT and *Waffen-SS* units had their own bands. Members of such musical detachments wore *Schwalbennester* ('swallow's nest') designs on their shoulders. Also known as 'musicians' wings', these decorations were half-circle pieces of cloth affixed to the tops of the sleeves on the tunic or shirt, at the ends of the shoulder straps. The SS version of this article consisted of silver-and-black vertical stripes. In addition, drum majors had silver fringes dangling from the bottom of the swallow's nests.

DIVISIONAL INSIGNIA

When *Waffen-SS* divisions were finally formed, shortly after the outbreak of World War II, each organization received its own insignia to put on battle tanks and other vehicles. The image adopted by the *Das Reich* Division was a rune that resembled a reversed N with a vertical line running down the middle of it. Known as the *Wolfsangel*, it was an ancient symbol that was supposed to protect those adorned with it from ravenous wolves. During World War II, the rune became the badge of an élite military organization that would fight in some of the most spectacular battles in the history of warfare.

Fighter's) chevron. Worn on the upper part of the right sleeve of a tunic or greatcoat, the V-shaped emblem indicated that the wearer had been a member of the NSDAP since before 30 January 1933, the day Hitler became Chancellor of Germany. Wearing this chevron was considered a great distinction, because it indicated a loyalty to the Nazi party going back to the days of struggle and before the seizure of power, when being a National Socialist offered few

CHAPTER THREE

FIRST ACTION

The invasion of Poland in 1939 was a key moment for the SS-VT and the *Waffen-SS*. If they did not perform well in action, they would lose favour with Hitler, and the prospects for an independent armed branch of the SS would be irredeemably harmed.

As the year 1939 progressed, Adolf Hitler engaged in a series of foreign-policy actions that moved Germany closer to a state of war with Great Britain and France. After acquiring the Sudetenland region and its mostly German-speaking population from Czechoslovakia, he violated his promise not to conquer any more territory, occupying the territories of Bohemia and Moravia in March. Furthermore, he encouraged Slovakia to proclaim its independence. By these actions, Hitler dismantled the nation of Czechoslovakia in a few swift strokes.

With Czech territory thus incorporated into the Third Reich, and Slovakia brought into existence as an obedient client state for Berlin, Hitler now turned his attention to Poland. Ostensibly, German territorial demands in Poland were as reasonable as they had been in Czechoslovakia. In order to provide the newly created nation of Poland with access to the sea, at the end of World War I the Allied nations had forced Germany to give up Danzig and a stretch of coastal land surrounding the port city at the mouth of the River Vistula. This Treaty of Versailles stipulation

Left: A German column enters a town in the Polish Corridor. Note the civilian giving a Hitler salute to the passing soldiers. The attack on Poland would see the SS-VT get its first taste of action.

partitioned Germany into two pieces, with East Prussia physically detached by land from the rest of the nation. Like many other provisions in the peace treaty, this was a great source of resentment for the German people.

PRESSURE ON POLAND

Even before the seizure of Prague, Hitler and his foreign minister, Joachim von Ribbentrop, were busy pressuring the Polish Government into consenting to the German take-over of Danzig. Because such a concession would have turned Poland into a land-locked country, Warsaw naturally baulked at the demand. When Hitler moved his forces into Bohemia and Moravia, the Polish Government realized that any of his diplomatic overtures were worthless, and remained firm in its refusal to deal with the Nazi dictator. This wary attitude seemed justifiable in light of the Führer's known contempt for Slavic-speaking peoples and, more importantly, his treacherous actions against them. Shortly after the fall of Prague, Hitler confirmed the Warsaw government's suspicions when German troops moved into Slovakia and massed along the south-west corner of Poland.

Indignant and alarmed by Hitler's deceitful behaviour over the Czechoslovakia crisis, the governments of France and Great Britain publicly proclaimed their

determination to support Poland in the event of a German invasion. Since 1921, France had been a ally of Warsaw. In March 1939, Prime Minister Neville Chamberlain brought Great Britain into this bloc when he delivered a speech before the House of Commons which guaranteed immediate military aid to Poland if war should break out with Germany.

In April Parliament supported this declaration by enacting a conscription law passed by an overwhelming majority. Although the British armed forces would require a great deal of time to develop a sizeable war machine, the significance of the measure was not lost on Hitler. He now realized that London and Paris had abandoned appeasement as a diplomatic policy in their dealings with Germany. In August 1939, a formal military alliance signed between Great Britain and Poland confirmed this.

If this end to appeasement caused any feelings of worry for Hitler in his conflict with Poland, his new

Above: Felix Steiner, commander of the *Deutschland* Regiment, observes the enemy during the invasion of Poland. The regiment was part of Army Group North's thrust into Poland from East Prussia.

alliances with Italy and the Union of Soviet Socialist Republics (USSR) quickly soothed such concerns. Repeatedly snubbed by London and Paris when he had sought a pact with the Western democracies, Josef Stalin was now keen to accept an overture from the rabidly anti-communist regime of Nazi Germany. Thus, in late August 1939, Berlin and Moscow signed a non-aggression pact which enabled Hitler to invade Poland without fear of starting a war with Russia. In return, Stalin would receive the eastern part of the country as far as the River Bug.

While Hitler played his diplomatic games with other European nations, the German military forces had been preparing for the increasing likelihood of war. Throughout the summer of 1939, soldiers in the *Wehrmacht* and the *SS-Verfügungstruppen* regiments carried on with their military exercises at areas near the Polish border. Stationed in East Prussia, Felix Steiner and members of his *Deutschland* Regiment practised their marksmanship. Later, they participated in a lavish parade commemorating the 25th anniversary of the Battle of Tannenberg, the site of a spectacular German victory over superior Russian forces during World War I.

GERMANY MOBILIZES

By mid-August, as relations between Germany and Poland deteriorated, SS-VT units and other German military forces mobilized and took up positions near the Polish border in preparation for an attack. Collectively, the Germans had approximately 1.5 million soldiers serving in five armies that were stationed in the area. To defend Poland against 55

German Army divisions, the Warsaw government had only 17 infantry divisions, three infantry brigades, and six cavalry brigades ready to fight. Despite receiving accurate intelligence reports confirming this massing of German forces in East Prussia, Silesia and Slovakia, the Polish armed forces were slow to mobilize more units to meet the threat.

The plan of invasion developed by the *Ober-kommando des Heeres* (OKH, or Army High Command) was a two-pronged pincer operation aimed at exploiting Germany's geographic advantage. With one army group stationed to the north along the Baltic Sea, and another to the south in Slovakia, the Germans were in a position to sweep through western Poland as if the

Below: A gun team from the SS-VT's artillery regiment during the invasion of Poland. Despite the speed of the much-vaunted *Blitzkrieg*, most of Germany's armed forces were still dependent on horsepower.

country were a large, vulnerable salient with a front line of roughly 2011km (1250 miles). Since this area contained both the capital and the most industrialized regions in Poland, its quick capture would constitute a decisive victory for the Third Reich. Poland was unprepared. To defend this area, as well as the Danzig Corridor, the Polish Army would be able to raise 45 divisions at the most.

On both sides of the Danzig Corridor, Army Group North (or 'A') was under the command of Field Marshal Fedor von Bock, and included two armies. In Pomerania, General Günther Hans von Kluge and his 4th Army contained six infantry divisions, two motorized divisions and one panzer division. His task was to sweep through the Corridor, destroy enemy forces in the area, and isolate the Polish 'Poznan' Army. East of

Above: German troops fording a river after the bridge has been blown by the retreating Poles on 11 September 1939. As the SS-VT discovered to its cost, the Poles were determined to make the Germans fight for their country.

Danzig, the 3rd Army, led by General Georg von Küchler, was poised to strike from Niedenburg and other areas in East Prussia. While some units within this organization would participate in the destruction of enemy forces in the Corridor, others would push roughly 160km (100 miles) due south, to Warsaw.

One of the formations under the command of General Küchler was an experimental unit in I Corps called Panzer Division *Kempf*. Named after its commander, Major General Werner Kempf, it contained only one infantry regiment, instead of two, the standard number. OKH had authorized this scheme to see if a large tank formation could function with only one unit of foot soldiers. The infantry regiment attached to Division *Kempf* was the *Deutschland* Regiment. Other SS-VT units serving under Kempf's command included the artillery regiment, the Flak machine-gun battalion, the reconnaissance battalion, and the signals battalion. The *Germania* Regiment, the *Leibstandarte* and other SS forces served in areas further south in other army groups.

In Slovakia and Silesia, Army Group South (or 'B') formed the other part of the German pincer. Commanded by Field Marshal Karl Rudolf Gerd von Rundstedt, this army group included three armies. Near Breslau and Glogau, General Johannes Blaskowitz and his 8th Army – which contained four infantry divisions along with the *Leibstandarte* and the SS pioneer battalion – prepared to engage Polish forces in the region of Poznan-Kutno, while the rest of the army group pushed upwards from the south.

East of Oppeln, the 10th Army, under the command of General Walther von Reichenau, served as the centre formation of Army Group B, and consisted of six infantry divisions, two motorized divisions, two Panzer divisions and other units. Their task was to move north-east and advance on Wielun, Lodz and Warsaw. From Slovakia, the 14th Army was to cross the Carpathian Mountains and trap enemy forces at Krakow and Przemysl. Led by General Sigmund Wilhelm List, the army contained six infantry divisions, two Panzer divisions and other units.

SS UNITS

Within Army Group B, the *Germania* Regiment was dispersed. Its units were attached to different sections within the 14th Army. In addition, the 'Dresden' Pioneer Battalion served in southern command and was attached to XV Corps. Meanwhile, the *Der Führer* Regiment remained in the Black Forest. With its recruits still in training, it would not see any action in Poland. Although Hitler and *Reichsführer*-SS Heinrich Himmler were both excited to see their SS formations prove themselves in battle, Hitler had chosen to divide them under different commands. This was

done as a concession to the *Wehrmacht*, which was opposed to the formation of an autonomous SS-VT division. Moreover, the sudden need for rapid mobilization for the upcoming invasion forced the Führer into postponing the creation of such a division, however determined he was to see it come to life.

At first, Hitler planned to launch *Fall Weiss* (Case White, the codename for the invasion of Poland) on 26 August. However, he abruptly postponed the date of the operation because he believed that Great Britain, France and Poland might agree to a last-minute diplomatic settlement over the Danzig issue. When this prospect proved impossible, he ordered his two army groups to resume their preparations for the invasion. By this time, the Polish Government noticed the threatening deployment of German forces along its borders and ordered a general mobilization of its own forces.

Across the border from East Prussia, the *Deutschland* Regiment and other units attached to the 3rd Army faced three major Polish formations, which were obstructing their advance to Warsaw. To the east, the Narew Army was arrayed in an area stretching from Suwalki and Bialystok to the River Bug. Its strength consisted of the 18th and 23rd infantry divisions and the Suwalki and Podlaska cavalry brigades. Along the east bank of the River Narew, the Wyskow Group occupied an area north-east of the capital and contained the 1st, 35th and 41st infantry divisions.

West of the River Narew, the Modlin Army covered an area that stretched from the German border at East Prussia to the town of Modlin, situated on the north bank of the River Vistula, with Warsaw directly on the other side. Well-entrenched in a network of fortifications, the army included the 8th and 20th infantry divisions and two cavalry brigades: Mazow and Nowogrod. In the north-west corner of Poland, from the Danzig Corridor to the River Warta, the Pomeranian and Poznan armies defended the region with nine infantry divisions and three cavalry brigades. Within the port of Danzig, a Polish garrison with fewer than 5000 men remained in a location that was vulnerable to isolation and encirclement by enemy forces.

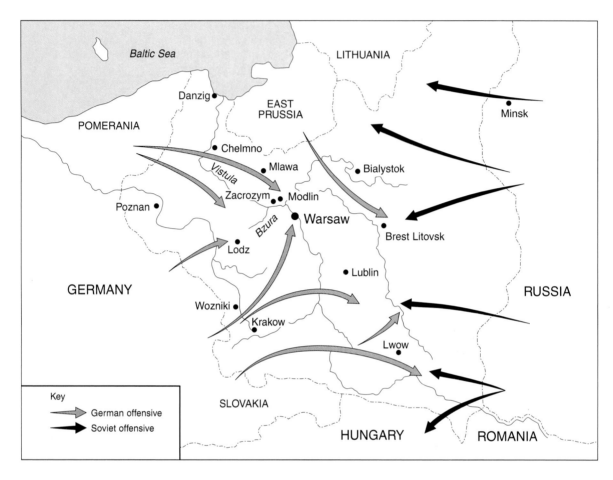

Map labels: Baltic Sea, LITHUANIA, Danzig, EAST PRUSSIA, Minsk, POMERANIA, Chelmno, Mlawa, Bialystok, Vistula, Zacrozym, Modlin, Poznan, Bzura, Warsaw, Brest Litovsk, Lodz, Lublin, GERMANY, RUSSIA, Wozniki, Krakow, Lwow, Key — German offensive, Soviet offensive, SLOVAKIA, HUNGARY, ROMANIA

In southern Poland, the *Germania* Regiment and other units attached to the 10th and 14th armies had to contend with three large enemy forces covering an area between the River San and the town of Wielun. Above eastern Slovakia, the Carpathian Army held a region west of the town of Przemysl with the 11th, 24th and 38th infantry divisions, along with the 2nd and 3rd mountain brigades. In the south-west corner of Poland, the Krakow Army occupied the city of Krakow and surrounding areas. Its strength included the 6th, 7th, 21st, 23rd, 45th and 55th infantry divisions, along with the Krakow Cavalry Brigade. Further north, the Lodz Army straddled both banks of the River Warta. Another large force, it possessed the 2nd, 10th, 28th, and 30th infantry divisions and two cavalry brigades, the Wolhynia and the Border.

Above: A map showing the German attack at the beginning of September 1939, and the Soviet Union's offensive a few weeks later, dividing up Poland in the manner that had been agreed by the earlier German–Soviet Pact.

Within the Polish interior, two more armies took up positions and prepared to block the German 10th and 14th armies in their march northwards to Warsaw. Between the Bug and Vistula Rivers, the Pyskor Group had a force consisting of the 39th Infantry Division and the Warsaw Armoured Brigade. At the city of Piotrkow, the Prussian Army occupied an area due south of the capital. This organization contained the 3rd, 12th, 13th, 19th, 29th and 36th infantry divisions, along with the Vilna Cavalry Brigade.

Although many of these armies seemed formidable on paper, they were not at full strength by the time the Nazi invasion started. In fact, the Polish Government did not even proclaim a general mobilization order until late morning on 31 August, just a few hours before the start of Case White. When the attack began, 13 Polish divisions were still moving into their concentration areas, while six more had not even finished mustering in their barracks. In addition, a poor communications system within the Polish armed forces prevented any effective coordination of these army groups.

Below: SS artillery opens fire on the Danzig post office, the scene of heaviest Polish resistance in the city. In practice there was little chance of the city's defenders holding out for long against overwhelming odds.

As participants in the invasion of Poland, the SS-VT units became involved in an experimental style of warfare that would be popularly known as the *Blitzkrieg* (or 'Lightning War'). Utilizing new fast-moving battle tanks, squadrons of warplanes flying at unprecedented speeds, and motorized infantry formations, the German armed forces used a strategy based upon speed and effective coordination among the diverse service branches. This type of combat was exactly what Felix Steiner and other SS officers wanted. At last, they seemed to have the opportunity to unleash their battalions of hunters and athletes to help demolish the Polish war machine before it could organise itself and mount an adequate defence against the invaders.

Thus, on the morning of 1 September 1939, the Germans launched their attack on Poland. From East

Prussia, Steiner and his *Deutschland* Regiment crossed the border with the *Kempf* Division. From the start of the invasion, the terrain and weather of Poland created problems for the *Deutschland* Regiment and other German units. In the daytime, the weather was unbearably hot and arid. At night, heavy rainfall and sharp drops in temperature forced the SS-VT soldiers to endure cold and damp conditions.

Lacking adequate roads, northern Poland was covered with crude tracks that were embedded into soil that had a loose, sandy texture. As a result, trucks and other vehicles were liable to get bogged down

Below: The Polish defenders of the Danzig post office seen being escorted from the scene by SS soldiers. Here, as elsewhere in Poland, the *Waffen-SS* acquitted themselves well, although with high casualty rates.

during the campaign. When the night rains soaked the landscape, this problem only worsened, as the dry, dusty trails became streams of mud puddles. Not surprisingly, the sandy terrain also caused mechanical problems for vehicles. Frequent breakdowns – along with fuel shortages – forced SS and regular Army soldiers alike to abandon their transports and advance into Poland on foot. Marching through the loose soil under the hot, summer sun, many of them began to feel tired and worn down even before they had engaged in combat.

Despite these hardships, the men of the *Deutschland* Regiment were eager to play their part in the *Kempf* Division when the organization reached its first objective. This was a group of defensive positions arrayed along the northern outskirts of the border towns of Zavadski and Dvierznis. At this site, the SS

regiment received the honour of spearheading the attack. On the left, 1st Battalion was to assail enemy positions at Zavadski while to the west, 3rd Battalion received the order to strike Polish forces at Dvierznis. After taking these towns, the two battalions were to proceed further south, attack enemy positions at the town of Mlava, and converge at a hill called Point 192.

FIRST CASUALTIES

In the wake of an artillery barrage that pounded enemy positions, the soldiers in 1st Battalion moved up a ridge leading to Zavadski. Georg Prell, a soldier in the battalion's No. 3 Company, noted, 'on the enemy side of the village there were barbed wire barricades and beyond that high ground from which the Poles had good observation'. Despite these obstacles, he asserted that 'the tempo of our attack could not be slowed down'. During the course of the battle,

Above: An NCO keeps a watchful eye on the enemy. As well as his KAR 98K rifle and German stick grenades, he has some captured Polish WZ 31 grenades with which to repel any Polish counterattacks.

Prell recalled, *'Unterscharführer* Luk Krieger worked his way through the barbed wire and stormed upon the heavily defended ridge. In the murderous enemy fire Luk was mortally wounded and we could not at first recover the body of ... the first comrade of our Company to be killed in action.'

After assailing another area within the Polish defence lines at Zavadski, the forward companies pushed through the Polish defences in a determined attack and seized the town. The men killed and wounded in this action were some of the first casualties of the *Waffen-SS*. On the right, 3rd Battalion experienced similar success at Dvierznis. With these border

47

positions thus captured, the SS soldiers proceeded south down a road leading to Mlava.

LITTLE OPPOSITION

Much to their surprise, the battalions of the *Deutschland* Regiment faced little opposition during their advance to Mlava, until they came close to a network of permanent fortifications established to the north of the settlement. Marching on a secondary road 2km (1.2 miles) to the west, 3rd Battalion carefully approached an outpost at the village of Bialuty, only to discover that the facility had been abandoned. When the regiment reached the Mlava Line, however, its members confronted a formidable obstacle blocking their drive to Warsaw. At the foot of a steep slope

Above: Troops entering Sochaczew in Poland. The white cross on the armoured car was the standard identification mark at this time, but it was changed in 1940, after it was discovered that the enemy used it as an aiming point.

in front of the Mlava Line, the SS battalions found themselves in an exposed position, vulnerable to punishing artillery- and rifle-fire from the Polish defenders occupying the crest of the ridge.

In another show of courageous behaviour, the *Deutschland* Regiment volunteers charged up the slope of the hill. This time, the Polish defenders were more tenacious, pouring down a hail of bullets that stopped the German advance in its tracks. After launching another unsuccessful attack, the SS regiment received an order from its division commander instructing it to dispatch reconnaissance patrols into the Polish defensive positions in an effort to find weak spots to exploit. Before Steiner could carry out this order, he received another order from I Corps headquarters which countermanded it and detailed a new plan. In the middle of the afternoon, all forces within the corps were to launch a combined assault on the Mlava Line.

In this attack, the *Deutschland* Regiment carried out its original task: the seizure of Point 192. After a massive artillery barrage on the hill, the SS troops moved up its slopes in a two-pronged assault, with battle tanks from the 1st Battalion, 7th Panzer Regiment accompanying them in the ascent. Unfortunately for the *Deutschland* Regiment, the artillery batteries proved to be ineffectual. Despite the intensity of the bombardment, the enemy bunkers positioned within the high ground of Point 192 suffered little more than minor scratches. In addition, the Luftwaffe failed in its promise to send a squadron of Ju 87 'Stuka' dive-bombers to soften the Polish defences

The tank crews did not fare any better during the assault. After travelling only short distances, most of them became ensnared in railway lines that had been implanted into concrete to act as anti-tank obstacles. Because the armoured battalion was operating PzKpfw I light- and PzKpfw II medium tanks that were not large or powerful enough to roll over these obstructions, it became an easy target for Polish artillery batteries, and withered under heavy shelling. During the course of the day, 39 German tanks were destroyed, heavily damaged or broken down.

Frustrated with the results of this assault, and alarmed at the amount of devastation inflicted upon his battalion, the commander of the 7th Panzer Regiment gained permission from I Corps headquarters to order a withdrawal of his remaining tank crews. The attack on the Mlava Line constituted an inauspicious beginning for tank warfare in World War II. During the Polish campaign, the tendency of these vehicles to break down frequently, as well as the lack of firepower mounted within their hulls, prevented them from performing as decisive a role in battles as

OKH had expected them to accomplish. The PzKpfw I contained only two machine guns within its turret, while the PzKpfw II had only one small 37mm (1.47in) cannon and one machine gun. Both tanks also had fairly thin armour, and did not have a particularly high top speed.

RARE SUCCESS

Despite the lack of support from artillery crews and armoured formations, and unable to use their motorized capabilities due to fuel shortages, the SS men of the *Deutschland* Regiment still acquitted themselves rather well during the battle for Mlava. Under constant fire from sharpshooters and artillery batteries, they travelled a good distance up Point 192, reaching a position less than 150m (164yd) from the first row of Polish bunkers, before their superior officers ordered them to retire at the end of the day. In its first day of battle, the SS formation was one of the few German units to do its job properly, and it did so under adverse circumstances.

The following day, the *Kempf* Division left the Mlava Line and headed towards Chorzele, a town situated 40km (25 miles) to the east. In this area, the fighting went well for the Germans. After another Army Corps had punched a gaping hole in the Polish lines, the combined strength of the *Deutschland* Regiment, a detachment from the 7th Panzer Regiment and other battle groups poured into the breach, routing enemy forces. In a furious pursuit, the Germans followed a corps-size group of Polish men, which was retreating to the River Narew. More than 48km (30 miles) south-east of Chorzele, at an area around the town of Rozan, the Poles took up positions within a complex comprising four old forts which had been built by the Russian Tsars.

Within these ancient fortifications, Polish resistance stiffened. In the ensuing battle – similar to the one fought at Mlava the previous day – the Polish defenders decimated the SS battalions and other German units which had been sent to attack them, relentlessly hitting these assailants with enfilade- and frontal gunfire. In addition, the Poles knocked out 11 battle tanks, while another 20 suffered from mechanical malfunctions. Although both sides sustained heavy losses, the Germans were getting the worst of it. Moreover, the battalions of the SS regiment eventually became too depleted to dislodge the Poles from their positions. After repulsing this offensive, the defenders launched a series of cavalry charges that forced the Germans to retire.

COSTLY VICTORY

The battle for Rozan turned out to be as unnecessary as it was costly. When the attacking German forces crossed the River Narew at a point further south, they threatened to encircle the town and its forts. As a result, the Polish units occupying the forts were forced to retreat in order to avoid being trapped. The Germans could have taken the area without firing a shot, simply by performing this flanking manoeuvre.

After this costly victory, the *Deutschland* Regiment resumed its pursuit of the retreating enemy forces. Marching south towards the River Bug, the SS battalions captured the towns of Loriza, Czervin and Nadbory. During this period of relative tranquility, the SS-VT troops had to contend with little more than the hot sun and the sandy dirt beneath their feet. Aided by the 7th Panzer Regiment, they beat back a feeble attack launched by a small Polish detachment sent from Lomza.

On 10 September, the *Kempf* Division crossed the river at the town of Brok and continued south in an attempt to intercept a detachment from the Pyskor Group, which was heading for Warsaw to aid in the defence of the capital. However, the *Kempf* Division failed to apprehend the Polish unit, as it was under the direction of skilled commanders and manned by motivated soldiers who successfully kept the Germans at bay. During this stage in the campaign, the German division was no longer acting as a monolithic organization: its units now operated in isolation as separate battle groups.

After this misadventure, the units in the *Kempf* Division moved further south and seized the towns of Kalosym and Zelechow before turning east and heading for Najiejowice. Fifty miles due east of Warsaw, the *Deutschland* Regiment captured Siedlce

and then began the march south-west toward Majieowicje. Travelling behind these formations, SS *Einsatztruppen* or 'death squads' performed their grisly work, liquidating any local Jews, communists and intellectuals that fell into their hands.

By the middle of the month, German forces in areas east of Warsaw had crushed most of the significant enemy opposition and were preparing to join the encirclement around the capital. On 16 September, *SS-Sturmbannführer* Matthias Kleinheisterkamp, the very talented commander of the *Deutschland* Regiment's 3rd Battalion, led his troops to the banks of the River Vistula and helped close the

Above: Inside a Polish fort after its fall at the end of September. The defence of the Modlin Line was effectively the last swansong for the Polish Army, and once it had been breached, there was no hope for Warsaw.

ring of German forces surrounding the city. Meanwhile, Steiner received a message ordering his SS regiment to participate in an attack on an enemy stronghold situated north-west of Warsaw.

Re-assembled into a unified organization, the *Kempf* Division moved south-west to the town of Naczpolsk, then headed north until it reached a long network of Polish defences known as the Modlin

Line. Arrayed across the northern outskirts of the town of Modlin in the east, and Zacrozym in the west, the line included two forts. Fort No. 1 was situated above Zacrozym, while Fort No. 2 occupied an area north-east of Modlin. Both of these structures were well-constructed citadels garrisoned with 35,000 soldiers who were highly motivated to take a last stand in defence of their country.

In the wake of the Battle of the River Bzura west of Warsaw, the Polish Army was in tatters. The conquest of the country was, by now, a foregone conclusion and simply a matter of time. However, Hitler and OKH wanted to capture the capital in a spectacular assault involving several divisions, regardless of the casualties suffered in such a dramatic action. To accomplish this feat, the Germans needed to overrun the Modlin Line, and so operations against this formidable defence complex began on 19 September.

CONSOLIDATION

For three days, the Germans consolidated their control of areas around Warsaw and the Modlin Line before initiating further aggressive action. On 22 September, reconnaissance detachments from the *Deutschland* Regiment probed enemy defences for vulnerable points, only to return with heavy casualties. Although this débâcle seemed to foreshadow a long and bloody battle for the city, Luftwaffe supremacy over the sky enabled the Germans to fight more effectively against their well-entrenched opponents. While Stuka dive-bombers (known as the 'flying artillery') softened up enemy positions, a pioneer company from the *Deutschland* Regiment managed to blast a hole in a line of barbed wire protecting the Modlin defence network.

Despite this breach, a general ground assault did not immediately ensue. Instead, senior German strategists waited for another week while more squadrons of Stukas swooped down on the forts and hammered the Polish defenders. Two days before the scheduled attack on Warsaw was to begin, on the evening of 27 September, an *Obersturmführer* (first lieutenant) from Steiner's First Battalion returned from a patrol and reported that the garrison at No. 1

Fort above Zacrozym appeared to be severely deplet-ed. The junior officer suggested seizing the structure in an attack similar to those launched by the storm battalions of World War I. The following night, Steiner led his own reconnaissance patrol into the area, agreed with this suggestion, and planned accordingly for a surprise attack.

Early the following morning, companies from the SS regiment infiltrated the outer line of the Polish defences arrayed in front of Zacrozym and waited for the order to attack, when the general offensive was to begin. At these positions, the SS men waited for another hour after the campaign's chief strategists had heard a rumour that the Poles might surrender without another battle. When this rumour turned out to be groundless, the final assault on Warsaw went ahead. At 06.15 hours on 29 September, an artillery bombardment began against the town of Zacrozym and No. 1 Fort.

Fifteen minutes later, the infiltration companies of the *Deutschland* Regiment sprang into action. Led by detachments armed with flame-throwers, these units quickly pushed their way through enemy defences and overran most of Zacrozym within 90 minutes, taking several thousand prisoners. By this time, the officer commanding the Polish garrison had ordered his troops to surrender. However, some of his soldiers either did not hear the order or defied it, and decid-ed to keep fighting.

MERCILESS BOMBARDMENT

Nearby, the Polish garrison at No. 1 Fort continued to resist, firing from their positions at German troops fighting in Zacrozym and elsewhere. However, the Germans soon unleashed a merciless artillery bombardment upon the citadel, forcing its surviving occupants to capitulate in the afternoon. By this time, Colonel Steiner was able to report that his SS regiment had achieved all of its objectives for the day.

Less than an hour after the fall of Zacrozym and No. 1 Fort, the general commanding Polish forces at the Modlin Line recognized the futility of continuing further resistance and ordered all the troops in his

command to surrender. The fall of this stronghold effectively ended the Polish campaign for the *Deutschland* Regiment. Despite the tensions between the *Wehrmacht* and the SS-VT, Steiner and his regi-ment had performed well enough to win the praise of the divisional commander, Werner Kempf, who promptly communicated his favourable impressions to OKH.

The general also declared his admiration for the SS Artillery Regiment as a unit that contained motivated soldiers who had carried out their duties

with skill and precision. In addition, he was impressed with the SS Reconnaissance Detachment which, in his view, was led by an officer imbued with energy and initiative. Kempf especially respected the type of training that the men in this battalion had accomplished and exhibited in action. Finally, the

Below: The victorious Führer drives past an armoured column on his way to Warsaw on 5 October 1939. The performance of the SS-VT had impressed Hitler, and he was persuaded to allow further expansion of the *Waffen-SS*.

general citied the SS Signals Unit for performing to a degree of perfection that he had never seen before.

The Polish campaign was also an invaluable educational experience for the *Deutschland* Regiment. During the month of September, the men in this unit learned to operate in a variety of situations that confronted infantry formations. Such experiences ranged from the assaults on enemy fortification, to cooperation with tank units. In Berlin, both Hitler and Himmler were pleased with the performance of their SS regiment and agreed that their *SS-Verfügungstruppen* units would perform better if they were assembled into their own autonomous division.

While the *Deutschland* Regiment swooped into northern Poland with the 3rd Army, the men of the *Germania* Regiment operated in separate detachments within the western and southern parts of the country. Primarily under the command of General List and thus attached to the 14th Army in Slovakia, some of Germania's battalions and companies spent much of their time guarding the left flank of XXII Corps during its push to the eastern town of Chelm. At the same time, the regiment's 2nd Battalion acted in cooperation with VIII Corps, while its Armoured Reconnaissance Platoon was attached to the 5th Panzer Division.

GOOD PERFORMANCE

Although these units were thinly spread over large areas, most of them performed well during the campaign. While blocking a road west of the town of Przemysl, No. 15 Company ambushed a battalion-size Polish column and took at least 500 prisoners. Later in the day, the company confronted a more serious problem when a unit of cadets and officers from the Polish War Academy at Krakow charged the Germans in an effort to push through the SS roadblock and reach Lemberg. After sustaining heavy casualties, the SS soldiers retreated north to join No. 1 Company. While the 7th Infantry Division attacked elements of the Carpathian Army at Przemysl, the two companies maintained precarious blocking positions to help prevent enemy troops from escaping the beleaguered town.

Meanwhile, *Germania*'s 2nd Battalion went with the 8th Infantry Division during an advance on the Brzoza–Stadnice–Linica railway line. Assigned the task of capturing a bridge crossing the River San at Kreszov, the battalion marched 130km (80 miles) in just two days and joined a detachment from the 5th Panzer Division en route to its destination. On the afternoon of the 12th September, the Germans reached the bridge at Kreszov, only to see it demolished by troops from the Carpathian Army stationed on the other side of the river.

Undeterred by this setback, a platoon from the battalion's No. 3 Company and another from No. 5 Company forded the River San under the cover of darkness during the ensuing evening. On the east bank, the SS men discovered that the Poles had withdrawn. By the end of the night, the Germans had secured both sides of the river just as the 8th Infantry Division reached the area. During a brief attempt to overtake the retreating enemy forces, the soldiers of No. 6 Company, 2nd Battalion, *Germania* Regiment came close to being hit by friendly fire when a squadron of Stuka dive-bombers swooped into the area and hammered the Poles with explosives and heavy machine-gun fire.

END OF THE CAMPAIGN

At the end of the month, when the devastated city of Warsaw had finally surrendered to the Germans, the Polish campaign effectively came to an end. Pummelled mercilessly by Luftwaffe bombers, the capital had lost its flour-mills, water facilities, and other important structures, forcing its defenders to capitulate. With Warsaw now in German hands, Polish resistance ended throughout the country, except for a small garrison occupying an area north of Danzig, which capitulated in early October. East of the River Bug, Soviet forces consolidated their control over the part of the country that Hitler had conceded to Russia in exchange for the non-aggression pact signed earlier in the year.

On 30 September, the Führer delivered a radio broadcast to his people, informing them of the great victory scored by the German Armed Forces in Poland. In his address, he noted that his armies had taken almost 700,000 prisoners of war, while suffering relatively low casualty rates. In the eastern part of the country, the Red Army captured another 217,000 Polish soldiers, while roughly 100,000 of them escaped to Romania to join the Allied war effort. During the campaign, total German losses included 10,572 killed, 30,322 wounded and 3400 missing.

Although most of the SS-VT regiments, battalions and companies had impressed their division commanders, high-ranking *Wehrmacht* officers maintained their opposition to SS military formations. Claiming that SS-VT officers and NCOs had exhibited inept leadership on the field, some Army generals also accused their unwanted auxiliaries of committing atrocities against unarmed civilians. However, the actual culprits in such actions were members of *SS-Totenkopf* (Death's Head) units, which had been charged with the specific task of eliminating intellectuals, Jews, communists and other undesirables from areas conquered by German forces. These killing squads also sent many civilians to concentration camps and engaged in extensive looting and property destruction throughout Poland.

Not surprisingly, Himmler considered such brutality to be justifiable, claiming that it was necessary to pacify the countryside and eliminate any potential threats to German control of the area. To him, and to other hardcore National Socialist ideologues, the alleged inferiority of the Slavic 'subhuman' races also made this cruel behaviour acceptable – and even appropriate – to advance the interests of the Aryan master race. Unfortunately for the soldiers of the *SS-Verfügungstruppen*, the atrocities performed by other elements of the SS organization quickly created the impression of guilt by association, even in the early stages of World War II.

Despite this blot on their reputation, the commanders of the SS-VT formations finally got what they wanted from their Führer. In mid-October, Hitler ordered these units, which were now stationed in Pilsen, to be joined into a single organization, the *SS-Verfügungs* Division, or the SS-VT Division. As an autonomous formation, the new division was to include the *Deutschland, Germania* and *Der Führer* infantry regiments, as well as the artillery regiment, and the signals, pioneer, reconnaissance, anti-tank and anti-aircraft machine-gun battalions. At the same time, he also authorized the creation of two more SS organizations, the *Totenkopf* and the *Polizei* divisions. To keep the *Wehrmacht* appeased, Hitler assured its senior commanders that these divisions would operate under Army control during campaigns.

Although Germany was now technically in a state of war with Great Britain and France, several months came and went without any real military hostilities taking place between them. As a result, the new SS divisions had an abundant amount of time during this 'Phoney War' to attract new members, acquire weapons, vehicles, and equipment, and learn how to fight and manoeuvre in unified formations. Before the invasion of Poland, the *SS-Verfügungstruppen* possessed roughly 18,000 men. In the months following the campaign, the newly named SS-VT Division grew to include 100,000 troops. During this time, the armed branch of the *Schutzstaffel* officially became known as the *Waffen-SS*.

Below: Sentries stand guard on the new frontier between German- and Soviet-occupied Poland. The success of the SS-VT led to its rapid expansion and re-fitting, ready to take part in Hitler's next gamble: the invasion of France.

CHAPTER FOUR

THE WEST

In May 1940 the SS-VT would fight together as a division on the battlefield for the first time. Although still unpopular with the *Wehrmacht* general staff, the division would nonetheless play a full part in Case Yellow, the invasion of the Low Countries and France.

Shortly after the conquest of Poland, the recently promoted *SS-Gruppenführer* (Lieutenant-General) Paul Hausser took charge of the *SS-Verfügungs* Division, becoming the first commander of the unit. A month later, he and his men left the city of Pilsen, in western Czechoslovakia, to spend roughly six months in western Germany. There they would engage in intense training and preparation for the coming war with Great Britain and France. For the first time, the soldiers in his command were learning to operate and fight as members of a unified division.

In April 1940, the new division received more support units that would strengthen the organization in time to participate effectively in the invasion of the Low Countries (Holland and Belgium). The addition of these fresh troops and the rigorous training regimen imposed upon the soldiers of the SS-VT Division indicated to them that they would play a significant role in the operation. Not surprisingly, the SS men were highly motivated to perform their duty. During this period of preparation, they had developed a strong sense of comradeship and loyalty to

Left: The commander of the *SS-Verfügungs* Division, *SS-Gruppenführer* Paul Hausser, discusses the battle situation with one of his officers in France, in May 1940. In the background are some of the division in foxholes.

their division commander, whom they affectionately referred to as 'Papa' Hausser.

While the men of the *SS-Verfügungs* Division laboured in western Germany, Adolf Hitler and the top military strategists of the Third Reich developed a plan for the conquest of Western Europe. Even before it began *Fall Gelb* (Case Yellow, the codename for the invasion of the Low Countries and northern France), in April 1940 the High Command of the German Armed Forces (OKW) launched an assault on Denmark and Norway. Concerned that these two countries might fall into Allied hands, Hitler and OKW had initiated this action in order to deprive British naval and air forces of possible bases. They also wanted to obtain areas that were rich in iron ore. Denmark fell to the Germans with little resistance, while Norway capitulated after a campaign that lasted until June.

GERMAN PLAN

The German plan of invasion for the Low Countries and northern France involved the use of three army groups. In the south, Army Group C occupied a collection of strongholds known as the Siegfried Line (or the Westwall), which stretched from Luxembourg to Switzerland. Led by Field Marshal Wilhelm Ritter von Leeb, this group contained two armies and was

positioned along the border directly opposite the famous Maginot Line, an impressive network of fortifications constructed by the French Army to prevent a German breakthrough into France across the River Rhine. While Army Group C remained at this location and kept Allied forces distracted in the south, the two other groups were to initiate offensive actions to the north.

Arrayed across a swathe of territory that extended from Aix-la-Chapelle to Luxembourg, Army Group A was under the command of Field Marshal Karl Rudolf Gerd von Rundstedt and included four armies. The task of this organization was to cross the Ardennes Forest and push through Luxembourg and southern

Belgium, then swing north-west until its panzer and motorized divisions reached the English Channel at an area north of the River Somme. OKW hoped that if Rundstedt's forces accomplished this feat, they might be able to trap several thousand Allied troops in a coastal area surrounding the port of Dunkirk.

On the northern end of the German invasion force, Army Group B served as the right wing of the operation. Commanded by Field Marshal Fedor von Bock, this organization contained 29 divisions distributed into two armies. While the 6th Army lunged across southern Holland, General Georg von Küchler and his 18th Army was to cross the River Meuse and help two airborne divisions to capture Rotterdam and

the Führer to commit more divisions to Army Group A, so that Rundstedt's armies could push deeper into France and prevent enemy forces from mounting an effective counter-offensive from the south. With this objective accomplished, Manstein argued, the Germans could then isolate Allied armies north of Sedan with less difficulty. Hitler's acceptance of this suggestion meant that the 18th Army would have fewer divisions to use in Holland and Belgium.

ALLIED ORGANIZATION

On the other side of the Low Countries, Allied forces were organized into three groups. Covering an area from Dunkirk to the town of Montmedy, the 1st Army Group included the French 1st, 2nd, 7th and 9th armies, along with the British Expeditionary Force (BEF), which was stationed at the city of Lille. Further south, the 2nd Army Group contained three French armies occupying the Maginot Line from Verdun to the town of Selestat. Near Switzerland, the 3rd Army Group faced the German 7th Army. In the event of a German attack, the 2nd and 3rd Army Groups were to maintain their defences, while the 1st Army Group was to attempt a counter-offensive through Belgium.

Months before the German army groups massed along their borders, the Dutch and Belgian governments knew that Hitler was planning to launch an invasion into their countries. In January 1940, this fact had become clear when a plane carrying two Luftwaffe officers crashed inside Belgium. When local soldiers took the two men into custody, they found on one of them a set of papers that included specific details of the invasion plan formulated by OKW. Undeterred by this mishap, Hitler and the German High Command were determined to launch Case Yellow on schedule, and made only a few minor changes to their attack. After this incident, the *SS-Verfügungs* Division and other units attached to the 18th Army would not be able to take their adversaries

The Hague. During Case Yellow, Hausser and his *SS-Verfügungs* Division would serve in this army. In addition to the Dutch and Belgian troops that they would have to fight during the invasion, Küchler's forces faced the prospect of 26 British and French divisions which were arrayed across an area from Dunkirk to the River Oise.

Originally, Hitler and OKW intended to provide Army Group B with the most divisions, believing that a strong right wing was necessary to drive across the Low Countries, smash enemy forces north of the River Somme, and seize Dunkirk and other Channel ports. However, Rundstedt's chief of staff, Lieutenant General Erich von Manstein, eventually persuaded

completely by surprise when the Germans eventually moved into Holland.

In the early morning of the 10th May, *Fall Gelb* began when two groups of German paratroopers jumped out of their Junkers Ju 52 transport airplanes, dropped from the sky, and landed on Dutch soil. Protected by squadrons of fighters and dive-bombers, the soldiers of the 22nd Infantry Division descended upon a designated landing zone near The Hague. With similar protection, the Luftwaffe 7th Airborne Division landed close to Rotterdam. Because the divisions were isolated within the two areas, the success of these airborne operations ultimately depended upon the timely arrival of the 18th Army before the Dutch could surround the paratroopers and crush them.

At the Dutch capital, the 22nd Division quickly got into trouble. Although the German paratroopers

Above: An SS-VT 37mm (1.47in) anti-tank gun pulled by what appears to be a Kettenrad half-track motorcycle during Case Yellow. However, the calibre of the gun was too small to threaten Allied tanks like the British Matilda.

captured three airfields surrounding The Hague, the Dutch I Corps soon arrived from its base near the North Sea and launched a brutal counter-attack. After retaking these facilities, the Dutch kept the German paratroopers at bay and took about 1000 prisoners, which were then sent to detention camps in England. For at least a short time, The Hague remained in Dutch hands.

At Rotterdam, the 7th Airborne Division enjoyed more success. After seizing part of the city and the Waalhaven airport, its paratroopers successfully repelled a Dutch counter-attack. Aided by close air-support, the division consolidated control over the areas it held and then seized a section of land to the east. This would open a corridor that would help the 18th Army march through the Netherlands. Within this area, the paratroopers occupied both banks of the River Maas at the city of Dordrecht. They also captured the strategically important Moerdijk bridges that crossed the estuary of the river before the Dutch could demolish them.

SS-VT IN ACTION

While the two groups of paratroopers assaulted The Hague and Rotterdam, the SS-VT Division and other formations of the 18th Army crossed the Dutch border to join the invasion of Holland. In this early stage of Case Yellow, the units within the SS division operated separately. Since December 1939, the *Der Führer*

Regiment, the 2nd Battalion of the division's artillery regiment, a pioneer company, and a vehicle column had been attached to the 207th Infantry Division. Meanwhile, *SS-Verfügungs* Division's reconnaissance detachment and the *Deutschland* Regiment's armoured car platoon served with the 254th Infantry Division.

To reach the paratroopers at Rotterdam, the 18th Army had to push through several lines of defence which the Dutch Army had established alongside numerous rivers and canals. The first such obstacle was a defensive position running between the Rivers Ijssel (or Yssel) and Maas at the cities of Arnhem,

Below: A map showing the main German thrusts during Case Yellow, and the locations where the SS-VT were involved in operations before the evacuation of the Allied troops from Dunkirk in June 1940.

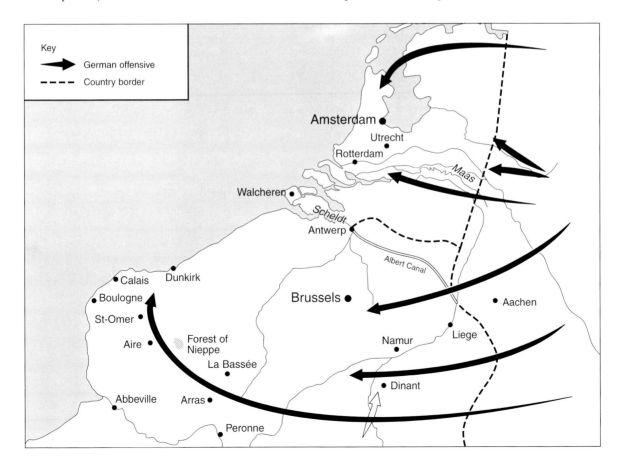

Nijmegen and Malden, near the German border. The second barrier constituted two sets of fortifications. From the Zuider Zee to the River Maas, the Dutch II and IV Corps held an area known as the Grebbe Line. Directly below this position, III Corps garrisoned the Peel Line, which extended as far south as the town of Weert. At this section, III Corps was not expected to halt the German advance for an indefinite period. Instead, its troops were stationed at the Peel Line simply to delay the 18th Army long enough for Allied forces to reach the area and mount a counter-attack.

The third line of defence established by the Dutch Army was known as *Vesting Holland,* or 'Fortress Holland'. This area consisted of several pillboxes and other strongholds positioned along a line that ran east of Amsterdam down to Hertogenbosch, then turned west along the River Waal, covering Dordrecht and Rotterdam before reaching the North Sea. As a last resort, to stall the German advance the Dutch Army planned to open several dikes in the region, thus flooding the countryside with sea water.

Hausser and other high-ranking officers in the 18th Army realized that speed would be crucial to the success of their drive through the Low Countries. If the Dutch succeeded in slowing Bock's armies long enough to destroy important bridges and dikes, they would isolate the 7th Airborne Division and buy enough time to enable French and British forces to reach the area. Just as the paratroopers landed on their zones near Rotterdam and The Hague, on 10 May Küchler's divisions poured across the border in an effort to reach the North Sea as quickly as possible.

At the front of the 18th Army, the *Der Führer* Regiment would receive its baptism of fire while attached to the 207th Infantry Division, X Corps. In fact, the regiment served as the spearhead for the invasion. Behind the *Der Führer* Regiment, the rest of the *SS-Verfügungs* Division waited with many other groups within the army, while the forward units of the 207th Division pushed into the Netherlands. Because the 18th Army was so large, when the invasion began, the rest of Hausser's command was still on the east bank of the River Rhine moving in one of the transport columns.

At the start of the invasion, the men of the *Der Führer* Regiment immediately showed their courage and enthusiasm for the task. Within two hours, the regiment's 3rd Battalion reached the east bank of the River Ijssel near Arnhem. Despite this rapid progress, it did not reach the area quickly enough to prevent the Dutch troops stationed across the river from destroying its bridges. Undeterred by this setback, *Der Führer's* 2nd Battalion crossed the River Ijssel and its pioneer company managed to establish a bridgehead by the afternoon. This feat accomplished, the regiment captured a stronghold at the town of Westervoort and later seized Arnhem.

POOR DUTCH MORALE

Senior military officers in the Dutch armed forces had hoped that their troops would hold this area for at least three days until Allied forces arrived. When the soldiers in the *Der Führer* Regiment seized Westervoort and Arnhem within a matter of hours, they shocked the Dutch Army with their tenacity and resourcefulness. By the end of the day, thanks in part to the actions of the SS unit, the 18th Army had advanced over 100km (62 miles) into Holland. Justifiably gratified by their achievements during the first day of Case Yellow, the *Der Führer* Regiment's troops bivouacked at an area near Renkum and prepared for their assault on the Grebbe Line. It was scheduled for the following morning.

While the *Der Führer* Regiment charged across the River Ijssel, Hausser's Reconnaissance Detachment operated in an area to the south in a formation known as the 'Grave Group'. In addition to this SS unit, the outfit included two *Wehrmacht* battalions from the 254th Infantry Division. One battalion was a machine-gun unit, the other an artillery battery. Separated into five assault detachments, the Grave Group was to perform a role similar to that of the *Der Führer* Regiment. To help the main part of the 18th Army in its drive across the Low Countries, these units were ordered to capture a bridge that crossed the River Waal at the city of Nijmegen, in addition to several canal bridges at Hatert, Heuman, Malden and Neerbosch.

Unlike the soldiers of the *Der Führer* Regiment, those of the SS Reconnaissance Detachment and their *Wehrmacht* colleagues had a rough day. Although one detachment from the Grave Group seized intact the canal bridge at Heuman, other units met stiff resistance at the remaining objectives , suffering high casualty rates. In the battle for the bridge at Hatert, every member of the German assault detachment involved in the action was either killed or wounded. However, the survivors did manage to take the structure after the retreating Dutch had inflicted considerable damage upon it.

At the other targeted areas, enemy forces had succeeded in destroying the bridges before they could fall into German hands. Despite this setback, the Germans managed to destroy a line of fortified bunkers situated near the town of Neerbosch, thereby enabling the 18th Army to ford the Meuse-Waal Canal without being delayed by well-placed Dutch troops. After the conclusion of this mission, the Reconnaissance Detachment returned to the main body of the *SS-Verfügungs* Division.

On the second day of the offensive, the *Der Führer* Regiment went back to work and continued to perform well. This time, it charged into the Dutch II and IV Corps and ripped open the Grebbe Line, the second row of defences established in Holland. Not

Below: Officers from the *Germania* Regiment of the SS-VT discuss their plan of action during the campaign in the West in May 1940. Note the camouflaged smock which had just been introduced.

surprisingly, as the 18th Army followed this vanguard and continued with its westward drive to the coast, conditions for the Allied armies in the Low Countries worsened. While the three Dutch corps pulled back from the Grebbe and Peel lines, the Belgian Army to the south withdrew from its defences along the Albert Canal and took up new positions at an area extending from Antwerp to the town of Louvain. These manoeuvres left the 1st Light Mechanized Division, French 7th Army isolated and vulnerable to attack by the German 6th and 18th Armies, and forced it to retreat from Holland.

On 12 May, the 9th Panzer Division breached the southern end of the 'Fortress Holland' network and made contact with the 7th Airborne Division at the Moerdijk bridges. To the north, other elements of the 18th Army headed for Amsterdam. Impressed with the

Above: An SS-VT artillery gun team in action in the Low Countries in May 1940. In the left foreground an officer with his back to the camera scans the surrounding area for potential targets.

performance of the *Der Führer* Regiment at the River Ijssel and the Grebbe Line, the commander of X Corps gave the SS unit the honour of spearheading the assault on the eastern line of Fortress Holland. This area was the only significant obstacle standing between the Germans and the old capital of the Netherlands.

With great enthusiasm, the men of the *Der Führer* Regiment led a furious attack upon the Dutch troops occupying the eastern end of Fortress Holland, and once again pushed through the enemy lines, enabling X Corps to sweep past Utrecht and into Amsterdam. After this achievement, the SS unit kept going until it reached the coastal towns of Ijmuiden and Zandvoort. Although the troops garrisoned at these towns defended themselves courageously, they could not prevent the *Der Führer* Regiment from overrunning their positions and taking the towns. Two days later, the regiment rejoined the rest of the *SS-Verfügungs* Division at Marienbourg.

Although the *Der Führer* Regiment had achieved a considerable amount of distinction for its actions in Holland, the rest of the *SS-Verfügungs* Division did not see much action in the country. During the early phase of Case Yellow, the main body of Hausser's forces was advancing in two motorized columns to Hilvarenbeck, a town north of Antwerp. Anticipating an Allied counter-attack, the German Army High Command had dispatched the division to the area in order to protect the left flank of the 18th Army. If such an assault were to occur, the division was to hold its position long enough to enable German infantry reinforcements to arrive.

When this expected counter-offensive failed to materialize, OKH ordered Hausser's division to attack Allied forces in northern Belgium in a quick *Blitzkrieg* fashion. However, the SS division soon found this feat impossible because of a military traffic jam that clogged the main roads running between Holland and Belgium. To find an alternative route into Belgium, Hausser sent reconnaissance patrols into the countryside. Their mission was to locate rural back-roads that might take the division to its destination. Although some patrols found such facilities, before it could move south, the division soon received new orders. The Army High Command now wanted the *SS-Verfügungs* Division to launch an attack upon the Allied troops occupying the western tip of Holland.

Located at the end of Beveland – a narrow peninsula north of the River Scheldt estuary – the island of Walcheren was the last part of Holland still in Allied hands by mid-May. With the rest of the country mostly overrun by the German 18th Army, the demoralized Dutch Army had capitulated, and Queen Wilhelmina and her government fled to Great Britain. Thus, the garrison at Walcheren was cut off

from the rest of the Allied armies, which were situated far to the south of Holland, and escape was possible only via the sea. Encouraged by the results of the battles fought elsewhere in the country, the Germans were confident that they could overwhelm this tiny outpost with air strikes and highly trained assault battalions, just as they had done in earlier battles.

Although threatened with the prospect of facing 21 battalions of heavy artillery and an air force consisting of six Stuka and five heavy bomber squadrons, the Walcheren garrison declined an offer by the Germans to surrender without bloodshed. Moreover, the Allied troops stationed on the island stayed there to fight rather than be evacuated by the Royal Navy: they wanted to force the Germans to earn this piece of land. Helped by artillery batteries in Antwerp and warships from the Royal Navy stationed off the coast of the Beveland Peninsula, the garrison commanders knew that their men could extract a terrible price for the island.

WALCHEREN DEFIANT

A favourable geographical situation also encouraged the garrison at Walcheren Island to hold its ground. Not only was the Beveland Peninsula a thin strip of land that prohibited any large-size attack force from assailing the island in a two- or three-pronged offensive, but also much of the terrain was flooded. This forced Hausser to send his battalions down a narrow, bottle-neck passage, where they were vulnerable to artillery- and machine-gun fire. At the end of the peninsula, the Germans had only one possible land-based route to the island. This passage was a strong, concrete dam running between the island and the peninsula, which was wide enough to allow an asphalt road and a single-track railway across the top.

For his attack upon Walcheren, Hausser selected two battalions from the *Deutschland* Regiment to use against the island garrison. *SS-Sturmbannführer* Fritz Witt led the 1st Battalion, while *SS-Sturmbannführer* Matthias Kleinheisterkamp commanded the 3rd Battalion. Although they had planned to approach the island in a two-pronged formation, the flooded terrain on the Beveland Peninsula forced the 1st

Battalion to close ranks behind Kleinheister-kamp's troops.

On the afternoon of the 16th May, as the SS battalions approached the island, they began to encounter stiff resistance from the garrison. At an area around Westerdijk, the men of the 3rd Battalion had to negotiate their way through a minefield that was covered with barbed-wire, while a group of enemy soldiers who were well-entrenched in permanent defensive positions along an embanked road fired into them. Meanwhile, artillery batteries based in Antwerp shelled the SS battalions, as did the British warships patrolling near the island. During this advance, the Germans lost 16 men.

ATTACK ON THE DAM

As a participant in the assault on Walcheren Dam, Paul Schürmann of No. 9 Company, 3rd Battalion, *Deutschland* Regiment, described the intensity of the fighting. 'I see one man fall,' he recalled, 'then two on the right and then another comrade who lies face down. Some men are using their teeth to tear open field dressings to bandage their shattered arms or chests.' Meanwhile, 'more and more of our machine-guns cease firing, with their crews silent, bloody and pale behind the weapons'.

During a pause in the advance, Schürmann noticed more carnage. At one point he observed a comrade wandering about with his shirt torn from him. On this wounded soldier, 'there is a gaping wound in his back and I can see the pumping movement of his lungs'. Schürmann recalled, 'To the left of me another comrade goes back almost marching, erect, ignoring the bullets flying through the air ... paying no attention to death. His throat and chest, covered in field dressings, are blood soaked. His unfocused eyes are wide open, his face is grey and he looks straight past me.' To the right, Schürmann noticed another fallen soldier 'lying on his back. His twitching fingers claw at the air.'

Despite this punishing counter-attack, the SS battalions pushed forwards and fought their way across the flooded, muddy ground to reach the Walcheren Dam. Here the German attack stalled in the face of more punishing resistance from the garrison. Finding protection in hastily excavated foxholes and behind railway cars, the SS troops held their ground as Allied machine-gun and artillery crews shot at them from the other side of the dam. During this engagement, the Germans lost another 17 men killed and 30 wounded. Satisfied with the amount of damage that they had inflicted upon the *Deutschland* Regiment, the Walcheren garrison finally evacuated the island.

While the *SS-Verfügungs* Division secured German control over the western end of Holland, the rest of Army Group B had captured Brussels, swept through Belgium and northern France, and had then pushed its way to the English Channel. When the Dutch Army capitulated, the main body of the 18th Army was able to join this offensive and help create a salient that separated Allied forces in northern France from those along the River Somme. During this action, the 18th Army was preoccupied with protecting the flanks of the salient, ensuring that Allied troops trapped in the area around Dunkirk would remain where they were, with their backs to the English Channel.

On the evening of the 22nd May, XIL Corps ordered the *SS-Verfügungs* Division to proceed with the 6th and 8th Panzer Divisions toward the port of Calais in order to help strengthen German positions west and south of the Dunkirk perimeter, as well as tighten the noose around this pocket of resistance. Specifically, the SS soldiers were supposed to cross the La Bassée Canal and intercept enemy forces attempting to break out of the pocket at a point on the waterway south of the town of Cassel. In addition, the *SS-Verfügungs* Division was to establish bridge-heads across the canal and push British troops out of the Nieppe Forest.

Although Hausser's men were now exhausted from several days of marching and fighting, they were still in high spirits and relished the prospect of playing a decisive role in the battle for Western Europe. During the march to the La Bassée Canal, the SS units covered the right flank of XIL Corps and headed for the town of Aire. Later in the night, Hausser received a message from 18th Army headquarters

ordering him to remain at his current position. The SS units bivouacked for the night at an area further south, near the town of Saint Hilaire.

Unfortunately for the soldiers in the *SS-Verfügungs* Division, enemy troops did not allow them to enjoy any relaxation. During the course of the night, scattered groups of French armoured and infantry units charged into Hausser's troops in an attempt to break out of the Dunkirk pocket. By the early morning hours of the 23rd May, an armoured battalion had overrun No. 9 Company, *Der Führer* Regiment, while other tank formations surrounded the regiment's No. 10 and No. 11 companies.

Later in the morning, the French attacked No. 5 and No. 7 companies and charged into an area near Blessy. Soldiers from 2nd Battalion, *Der Führer* Regiment and the 2nd Battalion of the SS Artillery

Above: Non-commissioned officers from the SS-VT take a break from the fighting around the Dunkirk perimeter to enjoy the sun and a bottle of wine. The speed of the German success meant there was much to celebrate.

Regiment had settled at this location for the evening, only to end up engaged in a confusing battle against desperate adversaries. They were fighting like cornered animals. During the battle, Karl Kreutz, a rising star in the SS-VT Division, witnessed the death of a careless battalion commander: 'I saw Erpsenmüller was standing beside me smoking a cigarette. He asked, "Kreutz, aren't you firing on prisoners of war?"' Kreutz recalled, 'The next second, while I was reloading, I saw him fall, shot through the head. He lay face downward with the cigarette still burning in his left hand.'

Reeling from the shock of the French surprise attack, the Germans rallied and began an orderly defensive action. Although surrounded by enemy battle tanks, a platoon of anti-tank gunners from *Der Führer*'s No. 7 Company destroyed at least 15 enemy vehicles. As the morning progressed, the French attack at Saint Hilaire gradually lost its momentum and the Germans seized the initiative, launching well-coordinated counter-assaults that involved infantry- and anti-tank units working in close cooperation. By the time the battle was over, *Der Führer*'s 3rd Battalion alone had destroyed 13 armoured vehicles and the division as a whole had taken about 500 prisoners. This battle was the first occasion in which the regiment had fought against battle tanks.

Other SS units distinguished themselves during the fighting that had broken out across the front of the division at the La Bassée Canal. While commanding a 30-man motorcycle patrol, *SS-Untersturmführer*

Fritz Vogt spotted a French armoured column heading east to the town of Mazinghem. As an officer in the 2nd Company, Reconnaissance Detachment, Vogt had already won distinction for his leadership in the attack on the Dutch garrison at the Meuse-Waal Canal. In France, his actions against this armoured column would earn him the Knight's Cross of the Iron Cross.

With his anti-tank crews prepared to fire upon the French column, Vogt directed his men to shoot at the soft-skinned vehicles moving at the tail of the convoy. After knocking out these targets, the anti-tank crews struck the battle tanks at the front of the formation. Panicked and demoralized by this assault, the soldiers

Below: Caught at the moment of firing, this SS-VT 75mm (2.95in) infantry gun and others like it gave the division its own source of artillery support. Unsuitable against tanks, it was used to knock out enemy positions.

in the battalion-size armoured unit surrendered to the 30-man reconnaissance team.

HARD FIGHTING

Eventually, the battle near Saint Hilaire ended when the surviving members of the French assault detachment retreated to the other side of the La Bassée Canal and fell back to the Dunkirk perimeter. Although the men of the SS-VT Division had successfully repelled the attack, they were frustrated by the difficulty they had encountered against the French-built Renault 35 and other, larger, battle tanks. The German anti-tank weapons were not powerful enough to penetrate the tanks' armour, except at close range. In some instances, enemy battle tanks had come within 5m (5.5yd) of anti-tank crewmen before being knocked out. This deficiency in firepower had contributed to the initial success of the French armoured formations in penetrating the division's lines.

On 24 May, the *SS-Verfügungs* Division crossed the La Bassée Canal, established bridgeheads across the waterway, and advanced 8 km (5 miles) behind enemy lines before being intercepted by British soldiers from the 2nd Infantry Division. Despite the tenacity of the British counter-attack, the Germans held their ground and maintained their bridgeheads. Even before this battle was over, the division received a message on 26 May ordering it to move north-west and begin an attack against British forces occupying the Nieppe Forest.

The following morning, the *SS-Verfügungs* Division started its assault on the forest. The *Germania* Regiment took the right wing of the advance, while the *Der Führer* Regiment marched on the left. Meanwhile, the Reconnaissance Detachment pressed forward at a position situated between *Der Führer*'s 1st and 3rd Battalions. Not surprisingly, the densely wooded terrain within the forest enabled the British defenders to fight effectively against this attack. They also enjoyed the protection of well-constructed field fortifications.

When the SS battalions launched their assault on the Nieppe Forest, they suffered high casualties from enemy marksmen. On the right wing of the attack, sharpshooters from the Queen's Own Royal West

Kent Regiment wreaked havoc upon the *Germania* Regiment. Despite this difficulty, the SS units made substantial progress in their effort to push the British garrison out of the forest, exploiting their numerical superiority and fighting in a very aggressive manner.

By the end of the day, the men of the *Germania* Regiment had advanced as far as the town of Haverskerque, while the *Der Führer* Regiment had pushed through the Bois d'Amont and reached the Canal de Nieppe. At these areas, the SS soldiers found anti-tank rifles which had been abandoned by retreating enemy forces. When the Germans tested these weapons on a makeshift firing range, they found that the barrels had been bent and thus rendered inaccurate, as other weapons would later be after Dunkirk.

On 28 May, the offensive against the Dunkirk pocket became easier for the armies of the Third Reich when King Leopold III and his Belgian Army surrendered, thereby enabling the German 6th and 18th Armies to close in on the eastern end of the Allied perimeter. This capitulation – combined with successful assaults launched by the Kleist and Hoth Panzer Groups to the south and the west of Dunkirk – pushed the remaining Allied forces back to a small and narrow area extending from Ypres in the east to the Franco–Belgian border. Because the Nieppe Forest was now situated on a salient that was vulnerable to isolation and encirclement, the British Expeditionary Force evacuated the Queen's Own and other regiments from the area, and took up positions closer to the English Channel.

While the *Germania* Regiment, the *Der Führer* Regiment, and the Reconnaissance Detachment saw action in the Nieppe Forest, Steiner and his *Deutschland* Regiment marched on Merville with the 3rd Panzer Division. On 27 May, the SS unit confronted a fresh line of British defences arrayed along the Lys Canal. After softening enemy positions with an artillery barrage, Steiner hurled his 3rd Battalion at the British defenders, driving them out of the area. Later in the day, two of his battalions were on the other side of the waterway forming bridgeheads for other German forces.

The *Totenkopf* Division was supposed to be in the area to help solidify German control over this part of the canal, but it was still several miles away when British armoured units launched a punishing counter-attack against the *Deutschland* Regiment. Although the SS soldiers fought valiantly, their rifles and grenades were not powerful enough to knock out the enemy battle tanks. After suffering heavy casualties, they were saved from the brink of annihilation when an anti-tank company from the *Totenkopf* Division arrived in the nick of time and repulsed the British armoured assault. Covered by protective artillery fire from nearby batteries, the surviving British tank crews withdrew from the area.

WELCOME REST

After the battles at the Lys Canal and the Nieppe Forest, the *SS-Verfügungs* Division was allowed to enjoy a short period of rest at Cambrai before resuming

Above: The move south begins for the SS-VT division during Case Red, the elimination of France from the conflict. As in Poland, mechanisation of units was only partial at best, and most soldiers were forced to march.

hostilities against retreating British units on 31 May. While the Germania Regiment marched across the Mont de Cats, the *Der Führer* Regiment moved into the town of Cassel. Standing on top of a hill within the town, its soldiers enjoyed an excellent view of the Dunkirk perimeter. They would not get the opportunity to participate in the final push aimed at closing the pocket and capturing the remaining Allied troops that awaited evacuation to England. On the evening of 1 June, the *SS-Verfügungs* Division received orders to pull back from the Dunkirk area and go to the town of Bapaume to be re-fitted with new equipment.

By this time, Hausser's division had received about 2000 officers and men to replace those who had been lost in battle during Case Yellow. These replacements brought most of his companies up to full strength and ensured that sentry duty and other unpleasant chores would be dispersed more widely through the ranks. When the Germans finally seized Dunkirk on 4 June, the *SS-Verfügungs* Division and other organizations prepared for the beginning of *Fall Rot* (Case Red), the plan developed by the OKH to conquer the rest of France.

This plan of invasion called for the three Army groups to march southward in a three-pronged offensive. North of Reims, Army Group B was to initiate Case Red on 5 June by advancing along a wide swathe of territory stretching from the Atlantic Coast to the River Aisne. Four days after Bock's forces began this action, Army Group A followed suit, proceeding down a corridor of land situated between the river

and the Franco–German border. While the French divisions garrisoning the Maginot Line turned their attention to this enemy juggernaut approaching from the west, Army Group C crossed the border and struck the line from the east. As a result, the French soldiers of the 2nd and 3rd Army Groups found themselves isolated and trapped in a vicelike grip between two large German formations.

Although the French Army still had at least 60 divisions deployed south of the River Somme, it was greatly outnumbered and vulnerable to air strikes from Luftwaffe warplanes. Because of these disadvantages,

Below: Himmler (right) congratulates Hausser (left) and Werner Ostendorff (centre) on the successful conclusion to the campaign in France. Yet again the SS-VT had emerged from a campaign with flying colours.

Army Groups A and B were able to shred the network of defences that had been hastily established by General Maxime Weygand along the river. With the Weygand Line quickly broken, the Germans pushed further south at a steady pace. On 14 June, troops from Army Group B marched unopposed into the city of Paris.

French Morale Collapses

Not surprisingly, the fall of the capital devastated the morale of the French armed forces and encouraged the Germans to press their advantages with more determination. Three days later, the beleaguered French Army of the East collapsed into a state of disorder, while Panzer groups from Army Groups A and C pushed it into a pocket located south of the city of Nancy. On 22 June, the French forces confined in this area surrendered.

During Case Red, the *SS-Verfügungs* Division was attached to Panzer Group Kleist and participated in the drive south of the River Somme as a part of Army Group B in the west. The night before the operation began, the division sustained a relentless but ineffective artillery bombardment that inflicted little damage. The following day, the SS regiments counterattacked. Undeterred by the destruction of a bridge that they were planning to use, gunners from the SS Artillery Regiment and various heavy weapons companies pounded enemy positions on the other side of the river. Meanwhile, the grenadiers from the *Deutschland* Regiment reached the opposite bank and sent the French defenders on a hasty retreat.

Closer to Paris, French resistance against the SS division became more stubborn. Although the *Der Führer* Regiment had succeeded in crossing the River Aisne, concentrated enemy fire forced Hausser to pull back his forces and lead them on a route further east, where the opposition was not as tenacious. When the capital fell to Army Group B, the

Right: Men of the *SS-Verfügungs* Division in a victory parade across a bridge at Hendaye on the Franco-Spanish border on 9 July 1940. Hitler and Franco, the Spanish dictator, were holding a conference in the town.

SS-Verfügungs Division and other units within Panzer Group Kleist continued their southern advance with much less difficulty. While XVI Panzer Corps headed south-east to Dijon, Hausser's units went with XIV Motorized Corps to south-western France.

Within this region, the *SS-Verfügungs* Division pursued enemy forces through Orléans, Tours and Poitiers before pausing for a brief rest. At this point, the invasion became anti-climactic for Hausser's troops as they proceeded closer to the Spanish border. Near the town of Angouleme, Felix Steiner, a company from the *Deutschland* Regiment and a group of SS artillerymen were surveying suitable locations to place their field pieces when a column of careless French soldiers stumbled into the area, thinking that the German soldiers were British.

After subduing these wayward troops, the SS units surrounded Angouleme. The German commanders then met with the mayor of the town and warned him that they would destroy the area with an artillery bom-

Above: Ludwig Kepplinger of the *Der Führer* Regiment receives the Knight's Cross of the Iron Cross from his divisional commander, Paul Hausser, in September 1940. The Knight's Cross was a highly prized decoration.

bardment if any resistance took place while the *SS-Verfügungs* Division moved in to occupy the town. After the mayor complied with this ultimatum, the Germans disarmed a small garrison stationed within the town and led the French prisoners of war back to Steiner's headquarters. The division spent the rest of the campaign engaging in more of these types of mopping-up operations. Collectively, the SS units had taken 30,000 prisoners and lost only 33 men during the sweep through south-western France.

On 25 June, Case Red came to a favourable conclusion when a new French Government formally agreed to a peace treaty imposed by the Axis powers. The resulting armistice partitioned France into two sections. The southern section remained unoccupied and would be ruled by Marshal Henri Philippe Pétain and his nominally independent pro-Axis regime. North of Vichy, the capital of this new government, the Germans maintained control over a much larger section of territory. In addition, the occupied zone included a sizeable swathe of land that ran along the Atlantic Coast all the way down to the Spanish border. Within this region, the *SS-Verfügungs* and *Totenkopf* divisions performed security duty until early July.

During the campaigns in Western Europe, the Germans had lost about 27,000 killed, 111,000 wounded and over 18,000 missing. French casualties included 92,000 killed, 250,000 wounded and at least 1.45 million taken prisoner, while the other Allied nations had somewhat lower casualty rates. The British had suffered 3457 killed and almost 16,000 wounded. The Dutch lost 2890 killed and 6889 wounded, while the Belgians had a casualty rate of 7500 men killed and 15,850 wounded in action.

For the men of the *Waffen-SS* divisions, the fighting in Western Europe had served as yet another opportunity for them to show their mettle in combat. After the conquest of France was complete, many received accolades for their bravery and leadership. Within the ranks of the *SS-Verfügungs* Division, Knight's Cross recipients included *SS-Obersturmführer* Fritz Vogt of the Reconnaissance Battalion, *SS-Sturmbannführer* Fritz Witt of the 1st Battalion, *Deutchland* Regiment, and *SS-Hauptscharführer* Ludwig Kepplinger of No. 11 Company, *Der Führer* Regiment. In addition, Felix Steiner earned this medal for his effective command of the *Deutschland* Regiment, as did Georg Keppler for his leadership of the *Der Führer* Regiment.

Below: Part of the preparations for Operation 'Sealion', the planned invasion of Britain. Here SS-VT men manhandle a 105mm (4.1in) leFH 18 gun on board a converted Rhine barge during an exercise.

CHAPTER FIVE

THE BALKANS

With a new name and now fully motorized, the division began preparations for an invasion of the Soviet Union. However Mussolini's interventions in the Balkans had destabilised the whole region, and Hitler was forced to order an attack on Yugoslavia to secure his flank.

After spending a brief period of time guarding the western coast of France near the Pyrenees Mountains, the *SS-Verfügungs* Division was relocated to Holland in early July to help oversee the demobilization of the Dutch armed forces. Although the bombing of Rotterdam had given many Dutch citizens good reason to resent their German conquerors, relations with the local population tended to be cordial, if not friendly. To help ensure a continuation of this amicability, the SS soldiers under Paul Hausser's command generally exhibited respectful behaviour while carrying out their duties.

During its stay in the Low Countries, the *SS-Verfügungs* Division experienced some changes in its structure. Although its Artillery Regiment received more battalions and equipment, the organization also lost important officers and units that were transferred to a new formation, the *SS-Wiking* Division. Specifically, this new division received personnel from the *Germania* Regiment, the 2nd Battalion of the Artillery Regiment, a unit from the Reconnaissance Detachment, and the No. 3 Company of the Anti-tank

Left: *Hauptsturmführer* **Fritz Klingenberg, 'the man who captured Belgrade', seen here preparing for his next mission. Klingenberg used a mix of dash and bravado to capture the city virtually single-handed.**

Battalion. These seasoned veterans were to serve as the foundation upon which the new division would be built.

The *SS-Verfügungs* Division also lost the resourceful commander of *Deutschland* Regiment, Felix Steiner, who became the leader of the *Wiking* Division. Fortunately for the soldiers of *Deutschland*, his replacement, Willi Bittrich, was a worthy successor. A capable Army officer and Air Force pilot during World War I, Bittrich had been the commander of the 1st Battalion, *Der Führer* Regiment. Within the ranks of the *Waffen-SS*, he was a rising star.

NAME CHANGES

Later in the year, the *SS-Verfügungs* Division returned to southern France and was stationed at the town of Visoul. In December 1940, *Reichsführer* headquarters changed the name of the organization to *SS-Deutschland* Division. A month later, the division underwent yet another name-change and would now be known as *SS-Reich* Division (Motorized). In addition, the renamed division received more troops, a motorcycle battalion and its divisional tactical sign. During this period of relative tranquility that ensued following the conquest of France, the men of the *Reich* Division trained vigorously and learned to operate effectively as a fully motorized organization.

Above: An artillery column from the *Waffen-SS* rolls into Yugoslavia in April 1941. The German forces were under pressure to neutralize both Yugoslavia and Greece as soon as possible in order to leave time to invade Russia.

By March 1941, the Army High Command (OKH) was satisfied that the *Reich* Division was ready for active service and ordered Hausser's regiments to relocate once again. Now the division was to join XLI Corps, which was under the command of General Georg-Hans Reinhardt and attached to Field Marshal Sigmund Wilhelm List's 12th Army. Stationed at the town of Temesvar, near Timisoara, in south-western Romania, the corps was preparing for an offensive in the Balkans. During their eight-day journey from southern France to south-western Romania, the men in the SS division were not entirely certain of their destination and wondered where their next campaign would take place.

BALKAN ADVENTURE

For several months, Hitler had been intending to launch an invasion of his one-time ally, the USSR. Originally, he planned to initiate this action in the spring of 1941. However, a series of events in the Balkans undermined Axis hegemony over Europe and thus distracted the Führer from his plan to conquer Russia and destroy its Bolshevik regime.

Before March, the diplomatic situation in South-East Europe appeared to be very favourable for Germany. During the previous year, Hungary, Romania and Slovakia had become allies of the Third Reich when their leaders signed the Axis Tripartite Pact. When Bulgaria signed the treaty in March 1941, the Germans seemed as if they might achieve total domination over the region without having to resort to the naked aggression that they had used in Western Europe or Poland.

After acquiring this new ally, the German 12th Army crossed the River Danube and took up positions near Greece and the Yugoslavian province of Serbia. Not surprisingly, this action caused a great deal of concern for the Belgrade government. Aware that Italy, Hungary and Bulgaria had territorial claims on neighbouring regions within Yugoslavia, Prime Minister Dragisa Cvetkovic and the Prince Regent Paul signed the Tripartite Pact. By joining the Axis powers, the Yugoslavian Government hoped to discourage these countries from using military force to satisfy their claims.

ITALIAN INTERVENTION

However, an ongoing conflict on the southern tip of the Balkans eventually provoked Hitler into taking more aggressive actions in the area. In October 1940, his ally, Fascist Italy, had invaded Greece from Albania, which had been under Italian rule since the spring of 1939. Unlike Hitler, Mussolini did not have many crack troops who were willing to fight, suffer and die in a war of conquest for their country. As a result, General Alexander Papagos and his Greek Army thrashed the Italians and even mounted a successful counter-offensive into south-eastern Albania.

Mussolini had failed in his effort to conquer Greece and also had lost about one-quarter of his Albanian territory to his would-be victims, who were now consolidating their control over the area. The outcome of this campaign ensured that the British and Commonwealth armed forces were able to maintain a presence in the Balkans. Unless Hitler did something to change this situation, he would have to confront the prospect of Allied control over the entire Mediterranean region. As a result, Axis forces operating in North Africa might become isolated from Europe and thus unable to receive supplies or reinforcements. Moreover, Italy would become increasingly vulnerable to British attacks from the sea and air.

Hitler finally decided to act when a political coup took place in neighbouring Yugoslavia. In late March, a clique of military officers overthrew Prime Minister Cvetkovic and the Regent Prince Paul, then installed Peter II as the titular ruler. Although the new Yugoslavian Government assured Hitler that it would not repudiate the Axis Tripartite Pact, the Führer distrusted this regime, and used the palace coup as a pretext for invading that country, along with Greece. Thus, he unleashed Operation 'Marita' in April 1941.

Without any difficulty, Hitler received full support from his regional allies by guaranteeing their territorial claims within Yugoslavia. Inside the country, the Germans and Italians also cultivated support among the disaffected elements of the Croat population. By encouraging Croat aspirations for self-government, the Axis powers hoped to turn this ethnic group against the Belgrade government and encourage widespread desertion in the Yugoslavian Army.

While this diplomatic manoeuvring was taking place, the Axis armies prepared to begin Operation 'Marita'. The plan of invasion essentially involved two main battle groups. The first group was concentrated in an area north-west of Yugoslavia and included the Italian 2nd Army, which was stationed at an area near Fiume, and the German 2nd Army, which was arrayed across an area stretching from Klagenfurt, Austria to Barcs in Hungary. This battle group was to destroy all enemy forces in its path and then march on the Yugoslavian capital from the west. Presumably, the fall of Belgrade would demoralize the nation's army and thus contribute to its disintegration.

The second battle group consisted of the German 12th Army and was mostly situated inside Bulgaria along the eastern border of Yugoslavia. While some divisions in this army were to press Belgrade from the south, others were to seize Serbian Macedonia and prepare for an assault on Greece. Several miles to the north, XLI Panzer Corps occupied an area on the western end of Romania and prepared to assail the capital from the north. The *Reich* Division was to join this organization after completing its journey from southern France.

The Germans presumed that conquering the Balkans would require less manpower than the invasion of France, and allocated fewer divisions to Operation 'Marita.' Collectively, the invasion would involve 32 divisions, with 10 of them armoured and four motorized. These units were allocated into 10 corps, four of which were armoured. When the campaign against Greece and Yugoslavia started on 6 April, eight divisions were not yet in their places or ready to participate in the attack.

At Fiume, the Italian 2nd Army consisted of 14 divisions, with two of them motorized and one armoured, allocated into four corps. In addition, the army commander, General Vittorio Ambrosio, had another division stationed in the port of Zara on the Dalmatian Coast. From the south, the Italian 11th Army was to sweep out of Albania and link up with the Germans in Serbian Macedonia. Although the ruler of Hungary, Admiral Miklos Horthy de Nagybanya, had signed a non-aggression pact with Yugoslavia a few weeks earlier, he too sent troops to participate in the invasion.

During their trip to Romania, the soldiers of the *Reich* Division moved quickly to ensure that they would reach XLI Panzer Corps in time to join the attack on Yugoslavia. However, they also had numerous conflicts with Army convoys that were rolling across the same roads and highways into the theatre of action. In the midst of one traffic jam, an SS officer placed landmines in front of a column of *Wehrmacht* vehicles and posted an armed guard to keep the Army convoy from moving while the SS column pulled away. In another episode of road rage, an SS commander threatened to open fire upon a group of *Wehrmacht* motorists who were attempting to overtake his column.

Despite these incidents, the division reached Temesvar on time, although the SS troops would have little time to rest before springing into action. To encourage rapid movement across the Yugoslav countryside, General Reinhardt issued a directive decreeing that the first division to reach the all-weather main road running from the town of Alibunar to Belgrade

Below: The advance to Belgrade was not a smooth procession to victory, thanks largely to the poor quality of the roads – a foretaste of conditions in the Soviet Union. Only a few all-weather roads existed in the country.

would be entitled to spearhead the drive into the capital. Not surprisingly, Hausser and his men were determined to see their division win this honour, although the soft, wet terrain that covered the ground between them and their objective would render this task rather difficult.

BOMBING CAMPAIGN

While the *SS-Reich* Division and other groups within XLI Panzer Corps prepared to attack Yugoslavia from the north, the Luftwaffe inaugurated the German invasion with a vicious bombing campaign against Belgrade. Meanwhile, the main part of Panzer Group Kleist initiated the ground assault by crossing the border from Sofia, Bulgaria and seizing the city of Nis. From this point, the group's XIV Motorized Corps travelled 194km (312 miles) towards Belgrade within a week.

Above: A car belonging to the *Reich* Division driving along the riverside in Belgrade after Klingenberg's spectacular coup. Organized resistance soon crumbled in the country after the fall of the captial.

To the west, the German 2nd Army swept in from southern Austria and Hungary. While the 8th Panzer and 16th Motorized Divisions of XLVI Panzer Corps headed east to capture the towns of Novi Sad and Ruma, the 14th Panzer Division moved west, seized Zagreb, and linked up with the Italian 2nd Army at Karlovac. Armed with obsolete weapons and caught in indefensible positions, the Yugoslavs stood little chance of resisting the German *Blitzkrieg*.

Five days after the invasion of Greece and Yugoslavia had begun, on the morning of 11 April, XLI Panzer Corps swept across the border from Romania. During the advance on Alibunar, the

SS-Reich Division immediately became bogged down in the muddy terrain. Many of the larger vehicles sank into the marshland, although others found dry patches of earth to carry them forward for at least a short distance. Fortunately for Hausser, the bikers in the *SS-Kradschutzen* (Motorcycle Reconnaissance Battalion) made great progress in the drive to the main road by riding along railway embankments and on top of dikes. Late in the afternoon, when these motorcyclists, along with elements of the *Deutschland* Regiment, reached the Alibunar–Belgrade highway before any other German unit, they ensured that the *SS-Reich* Division would have the honour of leading the charge into Belgrade.

By this time, there was little enemy opposition to prevent the Germans from moving into the capital.

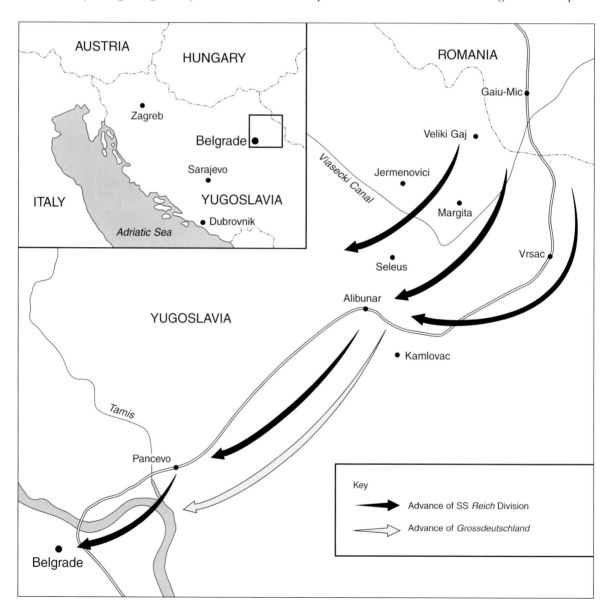

Because the Yugoslavian Army was preoccupied with attacks from the 2nd Army in the north-west and the rest of the 12th Army in the south-east, XLI Corps had relatively few enemy troops to deal with in the north-eastern part of the country. Luftwaffe bombing raids had wreaked havoc upon Belgrade and its garrison, rendering the city vulnerable to conquest.

REST ORDERED

To guarantee the quick seizure of Belgrade, General Reinhardt wanted to strike any enemy forces situated in front of his divisions before they had time to recover and re-group from the bombings. However, the soldiers in the SS formation were unable accomplish this task as they were so exhausted from the long march through mud that went up to their knees and, on some occasions, up to their thighs. Appreciative of this situation, Reinhardt rescinded his order to advance and directed the *Reich* Division to rest for the night on the north bank of the River Danube.

One officer in the division either did not receive this order to halt or simply ignored it. As the commander of No. 2 Company, Motorcycle Reconnaissance Battalion, *SS-Hauptsturmführer* Fritz Klingenberg had been one of the first Germans to reach the north bank of the river. Shortly after the arrival of his company, he led 10 men on a scouting patrol. Along the shoreline of the Danube, he and his troops requisitioned a motor boat, brought their vehicles to the opposite bank, and headed straight for the capital.

Riding through the streets of Belgrade without any opposition, Klingenberg and his small scouting party stopped near the government War Ministry at the centre of the city and established two machine-gun posts. While the SS soldiers performed this task, an official from the German Embassy arrived on the scene and requested protection for his facility. Klingenberg then went with the diplomat to the

Left: A map showing the invasion route of the *Reich* Division from Romania, itself a satellite ally of Nazi Germany. Although Yugoslavia was quickly subdued, Greece proved to be a tougher nut to crack.

Above: A soldier from the *Reich* Division in the Balkans in 1941. As well as a pair of binoculars, he carries what appears to be a despatch case on his webbing, and has a stick grenade tucked into his belt.

embassy and devised a simple plan to seize the entire capital without firing a shot or sacrificing any men.

First, he persuaded the German Military Attaché to demand that the Mayor of Belgrade attend a meeting at the embassy. When the mayor arrived, Klingenberg claimed to be the commander of a much larger military force and threatened to unleash another Luftwaffe strike unless he surrendered the city. Already weary from the devastation that had been inflicted on Belgrade, the mayor acceded to this ultimatum and capitulated. Several hours later, the soldiers in the advance guard of the 11th Panzer

Division entered the capital, astonished to see that it was under the secure control of fewer than a dozen SS troops.

With the panzer group now occupying Belgrade, Klingenberg returned with his small detachment to the *Reich* Division's headquarters to report his coup. Not surprisingly, the young company commander quickly became a celebrity within the Third Reich. On radio shows, he enthralled listeners with his description of the events that led to the capture of the Yugoslavian capital. A month later, Hitler expressed his gratitude for this *coup de main* by awarding Klingenberg the Knight's Cross of the Iron Cross. As the war progressed, Klingenberg's stature in the *Waffen-SS* continued to rise. After distinguishing himself in combat in Russia, he became the commander of the 17th *SS-Panzergrenadier-Division Götz von Berlichingen*. In the spring of 1945, his luck finally ran out when he was killed in action near Herxheim in the Palatinate.

Further German Success

As was expected, the fall of Belgrade seemed to hasten the disintegration of the Yugoslavian Army. On 15 April, the 14th Panzer Division entered Sarajevo unopposed. From the national capital, Panzer Group Kleist headed south to intercept a group of enemy troops attempting retreat from Bosnia to Macedonia. In the southernmost part of Yugoslavia, Skopje and other Macedonian population centres fell securely into German hands.

On 17 April, the Yugoslavian Foreign Minister, Aleksander Cincar-Markovic, and other dignitaries arrived in Belgrade to discuss the surrender of their country to the Axis powers. Noticeably absent from this delegation was King Peter II, who had fled to Egypt. The following day, the Yugoslavs formally signed a document of capitulation, enabling Hitler and his allies to dismember the country.

After a war that had lasted only 12 days, Yugoslavia ceased to exist as a nation. Italy and Germany annexed parts of Slovenia, while Hungary received territory north-west of Belgrade. To the east, Bulgaria acquired a large piece of land that included parts of Macedonia

and north-eastern Greece. Italy also received a section of the Dalmatian Coast and the Bay of Kotor.

The rest of Yugoslavia fell under the joint occupation of the Axis powers. Although Montenegro and Croatia became self-governing client states, they were very much under the influence of the Axis powers. The new King of Croatia (which also included Bosnia and Herzegovina) was an Italian aristocrat who never spent any time in his new domain. As a result, the actual administration of the government passed into the hands of Dr Ante Pavelic, a fanatical Croat nationalist who unleashed a reign of terror over the Serbs and Bosnian Muslims residing within the country. In other parts of the former Yugoslavia, the Hungarians also brutalized the local population living within their zone of occupation, as did the Bulgarians.

Along with land, Mussolini also acquired several warships. Because the Yugoslavian Navy had not scuttled its vessels or taken them to British-controlled waters, the Italians were able to seize these weapons intact. Despite this acquisition, the Fascist regime was not much of a naval power beyond the Adriatic Sea. After defeating the Italian Navy near Cape Matapan in late March, the British continued their domination over important parts of the Mediterranean Sea.

Not surprisingly, German casualties during the Yugoslav invasion were light. Collectively, they lost 151 killed, 392 wounded and 15 missing. By the end of the operation, the Axis armies had captured 337,684 enemy soldiers, along with 6028 officers. However, about 300,000 Serbs and other Yugoslavian loyalists managed to escape into remote areas and carry on a guerilla war. Led by Colonel Draza Mihailovic and Marshal Josip Broz Tito, they would participate in partisan campaigns against Axis troops and their local allies for the rest of the war.

To the south, the Germans also conquered Greece within a fairly short period of time, although they had to fight against tough Allied troops that were well-entrenched in the mountainous countryside. During this part of the Balkan *Blitzkrieg*, the soldiers of the *Leibstandarte-SS Adolf Hitler* distinguished themselves by leading assaults through rugged mountain passes, thus enabling the regular *Wehrmacht* divisions to push

British and Commonwealth forces further south until the Allied troops evacuated the country. By the end of the invasion, the Germans had taken more than 12,000 prisoners from the Greek Army.

EXPANSION OF THE WAFFEN-SS

Although the army maintained its opposition to any further expansion of the *Waffen-SS*, the performance of SS soldiers in the Balkans encouraged Hitler and Himmler to create more SS divisions. To avoid competition with the *Wehrmacht* for new recruits or conscripts, these divisions found new members beyond the borders of the German State. Since the regular armed forces were not allowed to recruit foreign nationals, the *Waffen-SS* sought young volunteers throughout the Nazi-controlled areas of Europe. Ethnic Germans living within these conquered territories were already rushing to SS recruiting stations. Flooded with volunteers from Holland, Belgium,

Norway, Denmark and other countries, Battle Group *Nord* became a full-size division by September 1941.

After fulfilling their role in the conquest of Yugoslavia, the soldiers of the *SS-Reich* Division returned to Romania and later moved on to an area near Salzburg, Austria for rest and more training. When the Greek Army capitulated to the Axis powers, organized warfare on the European continent had, at least for the moment, come to an end. Thus, the *Reich* troops expected to be sent to North Africa to aid Field Marshal Erwin Rommel in his campaign against the British. Instead, their next battle would take place to the east, within the vast countryside of the Soviet Union.

Below: An SdKfz 221 armoured car somewhere in Yugoslavia. Note the black uniform of the driver, and his special padded beret. Behind the driver his door lies open, giving an indication of the lack of space inside.

CHAPTER SIX

BARBAROSSA

The subjugation of the Soviet Union had always been Hitler's goal. Now, buoyed by his successes in Poland, Norway, the West and the Balkans, he threw Germany's armed might against Stalin. The *Reich* Division would again be leading from the front.

The conquest of the Soviet Union was a particularly significant objective for Adolf Hitler and the fanatical members of his National Socialist German Workers Party (NSDAP). They considered it to be a sacred crusade against what they saw as the two great evils of Western Civilization: Bolshevism and the Jewish 'race'. The invasion of Russia, known by the codename 'Operation Barbarossa', also represented to the Nazis the consummation of a long-held desire to seize the vast expanses of Eastern Europe from the Slavic 'subhumans' in order to provide the German people with new land. As the shock troops of the NSDAP, the soldiers of the *Reich* Division and other *Waffen-SS* formations were destined to play a major role in the operation.

The deep-seated ideological and racial animosities between the Soviets and the Nazis also meant that the war on the Eastern Front would be especially vicious for both sides. Unlike the battles of Western Europe in 1940, the campaigns in Russia and the Ukraine involved combatants who were unlikely to give or receive any quarter. This, combined with the harsh

Left: Men of the *Der Führer* Regiment wearing customized winter camouflage – usually sheets or blankets obtained from Russian houses – during the advance on Moscow in the late autumn of 1941.

Russian winters and the vast amount of manpower deployed by both belligerents, ensured that the war on the Eastern Front would see some of the greatest episodes of human cruelty, misery, death and privation in history.

GERMAN STRENGTH

German strength at the start of Operation 'Barbarossa' seemed to be formidable. Altogether, Hitler and his generals commanded three million men massed into 11 armies, including four large panzer formations and three Luftwaffe fleets. This impressive war machine collectively possessed almost 3600 battle tanks and about 600,000 other motorized vehicles. To aid the grenadiers in their drive to the east, the senior commanders of the German armed forces had almost 7200 artillery pieces and 1830 warplanes with which to pummel enemy positions.

The condition of the Soviet Red Army gave the Germans much encouragement for their coming invasion of Russia. For several years, the Soviet dictator Josef Stalin had purged and executed the most talented members of his officer corps to maintain his grip on power. Thus, although the Red Army was a large and formidable organization, it did not possess many talented high-ranking commanders to coordinate effective defensive strategies and mount

counter-offensives, at least in the early months of the war with Nazi Germany.

Despite these favourable conditions, some *Wehrmacht* and *Waffen-SS* soldiers harboured justifiable concerns about the upcoming offensive. At the start of the operation, the three German Army Groups were arrayed along a front that was 1600km (995 miles) in length. Eventually, this battle line would grow twice as long. This vastness created potential transportation and supply problems for the corps and divisions that were expected to cross several hundred kilometres to Moscow and other major cities. These would be exacerbated by the lack of decent roads and inhospitable terrain that covered the countryside between the River Bug and the Soviet capital. Most notably, a huge swamp known as the Pripet

Above: The opening of 'Barbarossa': men of the *Reich* division advance past a border marker on the German–Soviet frontier on 22 June 1941. The invasion came as a complete surprise to the Soviet border guards.

Marsh covered a huge area between Brest-Litovsk and Kiev, dividing the German forces.

Moreover, the OKW failed to contemplate the significance of the weather when planning Operation 'Barbarossa'. Jubilant over the rapid successes achieved in Poland, Western Europe, and the Balkans, senior military officers assumed that their armies would crush the Soviet war machine and reach Moscow before winter. Thus, OKW saw no need to worry about the incredibly cold climate that its troops might have to endure towards the end of the year.

Neither the vast size of the Russian countryside nor the transportation problems that might arise from its swampland, sandy soil or lack of roads led to any outward expressions of concern.

By June 1941, the *Waffen-SS* organization had grown to include roughly 60,000 men assigned to its divisions and other battle groups. At the start of Operation 'Barbarossa', OKW deployed these units at various places along the Nazi-Soviet demarcation line running through Poland. The *Leibstandarte* and the *Wiking* divisions went with Army Group South, which was under the command of Field Marshal Karl Rudolf Gerd von Rundstedt. In the far northern sector of the operation, the *Nord* Battle Group joined the Norway Mountain Corps. Near the Baltic Sea, the *Polizei* and *Totenkopf* Divisions served as reserve units for Field Marshal Wilhelm Ritter von Leeb and his Army Group North.

ARMY GROUP CENTRE

Stationed at an area west of Brest-Litovsk, the *Reich* Division fell under the command of Field Marshal Fedor von Bock and his Army Group Centre, an organization that included the 4th and 9th Armies, as well as the 2nd and 3rd Panzer Groups. Within this formation, the *Reich* Division was attached to XXIV Motorized Corps, 2nd Panzer Group. Commanded by General Heinz Guderian, the 2nd Panzer Group also included the 10th Panzer Division and an élite unit from XLVI Panzer Corps known as the *Grossdeutschland* Regiment. To signify their affiliation with Guderian's organization, the units of the Reich Division adorned their vehicles with the letter 'G'.

In May 1941, the unit commanders of the *Reich* Division attended a conference at Gmunden am Traunsee to discuss the upcoming invasion of the Soviet Union. Although many of those attending the meeting were apprehensive at the thought of such a huge operation, nonetheless they returned to Salzburg and led their formations from Austria to their starting positions in Poland. En route to the battle zone, the SS soldiers were kept in the dark about the mission they were about to undertake. After passing through a large wooded area in Poland, the division bivouacked near the River Bug. To ensure that the Soviet troops on the other side of the river would be taken by surprise the following morning, the SS officers forbade the building of campfires.

In the early morning of 22 June, Operation 'Barbarossa' began when the *Reich* Division's Artillery Regiment – with many other German batteries arrayed along the demarcation line – opened fire, pummelling Soviet defences on the other side of the border. Greatly outnumbered and taken completely by surprise, the Red Army troops garrisoned in the area were quickly overwhelmed by the Nazi *Blitzkrieg*. Unlike the *Leibstandarte*, the *Reich* Division did not participate in the initial ground assault across the River Bug, but spent most of the first week directing traffic along a line of advance established for the 2nd Panzer Group which ran from the Vistula to the Bug.

After performing this duty, the *Reich* Division experienced considerable difficulty in its advance to the battle zone. Because Army Group Centre had not allocated it any space on the road leading to the front line, most of its soldiers had to march on foot through the countryside, although some of them were able to hitch rides with Army convoys. On 28 June, the division finally received its first task to perform in the campaign. While the main part of the division was to force a river crossing between Citva and Dukora, a detachment consisting of motorcycle, reconnaissance, flak, and pioneer units were ordered to drive along Highway 1 and seize the village of Starzyca. In addition, Hausser's troops were to cover the northern flank of the Panzer Group during the advance along the main road running to Minsk and Smolensk.

At first, the assault on Starzyca went well when the SS detachment quickly pushed the Russians out of the village. However, a much larger enemy force soon arrived and surrounded the Germans. To save these men from annihilation, a relief column consisting of the 3rd Battalion, *Deutschland* Regiment and crewmen operating three self-propelled assault guns (SPs) headed for the area. En route to Starzyca, the rescue party overran a Russian roadblock by destroying one tank and chasing away another.

Just as the relief column entered the village and linked up with the Motorcycle Battalion, three more Russian tanks approached from the east. With little difficulty, one of the SP crews knocked out all three enemy vehicles. After sustaining minor damage from an anti-tank strike, the SS gunners obliterated four anti-tank weapons, then retired to obtain more ammunition and resupply. When the SP gun returned, it destroyed another Russian tank approaching from the north-west.

After performing this duty, the SP crew provided protection for an engineer detachment that was repairing a nearby bridge. While three of these weapons guarded the area, a fourth helped 1st Battalion, *Deutschland* Regiment in an assault on Serhioyevicza, which contained a bridge that was supposed to be taken intact. When the SS troops reached the area, they found that the Russians had already destroyed the objective. However, the SP crew managed to fire 20 rounds across the river into the retreating enemy column, destroying four tanks. The next morning, the Germans discovered eight more damaged and abandoned tanks on the other side of the river.

CLOSE COOPERATION

As these engagements indicate, the grenadiers, artillerymen and SP crews of the *Reich* Division were becoming very skilled at acting in close collaboration. Shortly afterwards, these troops continued to perform during an assault on high ground near Beresina. While the SP crews hammered enemy positions on the heights around the town, the infantrymen stormed up the slopes and seized their objective. From the crest of this high ground, the SP gunners bombarded a retreating group of Russian soldiers and vehicles attempting to cross a wooden bridge. In excited pursuit, one of the SP drivers actually moved his vehicle onto the bridge and rolled over throngs of fleeing soldiers. When the Germans were halfway across the bridge, Russian engineers on the opposite side detonated the structure, sending the self-propelled assault gun into the river. The crewmen emerged from the SP wet, but unhurt.

During their relentless drive into Soviet territory, the soldiers of the *Reich* Division were heavily dependent upon the skill and bravery of their engineering units. On many occasions, while under heavy enemy fire, these engineers repaired damaged bridges and even constructed temporary passages that enabled their comrades to cross rivers and other obstacles. At the River Pruth, No. 2 Company of the Engineering Battalion was ambushed while repairing a bridge. In the ensuing battle, the Soviets killed all 72 men in the SS unit. The engineers in the division also cleared minefields and performed other dangerous tasks to facilitate quick movement through an inhospitable country.

En route to Minsk, the *Reich* division passed through the northern edge of the Pripet Marsh, which covered an area almost as large as England. A member of the divisional artillery regiment named Heid Rühl recalled the problems encountered during this advance: 'Crossing the swamp was very difficult as we had to jump from one clump of grass to another and often had to put down our rifles and pull ourselves out of the swamp so that we did not get sucked under.' When they were not exchanging gunfire with the enemy, they were 'attacked by huge clouds of voracious mosquitoes'.

North of the swamp, other problems confronted the SS soldiers. As they travelled east, roads became increasingly scarce, forcing their vehicles over sandy dirt that often ruined engines and other vital parts. Marching for several kilometres per day under the hot, summer sun, many soldiers became severely fatigued and had difficulty fighting when the Russians attacked. Frequent instances of overflowing rivers only exacerbated transportation problems. Even in the early stages of Operation 'Barbarossa', the vast expanse of underdeveloped land situated between the River Bug and Moscow caused the fearsome German *Blitzkrieg* to bog down and stall in many areas along the Eastern Front.

As the *Reich* Division moved across the Beresina and Dnieper rivers in early July, it confronted scattered Soviet troops that harassed the Germans by staging ambushes and then melting into the countryside.

The SS units could hardly retaliate. East of Mogilev, a larger enemy force surrounded an isolated divisional artillery unit and destroyed a fuel truck with an anti-tank shell. After this action, Heid Rühl noted, 'from all sides came the chilling cry "Ooohrah!" and then a storm of small-arms fire'. When the Red Army moved in for the kill, 'our iron discipline manifested itself; the intensity of our training and of the everlasting drill paid dividends. We needed no orders. Like a fire-splitting hedgehog, we were soon in action laying down a heavy barrage and throwing hand-grenades just like infantry veterans.'

HARD RATIONS

By the end of the night, the SS artillery unit had repulsed the attack and then enjoyed a day of rest. During this hiatus, reconnaissance patrols obtained iron rations left behind by the Russians at a nearby

Above: Another break on the long march towards Moscow for these men of the *Reich* Division. The vast distances in the Soviet Union took their toll on men and machines alike, while supply problems multiplied with every mile.

village. According to Rühl, 'these consisted of a piece of hard brown bread as large as a fist and a similarly sized piece of cane sugar. The two together produced a feeling of fullness which our own rations never achieved.' Later in the day came another discovery; when 'some of the men found straw-covered bottles of vodka which proved to be too much even for hardened drinkers and which was undrinkable even when diluted with every sort of mix'.

The following day, the division resumed its task of guarding the northern flank of Army Group Centre's advance down the Minsk–Smolensk Highway. Not surprisingly, the Germans confronted tough opposition at Smolensk, although they captured the city in mid-July. To the south-east, the *Reich* Division received an order to capture Yelnya and a piece of high ground situated east of the town. This objective was important to the Germans because the town was located on a crossroad that they needed to control the main road to the Soviet capital, Moscow. The significance of this site meant that the Red Army would be very determined in its effort to keep the town from falling into enemy hands.

On 22 July, the attack on the heights near Yelnya began. Soldiers from the *Deutschland* Regiment and the *Der Führer* Regiment stormed up the slopes. Although the SS troops received assistance from tank crews of the 10th Panzer Division, they lacked artillery support because the ammunition trucks had not arrived with shells for the batteries. As a result, the Soviet troops in the trenches on the high ground fired relentlessly into the Germans. Despite this adversity, the soldiers from the *Deutschland* and *Der Führer* regiments maintained a steady, disciplined advance, and conquered the first ridge of the heights by the evening. After another day of intense combat, they seized the rest of the high ground. The Germans also captured the nearby village of Ushakova.

By this time, the hot, summer sun, the lack of shade-giving trees, and dwindling water supplies began to take their toll on the soldiers of the *Reich* Division, and after many SS troops collapsed from heat exhaustion, Guderian ordered the unit to abstain from further offensive action and consolidate its control over Yelnya. However, the Red Army did not allow the Germans to enjoy any rest at the town or the nearby heights that they had just conquered. In a savage counter-attack that began the following morning, the Soviets penetrated many German positions, although the SS defenders eventually threw the assailants off the high ground after several hours of hand-to-hand combat. This battle was just the beginning of a brutal contest over the area that would last for four weeks.

During this lengthy operation, the ammunition shortage became serious for the SS units. As a result, artillery commanders ordered their gunners to fire only upon visible targets. In his recollection of an armoured assault on his battery, Heid Rühl noted that 'one of our stretcher-bearers won the Iron Cross here by knocking out an enemy tank with a hand-grenade. He threw it into the open hatch. Finish! The gunners, working like fury, finally beat off the first Russian tank attacks, but these were then renewed in greater strength'.

On a nearby road, an SS anti-tank detachment experienced similar difficulties when confronted by eight Soviet armoured vehicles. After the Germans knocked out the leading tank, a flame-throwing vehicle emerged and 'projected huge gouts of flame at the anti-tank gunners'. According to a post-battle report, 'the Russian crew then leapt from their machine and raced towards the gunners, who grabbed entrenching tools and grenades, doubling forward to meet the Russian charge'. In the ensuing confrontation, 'a small knot of men ... fought for their lives and when, at last, the Russian tankmen had been killed, the SS gunners went back to their Pak [anti-tank gun] and carried on firing until all the Russian tanks had been destroyed'.

HEAVY LOSSES

As the ranks of the infantry battalions dwindled, soldiers in the pioneer units were obliged to pick up rifles and fight at the front line. After one assault, the Motorcycle Battalion had become severely depleted and was forced to retire while an Army engineer detachment stepped in to take its place. In human-wave attacks, some of the finest troops in the Soviet Army continued to punch holes in the German defences. Only through a great deal of exertion, discipline and determination were the SS soldiers able to beat back these assailants, with heavy losses inflicted upon both sides. North-west of Yelnya, the Red Army over-ran Ushakova. However, the Germans re-took the village the following day after launching a punishing dive-bomber assault.

Eventually, Guderian pulled the *Reich* Division out of the area and replaced it with *Wehrmacht* units, which would suffer just as badly during subsequent Soviet attacks. Within this pocket, mobile, mechanized

Above: SS troopers from the *Reich* Division advance through a burning Russian village. Stalin's scorched earth policy deprived the advancing Germans of both food and shelter on their march.

combat had degenerated into trench warfare similar to that seen in World War I. Although the Russians actually suffered higher casualty rates during the battle for Yelnya, they were able to replace their losses with much less difficulty than the Germans. The enormous amount of death and destruction that resulted from this struggle was an ominous indication of what the armies of the Third Reich would face throughout the Russian Front in coming years.

After enjoying a brief period of time to recuperate, the *Reich* Division went back into action. In September, Hausser's troops participated in an ambitious offensive that would become one of the greatest achievements in military history. After almost three months of combat, Army Group Centre had pushed deep into Soviet territory north of the Pripet Marshes, while Army Group South had made similar progress driving through the Ukraine. Between these two regions, which were now in German hands, at least five Soviet armies occupied an area that had become a large salient extending 150km (93 miles) into Nazi-held territory. The western tip of this salient was in an area surrounding Kiev.

For Hitler and his generals, here was the perfect opportunity to trap 50 or more enemy divisions and pound them into oblivion. To accomplish this feat, OKW developed a fairly simple plan. While the 6th Army kept the Soviets preoccupied at Kiev, the 2nd Army and the 2nd Panzer Group were to sweep in

from the north and take up blocking positions east of the city. From the south, the 17th Army and the 1st Panzer Group were to perform a similar manoeuvre and link up with the other two German formations, thus preventing the Soviet armies from evacuating the salient and retreating to the east.

Still attached to the 2nd Panzer Group, the *Reich* Division served as the right wing of XXIV Corps while it moved south-west and pushed through enemy lines. When the attack began on 6 September, the division made considerable progress and quickly captured an important junction at Sosnitsa. With this task accomplished, Guderian ordered Hausser to send his Motorcycle Battalion to Makoshim, the site of a railway bridge. After waiting for Stuka dive-bombers to soften Soviet defences, the SS motorcyclists were to capture the bridge and establish a bridgehead on the southern bank of the River Desna.

Above: Crossing one of the many rivers in central Russia in 1941. Rubber assault boats like the one above were used to cross such obstacles when the Soviets had blown up the bridges during their retreat.

Before the SS soldiers could even begin executing their assault, the operation went awry. The warplanes had failed to arrive on time. An hour later, Guderian grew impatient and ordered the Motorcycle Battalion to charge across the bridge without the air support that it desperately needed. Aware that the structure was probably wired with explosives that Soviet engineers on the other side of the river could detonate at any moment, the motorcyclists rushed across the bridge at top speed.

With this quick dash across the bridge, the SS motorcyclists took the Red Army defenders completely by surprise. While machine-gunners in the sidecars kept the Soviets pinned down with hot lead, the drivers crashed through the enemy barricades. As the SS soldiers wiped out the small garrison, *Wehrmacht* engineers followed the vanguard and defused the explosives placed within the bridge.

However, the motorcyclists didn't have long to savour their victory; a surprise attack was launched from an unexpected direction. While the SS soldiers were establishing their bridgeheads, the late 27 Stukas at last showed up. Mistaking the motorcyclists for enemy troops, the dive-bombers dropped their explosives upon the bridgehead, leaving 10 men dead and another 30 wounded. The warplanes also inflicted slight damage upon the railway bridge.

CROSSING THE UDAY

Although many SS soldiers in the *Reich* Division were upset about this carelessness and the losses that it brought, they knew that they had to put the incident behind them and continue performing their task. Thus, the main part of the division moved into the area and collected the survivors of the Motorcycle Battalion before resuming its journey southwards. It reached the River Uday in mid-September. As the SS advance guards approached the river's bridges, Soviet troops on the opposite bank destroyed the structures with explosives. Despite this setback, the division's infantry regiments managed to cross the river and attack enemy forces.

Aware that their armies were on the brink of being encircled and annihilated, the Soviet defenders on the south bank of the Uday fought tenaciously, inflicting heavy losses upon the Germans. Despite the intensity of this resistance, the division pushed back the Red Army and secured both banks of the river, along with the towns of Borsna and Priluki. When the *Reich* Division achieved these goals, it fulfilled its role in the encirclement of Kiev and received a letter of gratitude from Field Marshal Bock. Their mission completed, the SS soldiers took up positions at a point along the edge of the pocket and helped maintain the German gauntlet around Kiev.

By this time, the Red Army divisions trapped in the tight pocket had nothing left to do but fight desperately in an effort to break out. They assailed many points throughout the perimeter, only to be thrown back with heavy losses. At Putivl, the *Reich* Division's machine-gunners faced an attack launched by cadets from the Kharkov Military Academy. Singing as they charged into the German lines, the young pupils collapsed as sprays of bullets ripped into their ranks. Every one of the Soviet cadets perished in the frantic assault.

Later in the month, the surviving members of the Soviet armies trapped in the Kiev pocket surrendered. Collectively, the Red Army had lost about one million men killed, wounded, or captured in the area. By the end of the siege, the Nazi war machine had obliterated five enemy armies and shredded two more into tatters. With Kiev in their hands, the Germans were now in a good position to seize strategically important areas, such as the oil-producing Caucasus Mountains and the Donets Basin with its industrialized areas.

After the closure of the Kiev pocket, the soldiers of the *Reich* Division enjoyed a period of relaxation that lasted from 24 September to 2 October. During this interlude, it received replacements for the numerous troops lost during the opening actions of the Barbarossa campaign. Since the start of the invasion, the *Deutschland* Regiment alone had lost more than 1500 men killed, wounded, or missing. The *Der Führer* Regiment and other units within the *Reich* Division had suffered comparable losses. With several months of costly offensive and defensive operations still ahead of them, these formations would need all the men that they could find.

One of the new recruits sent to the *Reich* Division was Walter Schminke, who described his first impressions of life on the front line while serving with the Motorcycle Battalion: 'The atmosphere in the new unit was excellent. It was not exactly unmilitary but there was a complete absence of parade ground bullshit.' After sunset, he recalled learning the lyrics of the battalion anthem, 'unshaven and far from home', while lounging near River Volga: 'After we 36 men had sung our song, we heard applause coming from the other side of the Volga. Then they sang their song and we applauded. Is this really what the war was like?'

During the encirclement of Kiev, Hitler and his generals had devised a plan of attack aimed at capturing Moscow. Called Operation 'Typhoon', the action was to begin on 2 October and involved another quick *Blitzkrieg* thrust that was supposed to overwhelm the Soviets before the onset of winter. Aware that every male or female Russian citizen capable of wielding a weapon or a spade would be involved in either constructing or maintaining the defences around the capital, senior OKW strategists anticipated that the operation would be costly and difficult to accomplish.

On 4 October, the *Reich* Division joined Operation 'Typhoon' when its units moved with the 10th Panzer Division during an assault on the towns of Krichev and Ladishino. After the seizure of these two objectives, the SS division headed north-west to occupy an area between Gshatsk and Vyasma. This manoeuvre was part of an encirclement carried out by XLVI Corps to entrap enemy forces while capturing Gshatsk. Although hindered by autumn rain that had turned the soil of the Russian countryside into a sea of mud, the division reached the area within a few days.

OPERATION 'TYPHOON'

On the morning of 7 October, the *Deutschland* Regiment led the attack against Red Army positions near the town. Heavily supported by an SP platoon, the Artillery Regiment's 3rd Battalion, a light Flak battery and an anti-tank company, the *Deutschland* Regiment's 2nd Battalion made considerable progress and captured a piece of high ground north-west of Sharaponova in the afternoon. An hour later, the battalion pushed enemy forces further north to Mikeyeva and then captured Sloboda Potovskaya.

Later in the day, 1st Battalion, *Deutschland* Regiment leapfrogged past 2nd Battalion and then

Right: Dismounting ready for action, soldiers from the *Reich* Division advance towards a burning village somewhere in the Soviet Union. Note the divisional symbol on the back of the truck.

seized Komyenka at around midnight. Meanwhile, 3rd Battalion established a blocking position across the Smolensk-Moscow Highway. As a result of these actions performed by the battalions of the *Deutschland* Regiment, a sizeable Russian force was now cornered within Gshatsk. On 9 October, the regiment assailed the town in a two-pronged advance,

with 1st Battalion marching on a route right of the highway, while 3rd Battalion proceeded to the left.

The first task in this assault was to seize a railway embankment, which would then be left in the hands of 2nd Battalion. Although harassed by Soviet fighter-bombers, the assault battalions made steady progress. When 1st Battalion reached a wooded area that was

teeming with enemy snipers, the German advance on the right slowed down somewhat. While the grenadiers were performing this action, a reconnaissance patrol infiltrated the southern outskirts of Gshatsk and ambushed a group of transport trucks carrying Russian soldiers. Early in the afternoon, the rest of the SS attack force entered the town and

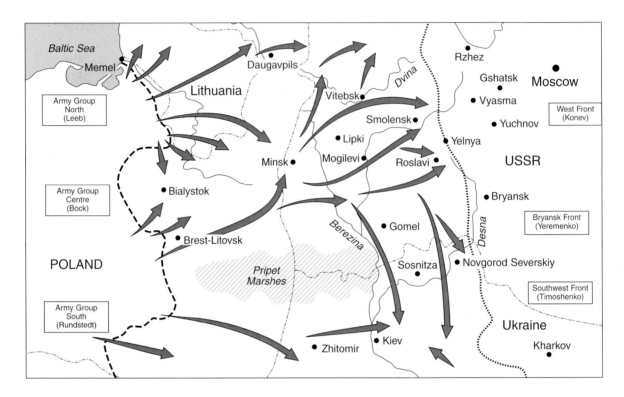

Above: A map depicting Army Group Centre's advance towards Moscow, with the diversion south to help their colleagues in Army Group South that cost the Germans a chance to take Moscow virtually unopposed.

found several dead civilians that had been hanged by the Red Army garrison shortly before it had retreated from the area.

Determined to re-take Gshatsk, the Soviets launched several counter-attacks against the *Deutschland* battalions. When informed of enemy troop build-ups in the area, the senior divisional commanders dispatched the *Der Führer* Regiment to an area east of the town in an effort to disrupt the movement of Soviet forces. After seizing an important piece of high ground near Slovoda, the regiment pushed through the Russian lines and moved up the Moscow highway until it reached the outer defences of the capital.

To stop the advance, Red Army artillerists bombarded the division with rockets fired from a weapon known as the 'Stalin Organ' or 'Katyusha', a device that could hurl 20 projectiles into the air at a time. On the receiving end of this barrage, an officer attached to divisional tactical headquarters recalled the effect created by the weapon: 'As I had not dug a slit trench, I just flung myself behind a tree and watched the terrifyingly beautiful display of exploding rocket shells.' From this vantage point, he noted, 'the memory of the smell of high-explosive and of black, red and violet colours as the shells detonated and took on the shape of tulip heads will always remain in my mind'. During the advance, Paul Hausser had been severely wounded in action and was replaced by the commander of the *Deutschland* Regiment, Willi Bittrich.

By mid-October, the *Reich* Division was launching a full-scale attack upon the outer defences of the Soviet

Right: *Reich* Division soldiers take cover in a shallow ditch as a building burns dramatically behind them. The division's progress was steady, but the weather was already beginning to worsen as autumn approached.

capital. Spearheading this assault, the battalions of *Der Führer* pushed through five roadblocks, dug-in tanks, and teams of flame-throwers and managed to destroy several concrete pillboxes. In a battle that lasted through the night, the SS grenadiers engaged in ferocious, hand-to-hand combat with crack troops from the 32nd Siberian Division. For two weeks, savage fighting persisted. Although the Germans had battered enemy defences relentlessly and captured the town of Mozhiask, they were becoming worn out from high casualty rates, fatigue, disease and a climate that was becoming increasingly cold.

North of the Moscow highway, the *Deutschland* Regiment confronted two Mongolian infantry battalions from the 82nd Motorized Division during a fight for Mikaelovkoya and Pushkin. Charging through a hail of rocket shells, the SS soldiers reached a village close to Mikaelovkoya. Supported by artillery and tank units, the Mongols counterattacked with human-wave assaults. In close-quarter fighting, many of the combatants killed each other with bayonets, grenades and entrenching tools. Eventually, the *Deutschland* Regiment's grenadiers beat back this offensive only with a great deal of effort and considerable help from SS artillery batteries.

POOR WEATHER

Several weeks after the start of Operation 'Barbarossa', the wet autumn weather played an important role in preventing the German war machine from taking Moscow. The inability of supply trucks to reach the *Reich* Division and other units situated on the front line of the offensive led to chronic shortages of ammunition, food and fuel. These only worsened as the season came to an end. In fact, weather conditions even hindered panzer units from moving forward to support the SS foot soldiers. Although the onset of winter eventually solidified the ground upon which the Germans travelled by freezing it, the new season created a new set of problems for the armies of the Third Reich.

Because Hitler and his generals were so confident that their armies would capture Moscow before the end of the year, they did not even consider equipping their soldiers with winter uniforms. When temperatures dropped to levels ranging from -30 to -50°C, numerous cases of frostbite broke out within the German ranks. In some instances, frozen limbs became racked with gangrene, leading to hasty amputation operations under unsanitary conditions and without anesthesia. To save themselves from their second enemy, 'General Winter', German soldiers acquired extra layers of clothing from the many dead comrades and adversaries that littered the countryside. When their boots rotted away after several months of continuous use, they wrapped their feet in rags.

Not surprisingly, the Red Army was far better prepared for the cold months of 1941 and 1942. As

Left: Making the most of their issued equipment, these SS panzergrenadiers from the *Reich* Division huddle around a small fire. The division was ill-equipped to cope with the sudden fall in temperatures caused by the onset of autumn.

natives of the area, many of them were already accustomed to the inhospitable climate and knew in advance how to dress for it. Some Soviet units were also equipped to travel across the deep snow quickly and easily using skis. With these advantages, the Red Army was able to launch numerous surprise counterattacks from mid-October until mid-November, while the Germans attempted to adjust to the demands of the winter weather and consolidate their control over conquered areas.

After absorbing these counter-punches, the Germans resumed their offensive on Moscow. On 18 November, XLVI Corps received an order to seize the city of Istra. In a two-pronged assault, the *Reich* Division constituted the right wing of the operation, while the 10th Panzer Division took the left. By capturing this city and other important areas around

Above: An ominous portent: soldiers of the *Reich* Division in the first snow of winter. They are marching past an abandoned Soviet field gun which has become bogged down to its axles in the Russian mud.

Moscow, the Germans hoped to encircle the capital and destroy its garrison in a manner similar to the manoeuvre carried out at Kiev.

Within a week, the SS units had fought their way to the River Istra and established a bridgehead there. After crossing the river, the *Reich* Division attacked approaching enemy forces and sent them into flight. Two days later, the SS troops seized Istra and attacked a nearby town that was situated on top of an important ridge. Although the Soviet garrison resisted tenaciously, after four days of combat the Germans finally took the heights, with tanks from the 10th Panzer

Division providing crucial assistance for the SS grenadiers storming up the slopes.

With this important cornerstone in the Russian defence network now in German hands, a fully fledged attack on Moscow began on 27 November. During this decisive phase in Operation 'Typhoon', the *Reich* Division seized Vyssokova within a day and closed in on the capital. Despite this continuous forward progress that seemed to be carrying the division to its destination, heavy losses from combat and the cold weather were depleting the SS units. The attack was steadily grinding to a halt.

By the end of the month, Bittrich was forced to disband the *Der Führer*'s severely depleted 2nd Battalion and assign its survivors to other parts of the regiment. He also had to break up *Deutschland*'s 3rd Battalion for the same reason. Meanwhile, the 10th

Above: So close – men of the *Reich* Division pose for the camera near the outer suburbs of Moscow. The solid nature of their bunker suggests that they have adopted a strictly defensive attitude in the face of winter.

Panzer Division had only seven tanks available to assist the SS division in future operations against the Moscow garrison. Only the sheer determination of the division's soldiers and their faith in their own fighting abilities seemed to hold the unit together and keep it on the field as a viable military force.

When Luftwaffe bombers flew overhead to carry out missions against the Soviet garrison at the capital, the SS soldiers found encouragement in their miserable state. Despite their predicament, they were still motivated to continue attacking the capital. In early December, the vanguard of the German offensive reached its easternmost point when No. 1 Company of the Motorcycle Battalion seized Lenino, a suburb situated only 17km (10.5 miles) from central Moscow. Occupying areas near the terminus of the Moscow tramway system, the SS soldiers could see the domed buildings of the Kremlin.

Before the *Reich* Division and other German formations could follow through with a decisive attack on the capital, worsening weather conditions forced them to stop in their tracks. Their final offensive was, so they thought, only delayed, but after a three-day pause in the fighting, the Soviets launched a counter-offensive. It was so great that the Germans had no chance to organize their attack. Collectively, the Red Army hurled 1.5 million troops into the Germans at areas throughout the Eastern Front. Organized into 17 armies, these hordes of Soviet soldiers pushed their enemies back, forcing the German Army High Command to order a general retreat to more defensible positions.

HUMAN WAVE ATTACKS

At its positions near Moscow, the *Reich* Division stood its ground as human-wave formations assailed its troops. With concentrated machine-gun fire, the *Deutschland* Regiment kept the Soviets at bay. The division finally received its order to retreat on 9 December 1941 and, although its soldiers were despondent at the thought of giving up so much territory which had been won with such tremendous sacrifice, it withdrew across the River Istra. Fortunately for the weary SS men, the Red Army was very cautious with its pursuit. Along the River Rusa, the division maintained its part of the new German defence line until the end of the year.

On 16 January 1942, the *Reich* Division received another order to retreat and thus pulled back to a position west of Gshatsk. During the execution of these strategic withdrawals, Soviet attacks along the front persisted. Later in the month, the SS division participated in a spectacular counter-attack around Rzhev, after the Russian 29th and 39th Armies had punched through German lines. Sweeping into an area west of the city, the Russian armies suddenly

became isolated after the German 9th Army had swung northwards and established blocking positions to their east.

For more than two weeks, the SS units and other German military formations battered the entrapped Soviet armies while the Russians fought desperately to break out of their pocket. In addition, the Germans contended with relief columns sent to rescue the cornered Soviets. Otto Kumm, the commander of the *Der Führer* Regiment, noted in these battles that 'the enemy dead formed walls of corpses in front of the companies' positions'. Although they continued to suffer high casualty rates, the SS soldiers remained enthusiastic, as long as they were able to perform offensive actions.

Meanwhile, the weather became even colder, actually freezing the oil that lubricated the German machine-guns and rendering these weapons useless. The merciless winter climate also disabled all of the SP vehicles of the *Reich* Division, causing Bittrich to disband the SP unit and transfer most of its members to the *Der Führer* Regiment. Some of them went back to Vienna to receive training in panzer warfare. Eventually, about 5000 Russians managed to slip through the Nazi gauntlet and reach friendly forces. However, they left behind 27,000 men dead and another 5000, who were to become prisoners of war.

Despite this setback, the Red Army renewed its pressure on the German lines throughout February. Near the end of that month, the *Reich* Division was placed on reserve. Because the division was so depleted, the German High Command temporarily renamed it the *Das Reich* Battle Group. After receiving 3000 new men to replenish its battalions, the *Der Führer* Regiment became a panzergrenadier unit.

In March, the SS battle group went back into action, taking up positions along the River Volga. Towards the end of the month, the soldiers in this organization had to contend with yet another enemy offensive, which lasted until early April. During this action, the *Deutschland* Regiment became involved in a particularly nasty battle at a place known as 'Jackboot Wood'. Georg Schwinke, a participant, noted that 'the whole terrain was brown with the

Above: A well-armed patrol from the _Der Führer_ Regiment. The cold was so severe that lubricating oil froze weapons solid, rendering them useless. Grenades were unaffected, which is why the men carry so many.

overcoats of the advancing Russian soldiers. This mass of men rolled towards us, terrifying because they came forward silently and without their usual shouting.'

During this battle, the soldiers in the _Deutschland_ Regiment repelled wave after wave of massed attacks. 'The Russians fell in rows,' Schwinke asserted, 'piling up into a great heap of dead. Most of that first wave had come forward without weapons – cannon-fodder – to use up our ammunition.' After running low on ammunition, the Germans were forced to beat back their opponents in brutal, hand-to-hand combat. 'Finally,' Schwinke observed, 'the Russians sent in tanks and like primeval beasts they came lumbering towards us.'

By this time, the _Deutschland_ Regiment seemed to be on the brink of annihilation. However, Stuka dive-bombers arrived in the nick of time. 'Those pilots really knew their job,' Schwinke asserted, noting that 'tank after tank was blown apart. Just before I pressed my face into the muddy snow I saw a bomb glide under the belly of one tank and blow it up.' Shortly afterward, friendly tanks and SPs appeared on the scene and helped the SS regiment smash the Russian assault on Jackboot Wood, thus enabling the division to stabilize its lines.

JACKBOOT WOOD

In the aftermath of battle, Schwinke noticed that he had been wounded by an artillery attack and recorded that he 'pulled the shell fragment out of my skull'. Also injured by a bullet in the right leg, he limped to his company headquarters, where his commander attempted to remove his jackboot. But the leg proved to be too swollen, so the officer 'cut the boot off and pus and blood poured out from the leg which was now coloured dark-blue and black ... frostbite'. Ordered to report to a field hospital, Schwinke noted that 'because there were no ambulances I had to make my own way back on foot and out of that damned "Jackboot Wood"'.

By early April, the Soviet counter-offensive had finally abated, allowing German forces along the Eastern Front to experience at least some rest and recuperation. Two months later, the _Reich_ Division returned to Germany to undergo reorganization and receive yet another name. In November, it became known as the SS Panzergrenadier Division _Das Reich_. It also acquired a panzer battalion that contained three companies and PzKpfw III and IV battle tanks. Protected with armour that was at least 50mm (1.9in) thick in some places, the PzKpfw III was capable of reaching a speed of 64km/h (40mph). The PzKpfw IV had similar characteristics but was equipped with a much larger gun mounted into the turret.

In addition, existing units within the division underwent changes for the better. The _Der Führer_ Regiment now became fully motorized. The Reconnaissance Battalion exchanged its motorcycles

for *Schwimmwagen* cars and became 1st Battalion of the newly established *Langemarck* Regiment. Meanwhile, the surviving remnants of the 4th SS-Regiment *Deutschland* constituted the regiment's 2nd Battalion. In early July, the *Der Führer* Regiment went to Le Mans. The rest of the division eventually followed and remained in that part of France until late in the year.

In November 1942, the *Das Reich* Division and several other German military formations moved south and occupied Vichy France, the part of the country that Hitler had spared from conquest back in 1940. The Führer had ordered action at this point because the Allies had invaded French North Africa, and were thus in a position to attack Western Europe from the south. For good reason, the Germans suspected that Marshal Pétain and his deputy, Pierre Laval, would not be able to mount a successful

Above: *Schwimmwagens* **from the** *Reich* **Division's Reconnaissance Battalion prepare to cross a river. A propeller at the rear of the vehicle meant that it could cross water at a maximum speed of 11km/h (7 mph).**

defence if the Allies were to land on the Mediterranean coast of France.

At the end of the year, the *Das Reich* Division underwent more changes. It received an SP battalion that contained three batteries, each one possessing seven guns. In addition, the *Langemarck* Regiment was disbanded. Some of its members were re-assigned to the Panzer Battalion, which was now large enough to be a full-size regiment, while 1st Battalion resumed its role as a separate reconnaissance unit. Thus reorganized, the division returned to the Soviet Union in January 1943, ready to help Army Group South repel a Red Army offensive in the Ukraine.

CHAPTER SEVEN

KURSK

Rested, rearmed and refitted as a fully-fledged panzergrenadier division, *Das Reich* was now a formidable fighting unit. However by early 1943 the German forces on the Eastern Front were so hard-pressed that the division was soon rushed back to the front line.

By late 1942, the tide of World War II began to turn against the Third Reich. In North Africa, German forces under the command of Field Marshal Erwin Rommel suffered a decisive defeat at El Alamein. On the Eastern Front, the Red Army dealt a more serious blow to the Nazi war effort when the Soviets launched a winter offensive that smashed several Romanian, Italian and Hungarian divisions, forcing Axis troops in the area to fall back to the River Dnieper. At Stalingrad, the Russians encircled the German 6th Army and repulsed all attempts to relieve the beleaguered garrison. By February 1943, the city and the surviving remnants of the German Army had fallen into Russian hands. Three months later, Allied forces swept their Axis adversaries completely out of North Africa.

To help blunt the Soviet assault against German positions on the Eastern Front, Adolf Hitler dispatched the recently organized I SS Panzer Corps into the area. After performing this mission, the SS troops were to initiate an aggressive counter-offensive, aimed at retaking the territory that had been lost to the Russians. Led by *SS-Obergruppenführer* Paul Hausser, the corps included three of the best divisions in the German armed forces: *Leibstandarte*, *Totenkopf*, and *Das Reich*, which was now under the command of *SS-Gruppenführer* Georg Keppler. All three of these divisions had been reorganized as panzergrenadier formations.

TOP PRIORITY MOVE

In January 1943, the SS corps went to the southern sector of the front to repel an attack that had been launched by the Soviet 3rd Guards Tank Army. Because their presence in the region was so desperately needed, the SS divisions received top priority in the use of road and rail transportation. After assembling at an area near the city of Kharkov, Hausser's forces were to maintain a bridgehead situated between Volokomovka and Kupiansk on the River Oskol. Although the SS corps was supposed to operate as a unified organization, the exigencies of war forced Army Group South to disperse its elements into different areas.

Das Reich was the first SS division to reach the front. Arriving in the middle of January, the *Der Führer* Regiment was in the area before the other elements of the division and immediately went to work against the Soviet war machine. West of the

Left: Heinrich Himmler congratulates members of the Panzer Regiment of *Das Reich* after their success in the retaking of Kharkov in the spring of 1943. The *Reichsführer-SS* was careful not to be too close to the front.

Above: A *Das Reich* armoured column with three PzKpfw IV tanks bringing up the rear during the operation to retake Kharkov in early 1943. Note the divisional symbol on the rear of the tank resembling an inverted *pi*.

River Oskol, the soldiers of the Red Army seemed as if they were about to achieve a breakthrough at Voroshilovgrad. To prevent such a disaster for the Germans, Army Group South formed a battle group that was comprised of *Der Führer*'s 1st Battalion, two field artillery batteries, one Flak battery, and two companies from other parts of the regiment. Attached to the 6th Panzer Division, this battle group was to aid in the defence of the town. On 22 January, the SS troops marched 205km (127 miles) to their battle zone and remained there until early March.

By the end of the month, the main part of I SS Panzer Corps had arrived and was arrayed at its assigned position on the River Oskol. While 2nd Battalion, *Der Führer* Regiment occupied a sector close to the river, the *Deutschland* Regiment covered a piece of woodland south-west of Kamenka, as well as areas west of Borki, Kosinka and Olovatka. As the SS troops moved into their positions, they encountered the

surviving remnants of the decimated Italian 8th Army retreating past the front lines and into safer areas. In addition, several depleted German units filed past the SS formations, including the 320th Division. Hausser's troops quickly learned from the demoralized state of these withdrawing forces that they would face formidable adversaries in the southern sector of the Eastern Front.

Shortly after taking up their positions along the River Oskol, the commanding officers in the SS corps learned that the Red Army had ripped large holes in the German defence line and recaptured a considerable amount of territory, including the important city of Kursk. The Russians were also in close pursuit of the rearguard elements of the Italian and Romanian armies that they had mauled. Moreover, intelligence sources soon revealed that the Soviets intended to push the Germans back to the River Dnieper and thus retake the city of Kharkov. As a result, Army Group South had to utilize the SS corps as a defensive group, despite the fact that Hitler had envisioned this new formation as an offensive weapon.

Fortunately for the soldiers in *Das Reich* and the other SS divisions, the Red Army winter offensive was just starting to lose its momentum by the time Hausser arrived. By late January, the Soviets had strained their logistical lines and lacked ammunition for their infantry, artillery and armoured units. Although the Red Army still had plenty of troops to hurl at the Germans, its dwindling firepower enabled the SS units to hold their ground more effectively and perhaps maintain enough strength to mount a punishing counter-offensive.

MASSED ATTACKS

As soon as the regiments and battalions of the *Das Reich* Division settled into their assigned positions, they had to beat back attacks being launched by division-size Soviet forces. By utilizing their overwhelming numerical superiority, the Red Army units gradually pushed back 2nd Battalion, *Der Führer* Regiment and forced it to withdraw from its bridgehead on the River Oskol in early February. As the Soviets approached the River Donetz and came closer to Kharkov, they created a salient that separated the main part of the *Das Reich* Division from its Reconnaissance Battalion.

On 7 February, the Red Army launched a new offensive that was aimed at taking Kharkov. To achieve this objective, Stavka (the High Command of the Soviet Armed Forces) developed a plan that called for a pincer movement that would force I SS Panzer Corps either to evacuate the city or remain entrapped in a pocket. The southern arm of this two-pronged assault covered a wide area located between the right flank of the *Leibstandarte* and the left flank of the 320th Division. The northern arm was less imposing and was situated north-east of Belgorod.

Although they were aware that this offensive would probably result in the encirclement of Kharkov, the Germans attempted to relocate to defensive positions on the western bank of the Donets which they hoped would be adequate enough to hold the city without being surrounded. Thus, the *Das Reich* Division pulled back from its area along the Oskol on 9 February during a heavy blizzard. Obscured by the weather conditions, Soviet snipers harassed the retreating Germans, who were forced to march across ground that was covered with deep snow. Not surprisingly, many vehicles got stuck during this retreat.

On the other side of the Donets, the SS soldiers were dismayed to find out that the Russians had already reached the area. As a result, the *Das Reich* Division pulled back even further and set up new positions much closer to Kharkov. To thwart the Soviet pincer action that threatened to entrap in the city, Hausser ordered a bold counter-attack against the southern arm of the Red Army advance. His plan called for a battle group to sweep southward and sever this appendage from the main part of the Soviet juggernaut.

To ensure that his battle group had enough men to accomplish this task, Hausser had to pull some of his troops from the front lines. He also moved his divisions further to the west to give the task force more time to perform its mission. This unit consisted of the *Der Führer* Regiment and the Motorcycle Battalion from the *Das Reich* Division, along with two units from the *Leibstandarte* Division. On 10 February, the battle group assembled at the town of Merefa to start its operation.

The following day, the SS units sprang into action. While the two *Das Reich* formations constituted the centre of the counter-attack, the other two SS units occupied the flanks. Although confronted with punishing snowstorms, the battle group travelled quickly until its armoured vehicles approached enemy rear echelon units 50km (31 miles) behind the Russian lines. While the SS took their opponents by surprise, Stuka dive-bombers hammered Red Army positions from the sky. Within a short period of time, the Germans amputated the southern pincer of the Soviet attack and obliterated the 7th Guard Cavalry Corps.

Left: Paul Hausser, now commander of the I SS Panzer Corps, seen here in the turret of a PzKpfw III tank of *Das Reich*'s Panzer Regiment when visiting his old division during an inspection in March 1943.

German panzer and artillery units also wreaked havoc upon the Red Army attack.

Despite these high casualty rates, the Soviets used their seemingly limitless supply of manpower to push the SS divisions back closer to Kharkov. Vastly outnumbered and severely depleted, the Germans relied upon their discipline, training, dedication and courage to keep the Red Army from collapsing their lines and sending them into a panicked rout. Although he had been ordered by Hitler to hold the city at all costs, Hausser found this task increasingly difficult when the Soviets seized Belgorod and were now moving north-west of the SS corps: the Germans were threatened with another possible encirclement.

To the north-east, the Russians were punching holes in the perimeter around Kharkov. By the evening of the 14th February, they had pushed into the suburbs and were penetrating rear echelon areas of the SS Panzer Corps. To buy more time, a group of battle tanks from the *Das Reich* Division launched a punishing counter-attack in the north-western part of the city. Although this action brought a temporary halt to the Soviet offensive on Kharkov, it seemed as if Hausser's troops were slipping into another pincer.

SUGGESTED WITHDRAWAL

Determined to see his division survive this ordeal, Hausser advised his superior officers in Army Group South to allow him to pull his corps out of Kharkov. To dramatize the futility of remaining in the city, he predicted that the Soviets would take it within two or three days, even if he sacrificed every man in his command. In response to this plea, the *Wehrmacht* strategists merely reiterated to Hausser that the order to hold Kharkov had come from Hitler himself. Thus, in order to save his command from annihilation, Hausser had to defy his Führer and, on 15 February, order an evacuation.

With Soviet troops closing in on Kharkov, the withdrawal from the city became a harrowing experience.

After performing this feat, the SS battle group continued moving south until it made contact with soldiers from the 320th Division. With this mission complete, Hausser broke apart the group and returned its units to their respective divisions. Although these units had suffered heavy losses during the counter-attack, their men were in high spirits and gratified by the result of the operation. By this time, Keppler had to step down as commander of the *Das Reich* Division because of a brain haemorrhage, and was replaced by Herbert Ernst Vahl.

Undeterred by this setback, the Red Army renewed its offensive on Kharkov. Although the SS divisions held their ground at Rogan and Ternovoya, the Soviets had more success to the south, and seized the suburb of Smiyev. Fortunately for the SS corps, overextended supply lines prevented enemy infantrymen from receiving adequate artillery support. As a result, they suffered terrible losses in wave after wave of assaults against positions that were protected by MG 42 machine guns. A new weapon in the German arsenal, the MG 42 had a rapid rate of fire and a deafening noise. The Soviets referred to it as 'Hitler's Saw'.

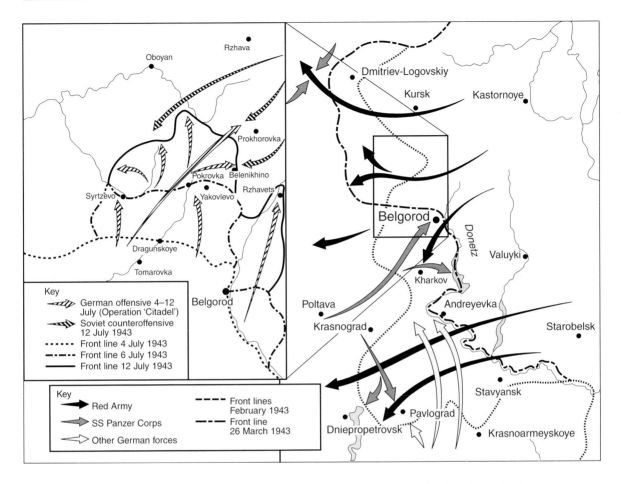

Above: The map on the right shows the German response to the Soviet offensive which resulted in the recapture of Kharkov, while the enlarged box show the I SS Panzer Corps' role in the German Kursk offensive of July 1943.

Although *Das Reich* panzer units had repulsed an enemy attack north-west of the city, Russian armoured groups managed to seize part of Rogan and thus tighten the gauntlet that seemed to be ensnaring the SS divisions. With the SS corps now confined to a narrow 1.6km- (1 mile-) wide corridor running from the centre of Kharkov to the German lines, the Russians were able to pour a rain of artillery shells into the city while the Germans evacuated.

As the Red Army tightened its grip, Hausser received two more orders to remain in Kharkov, even as his corps was preparing to retreat. Not surprisingly, he paid little attention to these messages. While the SS corps pulled out, Hitler personally visited the headquarters of Army Group South at Zaporozhye. Incensed that his order to hold Kharkov at all costs

had been disobeyed, he ordered the group commander, Field Marshal Erich von Manstein, to place Hausser's troops at the front of a counter-attack which would be aimed at re-taking the city.

Late in the afternoon, the Soviets pushed through the south-eastern suburbs. By this time, Hausser was leading his divisions south of the city until they re-grouped at an area on the opposite bank of the River Udy. The Russians were now able to capture Kharkov, but their success placed them in a salient that rendered them vulnerable to a punishing

offensive. This might produce a result similar to the one they had achieved against I SS Panzer Corps. Presented with such a promising opportunity, Manstein wasted no time planning a counter-attack. In his battle plan, the SS corps was to serve as the upper arm in a pincer movement around the city, while the rest of the 4th Panzer Army constituted the lower arm.

REORGANIZATION

During the preparation for this counter-attack, some elements of I SS Panzer Corps underwent reorganization to adjust for the severe losses suffered during the defence of Kharkov. Within the *Das Reich* Division, the surviving members of the Panzer Regiment were assembled into a single battalion. With more than half of its vehicles destroyed or disabled, the tank unit was incapable of functioning as a full-size regiment. Other depleted regiments within the corps experienced similar amalgamation. While the SS corps underwent these changes, Hausser congratulated his men for their willingness to work together under

Above: Soldiers from the SS-Panzergrenadier Division **Das Reich enter Kharkhov in March 1943. They are riding on a PzKpfw III Ausf M tank which has the more common divisional symbol on its right rear.**

extremely adverse conditions. He was particularly pleased with the ability of diverse units that had never worked together to cooperate and coordinate their offensive and defensive actions.

In late February, the Red Army was still pressing the German lines, but with much less speed or force. South of Kharkov, the Voronezh Front was heading due west. Meanwhile, the South-West and South Fronts moved south-west to establish bridgeheads on the Dnieper and seize the city of Dniepropetrovsk. Before he could re-take Kharkov, Manstein had to destroy these enemy forces that were advancing on Dniepropetrovsk. At the time, his Army Group South occupied an area between Rostov and Krasnograd.

From 19 February to 4 March, the Germans thus waged an aggressive counter-attack in an area between the Donets and Dnieper rivers. At the start of the operation, fog, snowfall and dampness bedevilled soldiers on both sides. Charged with the task of seizing Peretschepino and destroying all enemy forces west and south-west of Krasnograd, the *Das Reich* Division marched into battle with companies that had an average size of only 60 men. To get to their objective, the SS soldiers had to negotiate their way through a minefield.

Because the batteries in their mine detectors were dead, the men of the *Deutschland* Regiment were forced to locate the concealed explosives by sticking their bayonets into the snow. After they cleared a path for the division, 3rd Battalion, *Der Führer* Regiment rushed through and spearheaded the drive to Peretschepino. Supported by SP and tank units, the battalion ripped into the enemy flank and blocked a main road that the Red Army was using to reach the Dnieper. After repulsing several assaults on this position, the SS troops settled into the area for the night. During the course of the day, they had advanced roughly 90km (56 miles). When they received a letter of encouragement from Hitler, they were even more motivated to continue their mission.

The following day, the division received an order to proceed another 60km (37 miles) and seize a different objective, the town of Pavlograd. By this time, weather conditions had improved. During their advance to this new objective, the SS units noticed a Soviet force – comprising a regiment with five tanks – approaching the Dnieper. While the *Deutschland* Regiment prepared an ambush, a squadron of Stukas descended from the sky and knocked out four tanks. The SS regiment then destroyed the fifth, as well as two artillery pieces. After sweeping aside the surviving remnants of the Russian regiment, the division seized the town on 24 February.

At nearby sectors, other German divisions experienced similar success. As a result, Manstein's forces were able to blunt the Red Army's thrust to the Dnieper and push the Soviets out of areas south of Kharkov. With this task accomplished, the *Das Reich* Division headed north-east to capture the city. Determined to hold Kharkov at all costs, Stavka sent fresh reinforcements against the Germans. In addition, the Soviet High Command dispatched the 1st Guards Army and six tank formations into the region to launch another attack on Dniepropetrovsk.

Before the Russian Army could attempt this feat, it had to defend the important railway centre of Losovaya, which was being attacked by the *Das Reich* and *Totenkopf* divisions. After a three-day battle, the SS divisions routed the Red Army and captured the town. By the end of the month, the SS corps and other formations within the 4th Panzer Army had created a salient that was 100km (62 miles) wide and extended 120km (75 miles) east into Soviet-held territory.

NEW OPPORTUNITY

The next objective for the *Das Reich* Division was the seizure of the heights surrounding Yefremovka. In the late night of 1 March, the division began this operation amid a heavy downpour that turned roads into muddy creeks. During this sluggish move towards the objective, the Russian 3rd Tank Army moved into an area near Bereka so that it was now positioned between the *Das Reich* and *Leibstandarte* divisions. When notified of this, Hausser immediately recognized an opportunity to entrap the enemy force, and ordered the two SS divisions to swing around and cut off any retreat to the east.

In an ensuing battle that lasted for three days, the SS divisions had difficulty receiving adequate amounts of equipment. Foul weather and poor road conditions were preventing supply trucks from reaching combat units. Heinz Macher, a company commander in the *Das Reich* Pioneer Battalion, noted the problem created by the ensuing ammunition shortages during the fighting at Yefremovka. 'In a bomb crater only five metres from us two Russian soldiers were defending themselves bravely,' he recalled, 'fighting for their lives.' Because Macher and his battalion commander had no hand-grenades left, 'we each picked up pieces of ice and rock and threw them at the enemy. They naturally thought we were throwing hand-grenades and ducked. We leapt up, rushed forward and in a short charge had soon over-powered and disarmed them'.

Despite the problems created by chronic shortages of ammunition and supplies, the Germans relentlessly hammered the 3rd Tank Army. During the course of the battle, they obliterated three infantry divisions, three tank brigades, and a cavalry corps. Since the start of Manstein's counter-offensive, the actions carried out by the divisions of Army Group South had led to the death or capture of roughly 100,000 Soviet soldiers.

KHARKOV REGAINED

At Hitler's insistence, Manstein assigned to the SS Panzer Corps a major role in the recapture of the city. This task became somewhat easier when Red Army forces west and north-west of Kharkov withdrew to the east. In early March, the SS divisions moved towards their objective. During the advance, the *Der Führer* Regiment guarded the eastern flank of the corps. As he approached Kharkov, Hausser assembled a battle group consisting of 3rd Battalion, *Deutschland* Regiment and a panzer battalion from the *Totenkopf* Division. With little effort, this battle group seized a suburban area west of the city and prepared for the German attack that was to begin on the morning of the 11th March.

The attack on Kharkov began as scheduled, and a savage battle for possession of the city quickly ensued. By mid-afternoon, SS troops had taken the Salyutine railway station and were beating back the Soviet attempts to re-take the facility. Fighting within the southern section of the city, the *Der Führer* Regiment pushed through well-defended enemy positions and blocked the Udy–Merefa Road. In the northern part of Kharkov, the *Deutschland* Regiment encountered more stubborn resistance until its 3rd Battalion outflanked the Russians and forced them to retreat.

Later in the day, the commander of the 4th Panzer Army ordered the *Das Reich* Division to spearhead an assault into the centre of Kharkov and entrap an enemy garrison occupying the industrial district, which was located in the south-eastern part of the city. To accomplish this task, the *Deutschland* Regiment's 16th (Pioneer) Company had to capture an anti-tank ditch and establish a bridgehead that would enable the division's heavy vehicles to reach the objective.

Led by *SS-Untersturmführer* Heinz Macher, the pioneer company was to deal with the enemy troops which were now occupying houses located behind the ditch. The Russians had the advantage of a good view from which they were able to shoot at the Germans.

In the early morning of 13 March, Macher led his troops to the ditch under a covering barrage from an artillery battery. Despite this aid, the pioneers drew fire from several directions as they crossed the obstacle. Undeterred, the SS unit fought its way past mortar- and machine-gun fire and seized a group of houses adjacent to the anti-tank trench. With their bridgehead secure, the rest of the regiment moved across and pressed on to the city centre. To enable the SPs to move forward, the pioneers broke down the walls of the ditch. Eventually, the *Der Führer/ Totenkopf* panzer battle group arrived to join the drive deep into the city.

By this time, enemy resistance had begun to waver. Although the Russians within Kharkov still had superior numbers and firepower, they were becoming disorganized, demoralized and worn down from the continuous fighting. As the SS divisions drove further into the city, their troops fought and decimated the 1st and 2nd Tank Guard Corps, as well as four infantry divisions. On 15 March, the Germans destroyed the last remnants of the Red Army garrison at a tractor factory located 6km (3.7 miles) east of the city. With this feat accomplished, Kharkov once again fell into Manstein's hands.

Without spending much time savouring his achievement, the Field Marshal resolved to press his advantage. Sensing the potential to do yet more damage to the Soviet war machine, he planned further attacks that were aimed at re-taking more of the territory that the Germans had lost to the Red Army winter offensive of 1942–43. Ultimately, he and other senior strategists in Army Group South hoped to destroy Soviet forces occupying a large salient around Kursk, and then recapture the city.

Right: A patrol from I SS Panzer Corps inside the recaptured city of Kharkov in March 1943. Manstein's counterattack was timed to catch the Soviet forces when they were over-extended and short of supplies.

On 19 March, the Germans seized the town of Belgorod, thus securing uncontested control over all land situated between the Dnieper and Donets Rivers. By this time, the spring thaw had swept across the Ukrainian landscape, melting the snow and covering the ground with large amounts of mud. Motorized transportation was hindered by the weather and as a result, the attack on Kursk had to wait.

FURTHER CHANGES

During this break in the fighting, the *Das Reich* Division underwent more reorganization and re-supply to adjust for the losses suffered during the fight for Kharkov. Most notably, many artillery batteries traded in their static field pieces for SP guns. In addition, Hausser's organization acquired a

Above: Men from *Das Reich* take up positions in front of an unidentified village during the opening stages of Operation 'Citadel', the attack on the salient around Kursk in July 1943.

new name and would now be known as II SS Panzer Corps. The *Das Reich* Division also experienced changes in leadership. Its commander, Herbert Ernst Vahl, had been severely wounded in action and was temporarily replaced by *SS-Oberführer* Kurt Brasack. Finally, the commander of the *Der Führer* Regiment, Otto Kumm, received the Oak Leaves Medal and a promotion that transferred him out of the division. Eventually, he went to Yugoslavia and became the commander of 7th *SS Freiwilligen-Gebirgs* Division *Prinz Eugen*.

Meanwhile, most of the soldiers of *Das Reich* and other divisions stationed in the area did their best to co-exist peacefully with the local population. To facilitate cordial relations, some German units provided the malnourished residents of Kharkov and nearby areas with bread and soup. Soldiers from *Das Reich* who were quartered in Soviet houses generally treated their hosts with respect. The Germans also employed cobblers and skilled artisans who were able to make decent money mending boots and other useful equipment.

Indoctrination Ignored

In many instances, the SS soldiers ignored their Nazi racial indoctrination and openly fraternized with the Slavic 'subhumans'. Before the attack on Kursk, the Germans and their Ukrainian hosts even staged dances and feasts to pass the time. Despite its origin

as an armed branch of the NSDAP, the *Waffen-SS* was becoming less political and developing an affinity with the *Wehrmacht*. Like their Army counterparts, many SS soldiers were more interested in waging a successful war against a Bolshevik regime than in imposing an oppressive racial order upon Eastern Europe. The Aryan 'supermen' of the *Waffen-SS* were all too willing to accept anti-communist Russians, Ukrainians and other Slavic groups into its ranks.

Ironically, the most noticeable tension to emerge during this brief pause in the fighting took place between the frontline soldiers and the Nazi officials

Below: A company of *Das Reich* PzKpfw V Panther tanks are given the order to attack. The offensive had been delayed to allow more Panthers to reach the front lines, but the early models proved to be unreliable.

returning to restore order to the area. When these bureaucrats found SS and Army troops occupying facilities that had belonged to the bureaucrats before the Soviet winter offensive, fighting often broke out. Not surprisingly, the combat veterans usually prevailed in these brawls.

KURSK THE OBJECTIVE

By the summer of 1943, both sides knew that Kursk would be the next target for the German armed forces in the Eastern Front. Because Hitler and OKH anticipated that an invasion somewhere in Western Europe would be launched by British and American forces, they sought to score a decisive victory in the Soviet Union. If the Germans succeeded in collapsing the Russian salient around Kursk, they could shorten their front line by about 500km (311 miles). With less territory to cover, OKH could send more divisions to France, Italy and other possible sites of an Allied landing. Moreover, such an achievement might inflict

Above: A StuG III assault gun from *Das Reich* waits for the order to attack again with its accompanying section of panzergrenadiers. Its *Schurzen* or 'side skirts' of armour have either been removed or ripped off in battle.

severe damage and even destroy the Red Army, thus enabling the Axis powers to deal with this threat to the west more effectively.

Like earlier offensives in the region, Operation 'Citadel' was to be a pincer action against Soviet forces at Kursk. North of the city, Field Marshal Walther Model was to lead his 9th Army into the upper wall of the salient with three panzer corps. On the other side of the salient, General Hermann Hoth and the three panzer corps within his 4th Panzer Army were to strike from the south. Hausser's SS divisions were attached to this latter organization. Essentially, the objective of the operation was similar to that which had been accomplished at Kiev. The two armies were to drive inwards until they linked up, thus pinching off the salient and turning it into an isolated pocket filled with trapped Soviet forces.

When Communist agents confirmed that the next German offensive would take place at Kursk, the Red Army prepared an elaborate network of defences around the salient. Its troops excavated several layers of trenches and laid minefields at important locations. Soviet commanders also positioned anti-tank units throughout the salient to blunt the panzer formations. Stavka hoped that if the Germans suffered a decisive defeat in Operation 'Citadel', then the Red Army might be able to launch a punishing counter-offensive and break the back of the Nazi war machine.

SOVIET ATTACK

To deprive the Germans of much-needed manpower for the offensive, the Red Army launched an attack against the 2nd Panzer Army, which was situated north of the 9th Army. By performing this manoeuvre, Stavka intended to expose the left flank of the 9th Army, thus forcing Model to divert some of his forces from the Kursk attack. Although this action seemed to be a sensible tactic, it was based upon an erroneous assumption. The Soviets thought that the main part of the German offensive would be at the northern wall of the salient, when the larger concentration of forces was actually in the south.

On 28 June, Hoth and his staff received an intelligence report indicating that the Red Army had four infantry divisions arrayed across the first line of trenches in the sector facing his army, as well as two more divisions on the second line. The senior commanders of the 4th Panzer Army also suspected that the Soviets had at least two armoured corps in the area. Aware that a penetration of these lines of defence would bring a swift counter-attack upon both of their flanks, Hoth and his strategists issued instructions to their divisions.

First, the three corps under Hoth's command were to break through the first two lines of defence at an area near Belgorod. On the left, XLVIII Panzer Corps was to head towards the town of Syrtzevo, while an armoured formation known as Operational Group

Kempf drove across an area east of Belgorod. Between these two organizations, II SS Panzer Corps was to play the most important role in the southern pincer of the offensive. Hausser's divisions were to head toward the towns of Pokrovka and Yakovlevo, then turn north-east and capture strategic high ground near Prokhorovka. The 4th Panzer Army identified the seizure of this piece of land as a crucial step to ensure the closure of the Kursk pocket.

During this action, the Kempf group was supposed to protect the eastern flank of the SS divisions. If the advance into enemy territory went as planned, the SS corps and the Kempf group would effectively create a pincer formation that could destroy the Soviet troops within its grasp. After accomplishing this feat, the two formations were to unite at Prokhorovka and charge into Kursk.

At their starting positions, the SS divisions covered a sector that was 20km (12 miles) wide. The *Totenkopf* occupied the left flank of the advance, while the *Leibstandarte* was in the centre and *Das Reich* held the right. Several hours before the attack was to begin on the morning of 5 July, 3rd Battalion and a group of pioneers armed with flame-throwers from the *Deutschland* Regiment infiltrated enemy lines. After striking Russian outposts from behind, the battle group swung around and attacked the main line positions in front of them. These actions softened up the Red Army defences in front of the SS corps and helped its divisions over-run the first line of trenches.

When the main attack began, *Deutschland*'s 2nd and 3rd Battalions constituted the spearhead of the SS advance. Because of an intense downpour that had turned the countryside into a gigantic quagmire of mud and swampland, tank and SP units were unable to provide adequate support for the infantrymen, who soon became involved in brutal, hand-to-hand combat. Hans Huber, a member of a flame-throwing unit attached to 3rd Battalion, described his role in the assault: 'I fired a burst of flame as we approached every zig-zag in the trench and at every strong point. It was a strange feeling to serve this destructive weapon and it was terrifying to see the flames eat their way forward and envelop the Russian defenders.'

While utilizing his flame-thrower, Huber recalled, 'soon I was coloured black from head to foot from the fuel oil and my face was burnt from the flames which bounced back off the trench walls or which were blown back at us by the strong wind. I could hardly see'. However, he conceded that the weapon was an effective instrument in ensuring the success of the German attack, noting that 'the enemy could not fight against flame-throwers and so we made good progress, taking many prisoners'.

EXHAUSTION

Eventually, Stuka dive-bombers appeared on the scene and hammered enemy positions relentlessly, enabling 3rd Battalion to capture Beresov. The battalion was also supposed to seize a ridge known as Point 233, which was situated north of the town. However, the SS men were too exhausted and depleted from high casualty rates. To complete the mission, 1st Battalion leapfrogged past them and pushed the Russians off the ridge. By mid-afternoon, the *Das Reich* Division had met all of its objectives for the day but still pressed forward in an effort to over-run the second line of trenches in the Kursk salient.

Although the division made considerable progress, its troops could not dislodge the Soviet forces occupying the defences because poor road conditions and minefields had prevented SS tank and SP units from reaching the area and providing necessary coverage for the grenadiers. Thus, the division waited until the next morning before continuing with its advance. During the course of the night, SS units carried out small-scale attacks against enemy outposts.

On the second day of Operation Citadel, the *Der Führer* Regiment replaced *Deutschland* as the spearhead of the SS offensive. In an attack upon another piece of high ground that had been designated Point 243, the regiment had difficulty ascending the muddy slopes of the objective. Enemy artillery and machine-gun fire ripped into its battalions. Later in the morning, the division pounded the Russians with artillery shells, enabling the *Der Führer* Regiment to seize the

heights. This piece of territory provided the SS corps with access to a road that ran to Lutschki.

By this time, Stavka was aware that the main thrust of the German offensive was in the south, rather than the north, and so shifted its defences to deal more effectively with II SS Panzer Corps and other nearby German formations. As a result, the 5th Guards Tank Army and other reserve units in the Red Army headed towards Prokhorovka to blunt the Nazi advance. Stavka also planned to launch punishing counterattacks at the German divisions in order to bleed them white.

Meanwhile, the *Das Reich* Division initiated another assault in order to capture an elevated area containing several villages situated north of Prokhorovka, as well as a railway line at Belenichino. Spearheaded by 3rd Battalion, *Der Führer* Regiment, the assault began badly. Soviet warplanes and artillery batteries tore into the SS troops. In a battle report, a battalion commander described the heroic leadership exhibited by a junior officer named Krüger serving in his command. During the attack, the battalion commander recalled, 'a rifle bullet struck his pocket and ignited an incendiary grenade he was carrying. *Untersturmführer* Krüger tore off his trousers and continued to fight completely naked. He fought at the head of the Company until the objective was gained.' A week later, Krüger died in combat.

REGAINED MOMENTUM

When the rest of the regiment joined the fight, the attack gained more momentum and the Germans managed to open a substantial gap in the enemy lines. On 8 July, the Red Army threw more armoured units at the advancing SS divisions. By this time, the focus of the battle for Kursk had clearly shifted to the southern sector. When it seemed as if the SS corps and the Kempf group were going to surround the Soviet garrison at Prokhorovka, the Red Army responded with a savage counter-attack. At Teterevino, 3rd Battalion, *Der Führer* Regiment held its ground against an armoured assault until every unit in the *Das Reich* Division reached the area to participate in the fight for this and other villages and the ridges upon which they sat.

With the help of Stukas fitted with anti-tank cannons, attacks upon the SS divisions were kept off for a brief period. But before Hausser's troops could resume offensive actions, the Red Army hurled more infantry and armoured units at them. Most notably, a formation of 60 Russian battle tanks threatened SS supply lines by trying to block the main road running from Belgorod to Oboyan. However, this threat soon abated when several Luftwaffe warplanes arrived, knocked out about 50 tanks, and killed several foot soldiers. At the same time, *Das Reich* and the other SS divisions repelled a series of armoured assaults at Teterevino, destroying almost 300 enemy armoured vehicles during the course of the day.

On 9 July, the three SS divisions concentrated their forces in order to renew their offensive against the Red Army. To prevent this action, several corps from the Russian 1st Tank Army attacked the Germans from three directions. In the ensuing battle, the SS divisions took many heavy blows, but they held their ground against extreme Russian pressure. Although Hausser's forces were in danger of being encircled, they received orders from 4th Panzer Army headquarters to push forward and attack Soviet troops north-east of Beregovoy.

Below: A 75mm (2.95in) infantry gun from *Das Reich* in action against Soviet artillery positions. Their exposed position suggests that they are not expecting to come under fire from the enemy themselves.

During this operation, *Das Reich* guarded the eastern flank of the other two SS divisions. En route to its objective, II SS Panzer Corps became involved in a massive tank battle in the hills around Prokhorovka on 12 July. This engagement would be the climax of Operation 'Citadel'. While the *Leibstandarte* and the *Totenkopf* divisions went on the offensive, *Das Reich* remained on the defensive, repelling several infantry and armoured attacks. On the second day of the

battle, Hausser put the *Das Reich* Division into action and it fought a duel with II Guards Tank Corps. After several hours of combat, the battle reached an indecisive conclusion. By nightfall, the two belligerents retired in a state of exhaustion.

Although both sides had lost several hundred tanks and thousands of troops, the Red Army was able either to repair or replace its losses, while the SS divisions were becoming worn down. Meanwhile, the

Below: (left to right) *SS-Standartenführer* **Heinz Harmel,** *SS-Sturmbannführer* **Helmut Schreiber and an unknown** *SS-Untersturmführer* **celebrate their latest decorations with champagne on the Mius front in August 1943.**

Right: A *Nebelwerfer* **rocket launcher prepares to fire a salvo against the Soviets in September 1943. After the failure of Operation 'Citadel', the men of** *Das Reich* **were once again relegated to plugging gaps in the German lines.**

entire offensive against Kursk seemed to be falling apart. On the northern wall of the salient, the 9th Army was unable to make much progress; Field Marshal Model had to deal with a Russian counter-offensive that had been launched above the Kursk area. Moreover, the Allied landings on Sicily forced Hitler and OKW to contemplate the possibility of diverting much-needed troops from the Eastern Front down to Italy.

Despite this bleak situation, the SS divisions continued to fight like wildcats. On 14 July, *Das Reich* launched another attack on Belenichino. In a battle that raged from house to house, the 1st and 3rd Battalions of the *Der Führer* Regiment destroyed 12 tanks while Stuka squadrons bombed and strafed enemy forces in and near the village. By the end of the day, Belenichino was in German hands. While the *Der Führer* Regiment consolidated its control over the area, *Das Reich*'s Panzer Regiment repelled an armoured assault that was aimed at re-taking the village.

LAST HURRAH

Unfortunately for the Third Reich, the victory at Belenichino turned out to be the last hurrah of Operation 'Citadel'. Although the 4th Panzer Army had taken a considerable amount of territory, it was still 130km (81 miles) south of the 9th Army. Thus, the Red Army still controlled a large piece of territory that connected the city of Kursk to the rest of the Soviet battle lines. After several days of fighting, the two German armies had barely dented the salient and were in no condition to launch more assaults against it. Not surprisingly, both sides had sustained heavy losses. The Germans had suffered about 100,000 casualties, while the Soviets lost 250,000 men killed and 600,000 wounded. The Red Army had also sacrificed roughly 50 per cent of its armoured vehicles.

Although Hitler had not officially ended Operation 'Citadel', the campaign would soon come to an end for II SS Panzer Corps. Removed from the area, the *Das Reich* Division was to participate in a series of battles against a counter-offensive that the Red Army had launched along the River Mius. By this time, the *Leibstandarte* Division had departed for Italy. When it left the Eastern Front, it turned over its armoured fighting vehicles to *Das Reich*. Its departure also led to the dissolution of II SS Panzer Corps. In place of this formation, Army Group South assembled a new corps that consisted of *Das Reich*, the *Totenkopf*, and the 3rd Army Panzer Division.

At the end of the month, this new organization reached the Mius and engaged enemy forces that were moving into the area. As usual, the *Das Reich* troops distinguished themselves with their bravery. At the town of Stepanovka, Heinz Macher noted that 'a small piece of shrapnel from a 17.2 shell hit me in the left forearm and our platoon stretcher-bearer put on a field dressing. For a scratch like that one did not abandon one's mates'. A few minutes later, another shell fragment 'severed the nerve in my upper left arm. End of the Act'.

SOVIET ATTACK BLUNTED

At another location along the Mius, Heid Rühl and a comrade relaxed briefly after repelling a Soviet armoured unit: '*Oberscharführer* Töpfer, an infantry platoon commander, stopped with me and we both lit cigarettes. He died in my arms,' Rühl recalled, 'but no shot had been fired. The doctor found that the cause of death was a hand-grenade splinter which had struck and penetrated his temple. He had been wounded on the previous day but had refused to go back. He was determined to stay with the attack until it was finished.' After three days of combat, the SS units blunted the Red Army drive, pushing the Russians back across the river.

In mid-August, the *Das Reich* Division returned to Kharkov when Stavka launched another attack on the city. While the Soviet 53rd rushed the city from the north, the 57th Army assailed its objective from the south. At first, the Red Army offensive stalled in the face of well-prepared defences established by Army Group South. In the first two days of battle, the Russians lost 184 battle tanks. However, on 22 August Manstein had to evacuate his forces – once again in defiance of Hitler's order – when the Soviets seemed as if they were about to encircle Kharkov yet again.

Above: An armoured column belonging to *Das Reich* prepares to move off in Russia in October 1943. On the left is a PzKpfw VI Tiger tank, armed with an 88mm (3.45in) gun capable of knocking out any Soviet tank.

Now recaptured by the Russians, the city had changed hands for the last time in the war.

TANK VICTORIES

By this time, the *Das Reich* Division had already been pulled out of the area in order to intercept enemy forces that were driving towards the River Dnieper. On the same day of the Kharkov evacuation, a company of Panther tanks destroyed 53 enemy vehicles during a three-hour battle with a large Soviet armoured formation. This engagement inaugurated a series of similar victories for the SS division that lasted until the end of the month, when its commanders received an order to withdraw to the western bank of the Dnieper.

During the month of September, the *Das Reich* Division pulled back to the river, fighting Soviet troops along the way on many occasions. On 12 September, the Reconnaissance Battalion and an armoured unit consisting of 14 Panther tanks ambushed a Red Army armoured formation that had overrun the division's positions. In the ensuing battle, the SS Panzer and Reconnaissance troops destroyed a total of 78 T-34 battle tanks. A week later, the division reached the Dnieper at an area near Kremechug, only to find that the Russians had already successfully crossed the river.

At the end of September, in an effort to prevent large numbers of enemy forces from consolidating control of areas west of the Dnieper, the *Das Reich* division attacked the village of Grebeni, where the

Above: (left to right) Schlink, *Gruppenführer* Krüger (divisional commander), *Obersturmbannführer* Sarg, and *Obersturmbannführer* Sylvester Stadler, commander of the *Der Führer* Regiment, photographed in December 1943.

Red Army had established several small bridgeheads. With a great deal of help from two flame-throwing armoured vehicles, the *Der Führer* Regiment seized the town. By this time, the regiment had only 500 surviving soldiers in its ranks. Fighting for these bridgeheads continued until early October.

SOVIET PRESSURE

Despite these successes, the overwhelming power of the Soviet armed forces continued to push the Germans westward. In early November, Army Group South had to abandon Kiev. South-west of the city, the *Das Reich* Division and other German formations did what they could to keep the Red Army from marching across the western Ukraine. In this region, the division fought several inconclusive battles that depleted its regiments and battalions even further. By December, *Das Reich* was no longer able to function as a full-size division and had to be re-formed into a

smaller organization that would be known as the Panzer Battle Group *Das Reich.*

The new panzer battle group contained 5000 troops and included an infantry regiment comprised of 1st Battalion, *Deutschland* Regiment and 2nd Battalion, *Der Führer* Regiment. It also contained an armoured battalion that included two tank companies, as well as the Reconnaissance Battalion, two SP companies, a pioneer company, and various heavy weapons units. While this group remained in the Eastern Front as a component of XLII Corps, the other surviving elements of the *Das Reich* Division returned to Germany after roughly 10 months of almost continuous service in the battlefield.

On Christmas Eve, the Red Army launched another offensive and quickly created two salients in the German lines, forcing Army Group, South to pull back its forces to new positions east of Zhitomir. Near Studenizza, a *Das Reich* SP unit kept several T-34 tanks at bay while the rest of the division retreated. After beating back the Soviet forces in this area, an SP crewman named Hans Woltersdorf peered into the first vehicle that his group had knocked out, noting that 'the interior was sickening. A headless torso, bleeding flesh and guts splattered the walls'. Outside the T-34, the Soviet tank driver died in SS captivity. 'The back of his head had been smashed, exposing his bloodied brains. There was froth on his lips,' Woltersdorf recalled, 'typical of this type of wound where the brain is dead but the lungs are still working.'

REARGUARD ACTION

To reach its new line of defence, Battle Group *Das Reich* had to cross the River Tetrev. While the unit's infantrymen and SP units carried out a holding action that kept the Soviets at bay, the pioneers hastily constructed a temporary bridge that enabled the SS vehicles to cross the river. When the last of the Germans reached the other bank, the pioneers detonated the bridge, preventing the Russians from continuing the attack, at least for a short time.

For the rest of the winter, the SS battle group saw more action as the Red Army continued to push the

Germans westward and out of the Ukraine. By January 1944, the unit had lost more than 1000 of its 5000 troops. In March, these survivors had to fight their way through enemy forces out of a pocket before reaching the relative safety of the 4th Panzer Army at Buszacz.

On 8 April, the soldiers of *Das Reich* at last departed the front lines and marched 80km (49 miles) across Galicia to climb on board a train that would take them back to Germany. After 13 hard months of service in the Eastern Front, at the end of April, the 800 survivors from Panzer Battle Group *Das Reich* reached Toulouse in south-west France and rejoined the rest of their division.

Below: An improvised self-propelled gun mounting an anti-tank gun on a half-track chassis commanded by Hans Woltersdorf, part of the *Das Reich* battlegroup on the Eastern Front in early 1944.

CHAPTER EIGHT

NORMANDY

Sent to the south of France to refit, the division was still there when the Allies invaded in June 1944. Despatched north to throw the invaders back into the sea, what happened on the way to Normandy would bring the division to the world's attention.

In April 1944, the elements of the *Das Reich* Division reassembled at an area north of Toulouse. Under the command of Heinz Bernard Lammerding since the beginning of the year, the battered and depleted organization had become a reserve force attached to LVIII Corps. Stationed at the city of Montauban, the division was to aid in the defence of southern France if, or when, the anticipated Allied invasion took place there. For several weeks, the surviving veterans of the *Das Reich* Division also passed the time training the 9000 recruits who had recently joined them.

Although many of these volunteers would not have been considered fit for service in the earlier years of the *Waffen-SS*, the course of the war and the need for fresh troops forced the SS Recruiting Office to be less selective about potential candidates. At Montauban, these recruits exhibited a great deal of enthusiasm during their training and soon proved themselves disciplined and dedicated soldiers. Several of these young novices were actually *Volksdeutschen* from Hungary, Romania and many other parts of Europe. Some of them also hailed from the French-speaking

Left: Panzergrenadiers inspect the contents of a container dropped by the US air force for the French Resistance. The Resistance proved to be far more active in the south than the *Das Reich* Division had expected.

region of Alsace-Lorraine, which Hitler had annexed into the Third Reich after the defeat of France in 1940.

With this new transfusion of manpower, *Das Reich* once again became a functioning, full-size division with more than 15,000 troops and 200 armoured fighting vehicles in its ranks. Like most other SS panzer divisions at the time, Lammerding's organization was almost twice as large as a typical *Wehrmacht* panzer division. In fact, *Das Reich* possessed 10 per cent of the total armoured strength of the German armed forces in Western Europe.

RESISTANCE THREAT

After spending several months on the Eastern Front, training recruits in a wooded area in south-west France seemed to be a welcome break for the veterans of *Das Reich*. However, the political situation in the country had changed considerably since the last time the division had been there. By 1944, anti-Nazi Resistance groups had grown and become more active, threatening German soldiers who dared travel beyond garrisons or urban centres. Although such 'terrorist' bands could not possibly defeat *Das Reich* or any other sizeable military organization stationed in the country, they were able to carry out sabotage operations against railroads, bridges and other important facilities that the Germans needed in order to move and communicate.

Above: On the hunt for secret caches of weapons or hideouts with Alsatian dogs. The activities of the Resistance hampered the Germans' training programmes and led to brutal reprisals.

The members of *Das Reich* and most other *Waffen-SS* organizations rarely participated in the genocidal policies that had been implemented by the *Allgemeine-SS* and carried out by the *Einsatzgruppen* killing squads and other units. However, these soldiers had no qualms about enacting brutal reprisals against any groups of civilians suspected of providing aid and comfort to guerrillas and saboteurs. In fact, Lammerding himself had a great deal of experience carrying out ruthless anti-partisan operations in the Soviet Union. As the activities of the French Resistance intensified within the countryside around Toulouse, the Germans became increasingly harsh in their treatment of local communities.

While the SS division was trying to mould its raw recruits into effective soldiers, Resistance groups assassinated Germans, blocked roads and engaged in other forms of harassment. During the month of May,

these guerrillas killed 20 *Das Reich* soldiers and destroyed about 100 vehicles. In response to such activity, detachments from the division swept through the region, burning down many houses and killing scores of villagers. The SS troops also deported thousands of civilians to Germany to work as labourers in concentration camps. When the Germans found several rifles, bazookas and British-made machine-guns stashed within the town of Figeac, they executed 41 inhabitants and exiled several hundred others.

On 6 June 1944, the Allied invasion of France began when 176,000 British, Commonwealth and American soldiers landed upon the coast of

Normandy. That evening, General Charles de Gaulle delivered a radio broadcast to the people of France, proclaiming the start of a great battle for the liberation of the country and calling upon his supporters to join the fight against the Germans. Although the Germans had managed to jam this message on the short-wave frequency, many listeners heard it on the medium wave. The landings on Normandy coupled with this announcement indicated to many Resistance groups that the time had arrived for them to engage the enemy in open battle.

NORMANDY LANDINGS

At the time of the landings on Normandy, the *Das Reich* Division was located 724km (450 miles) from the site of battle. To help the German armies in the area repel – or at least contain – the invasion, Lammerding's forces needed to move quickly. If the division reached north-east France in time, the SS units might provide enough armour and manpower to bring a German victory. Although the officers and men in *Das Reich* anticipated trouble from Allied aircraft during their journey across France, they did not expect any serious interference with their movement until they reached the River Loire.

For an entire day, the SS soldiers waited for orders directing them to head for Normandy. However, Hitler and his generals procrastinated because they suspected that the Allied landing there might be a diversion, and they expected another invasion to take place in another part of France. Meanwhile, *Das Reich* and other German military units stationed in southwest France received reports of Resistance activity taking place throughout the region. Fearful that the entire area might explode in open rebellion, OKW kept several divisions there rather than sending them north to help Field Marshal Rommel deal with the Allied armies.

On 7 June, after being transferred to LXVI Reserve Corps, the *Das Reich* Division received orders directing it to proceed north and suppress Resistance groups that were operating in an area between Tulle and Limoges. However, the division had difficulty in reaching the area because Resistance saboteurs had destroyed railway lines running to Limoges, forcing the SS troops to drive their slow-moving armoured vehicles to the area on their own. Leaving behind a 600-man battle group to maintain security at Montauban, the bulk of the division headed for Limoges the following morning.

Near the town of Gourdon, 1st Battalion, *Der Führer* Regiment turned left and headed toward Sarlat, while the rest of the *Das Reich* Division continued moving due north in the direction of Brive-la-Gaillarde. At the hamlet of Groslejac, the battalion fought a brief skirmish with 15 members of *Armee Secrete* (AS), a resistance organization that supported De Gaulle and was affiliated with the British Special Operations Executive (SOE). After killing five rebels and chasing the rest of the gang out of the area, the Germans continued on their journey. On later occasions, the battalion encountered roadblocks that had been thrown together by AS operatives. Satisfied that the area around Groslejac was a hotbed of resistance activity, the SS troops fired upon all civilians that they saw en route to Limoges, presuming that such bystanders were 'terrorists'.

At Souillac, the battalion rejoined the rest of the division on the main road to Limoges. As the division approached the village of Cressensac, another resistance band fired into the lead vehicles of the convoy. When the Germans returned fire and destroyed several houses with a 75mm (2.95in) Pak gun, the guerillas fled. Another skirmish took place further north as the division passed through Noailles, producing a similar result. Although the AS operatives had inflicted only minimal damage on the SS convoy, they had already delayed its advance by several hours.

The following morning, a three-hour battle broke out at the town of Bretenoux. After destroying three German vehicles, the partisans withdrew, losing 18 of their men in the exchange of gunfire. Apart from a brief skirmish at Beaulieu, the division did not encounter any more trouble as it rolled into Brive. However, a band of guerrillas later fell upon, and killed, the members of a maintenance crew that had been left behind to repair a disabled vehicle.

Above: *SS-Sturmbannführer* **Heinrich Wulf, the commander of** *Das Reich*'s **Reconnaissance Battalion, who was responsible for ordering the mass execution of civilians carried out in Tulle in reprisal for the division's losses.**

By the time *Das Reich* reached Tulle, it had lost 15 men killed and more than 30 wounded during its trip from Montauban. French casualties included more than 100 men and women killed. Outraged at the rebellious behaviour that seemed to be breaking out in the area, OKW authorized all divisions attached to LXVI Reserve Corps to enact punitive measures against suspected resistance operatives.

When the division reached Brive, its officers found the local German garrison almost in a state of panic over rumours of an impending uprising. Comprised of reservists that were considerably older than the SS troops, the soldiers assigned to guard the city had allowed Resistance cells to grow and become active in

the nearby countryside. Many other garrisons in neighbouring towns had been just as derelict. Unlike these green conscripts, the SS soldiers felt nothing but contempt for the AS and other 'terrorist' bands, and chided these reservists for failing to send out regular patrols that would have kept the area pacified.

COMMUNIST RESISTANCE

While the main part of the division continued moving due north to Limoges, *SS-Sturmbannführer* Heinrich Wulf led his 500-man Reconnaissance Battalion east to aid a beleaguered garrison at Tulle. At this town, a pitched battle between the Germans and members of the *Francs-Tireurs et Partisans* (FTP), a Communist resistance organization, was underway. When the SS battalion reached Tulle, the FTP was in control over most of the area. Meanwhile, the German soldiers attached to the town garrison had barricaded themselves in an arms factory and a nearby school and were waiting for help to arrive. As the 100 trucks and half-tracks of the Reconnaissance Battalion rolled into Tulle, the Communists executed a hasty retreat.

After consolidating his control over the town, Wulf ordered two companies to conduct a house-to-house search for hidden weapons. He also directed his men to bring every male citizen to a courtyard in front of the arms factory for an identity check. Presumably, those with valid identity papers would be released. On the morning of 9 June, 3000 confused villagers of various ages stood at this assigned location, wondering what the SS soldiers planned to do with them.

Although Wulf had lost only three men killed and nine wounded during the re-taking of Tulle, he and other SS officers were fed up with Resistance activity and thus decided to carry out systematic reprisals for what they considered to be terrorist actions. This sentiment became much stronger when the Germans learned that the Communist guerillas had killed 139 and wounded 40 members of the garrison. Officers in the SS division also claimed that the FTP had murdered and mutilated at least 40 German soldiers who had surrendered to the Communists.

At the courtyard, SS soldiers went through the large crowd of Tulle residents and singled out who they

considered to be suspicious-looking men as candidates for a mass execution. During the course of the afternoon, the Germans hanged almost 100 of these unfortunate civilians, despite the lack of proof linking these victims to the FTP or the AS. After three hours of performing this grisly work, the executioners decided to spare the 21 remaining villagers who had been marked for death. Wulf and other officers at Tulle claimed that Lammerding had approved of this reprisal, although the division commander later asserted that he had not known about the action until after it was over.

Before pulling out of Tulle, the Reconnaissance Battalion loaded 311 men into trucks and sent them to Limoges. There, the SS troops released 162 prisoners and sent the rest to Dachau and other concentration camps in Germany. En route to their destinations, many prisoners perished on board unsanitary railroad cars. By the end of the war, only 49 of these

Above: An SS officer captured by the Resistance is handed over to the Allies after the invasion on 6 June 1944. However it is likely that many SS prisoners were not handed over but simply killed by the Resistance.

149 Tulles residents had survived their imprisonment. North of Limoges, 3rd Battalion, *Der Führer* Regiment swept into other towns that had fallen into the hands of resistance groups. At Argenton-sur-Creuse, No. 15 Company chased away 50 FTP activists and shot several residents. To the east, *SS-Sturmbannführer* Helmut Kampfe led the rest of the battalion toward Gueret. After executing 29 captured guerillas en route to the town, the battalion reached the area, only to find that *Wehrmacht* units had already re-established German control.

Leaving two platoons behind to help maintain German control of the town, the battalion commander

led the rest of his unit back to Limoges. In the early evening, after Kampfe had pulled far ahead of his troops in his staff car, a small band of FTP partisans stopped him on the main road and hauled him away in a truck. When the Germans found his empty vehicle, they initiated a thorough search throughout the Limousin area. Despite this effort, the battalion commander was never seen alive again and was probably executed by the Resistance. Not surprisingly, this incident caused the officers and men of *Das Reich* to become very bitter and led to more reprisals against the civilian population of southern France.

On 10 June, Lammerding finally received a message from OKW ordering the *Das Reich* Division to aid in the defence of Normandy. Weary of engaging in police actions against resistance groups, most SS soldiers were pleased at the idea of resuming their role as

Above: The ruins of Oradour-sur-Glane, destroyed on 10 June 1944 by Otto Dickmann and subordinates from *Das Reich*. Dickmann believed that his friend Helmut Kampfe was being held in the town by the Resistance.

combat soldiers. However, the division still had difficulty carrying out this new order because many of its battle tanks and SP guns were breaking down en route to the destination. The lack of available spare parts for these disabled vehicles and insufficient fuel supplies exacerbated this problem. Finally, the members of the French Resistance and their confederates in the British SOE and American Office of Strategic Services (OSS) remained determined in their effort to hinder the progress of the division in its move northwards.

While the SS division struggled with its transportation problems, partisan activity continued to flare up in towns throughout southern France. West of Brive, elements of *Das Reich* pushed a band of 100 FTP guerillas out of Terrasson. Although they promptly hanged a Communist that had fallen into their hands and torched a house that was flying a red Communist flag, the Germans left the town without killing any of its residents.

OTTO DICKMANN

Meanwhile, 1st Battalion, *Der Führer* Regiment swept into Saint Junien, a town located north-west of Limoges. The commander of this unit, *SS-Sturmbannführer* Otto Dickmann, had been a close friend of Helmut Kampfe and was thus in a very vindictive mood. Two days before the battalion moved into the town, Resistance partisans had killed two German soldiers during an ambush at the train station. While Dickmann was helping a group of Gestapo and Vichy officials restore order in Saint Junien, two residents informed him that the FTP was holding a German military officer in a town called Oradour-sur-Glane and intended to execute the captive.

Not surprisingly, Dickmann assumed that this officer was his friend Kampfe and immediately requested permission from his regimental commander to take 1st Battalion to Oradour-sur-Glane, situated a short distance east of Saint Junien. After receiving permission from his superior, Dickmann led his No. 3 Company into Oradour on the afternoon of 10 June. Although the town normally contained only 330 inhabitants, it was now almost twice this size because of refugees that had been moving in from other parts of France. Contrary to German intelligence reports, Oradour was not a hotbed of Resistance activity and did not even seem as if it had been affected by the war.

After entering the town, Dickmann and his 120 SS soldiers herded most of its population into the central square. Kampfe was nowhere to be found. The Germans then declared that they intended to perform a house-to-house search for hidden weapons and led the male residents of Oradour out of the area. Dividing these men into six groups, the SS soldiers led their docile captives into barns and

garages located at various points along the main road. At these sites, the German guards suddenly opened fire, pouring hundreds of machine-gun bullets into their prisoners.

When the Frenchmen collapsed into bloody piles in the execution chambers, the SS troops stopped firing their machine-guns and walked among the victims, shooting survivors with pistols. The Germans then set fire to the buildings, incinerating most of those who had not been killed by gunfire. In other parts of Oradour, Dickmann's soldiers torched houses and murdered fugitives who had not complied with the order to gather at the central square.

Meanwhile, other soldiers in No. 3 Company herded the women and children of Oradour into a large church situated at the southern end of the town. With about 400 people crowded into the building, the Germans continued with their reign of terror, shooting and tossing grenades into the crowd before closing all exits and starting another fire. As clouds of smoke drifted into the sky, a tram filled with passengers returning from Limoges approached the edge of the town. Before the tram could proceed any further, a group of German guards stopped it and warned its occupants to stay away from the area.

Dickmann and his troops finally left Oradour the following morning, bringing looted valuables and livestock with them. Collectively, they had liquidated 642 residents. During the killings, the Germans had lost only one man: a junior officer who was crushed by collapsing masonry at the church. When *SS-Standartenführer* Sylvester Stadler, the commander of the *Der Führer* Regiment, heard about the atrocity, he became furious and planned to initiate court-martial proceedings against Dickmann. As news of the incident spread across France, Vichy officials and *Wehrmacht* officers called for an inquiry. Despite this pressure, the battalion commander never forfeited his command and would perish in battle at Normandy before he could be brought to justice.

Not surprisingly, the harsh reprisals committed at Tulle and Oradour-sur-Glane helped foster an unsavoury reputation for the *Waffen-SS*, blurring the distinction between this organization and the

Gestapo, *Sicherheitsdienst* (SD), *Einsatzgruppen,* and other notorious departments within the *Allgemeine-SS.* However, these violent actions also lead to a dramatic reduction in Resistance activity. As the *Das Reich* Division left Limoges and continued moving northwards, local AS commanders decided that further acts of sabotage and assassination carried a price that was too high.

FINAL ACT

Even FTP activists curtailed their actions to a considerable extent, although a small band of these partisans did stage one more raid against the SS division. Near Bellac, the Communists charged a German truck, believing that the vehicle and its occupants were isolated. As the Frenchmen closed in on their target, hundreds of soldiers from the Reconnaissance Battalion returned fire, killing five partisans and sending the rest fleeing into the woods. This engagement was the last battle fought between the *Das Reich*

Above: The last class photograph of the schoolgirls of Oradour-sur-Glane. All of those pictured here were barricaded in the church by the Germans. The building was then set on fire: none of the children survived.

Division and the French Resistance. Collectively, the SS units had lost no more than 40 men during their trip from Montauban to Normandy.

As they approached the site of the Allied invasion, the SS soldiers faced much more powerful and better organized adversaries. Most notably, they had their first encounter with Allied air power. North of the River Loire, British and American fighter-bombers wreaked havoc upon the vehicles of *Das Reich.* On 14 June, as the division moved toward its concentration area near Domfront, these warplanes struck hard with machine-guns rounds, bombs and rockets, destroying 16 trucks. After this costly lesson, the SS units quickly learned the necessity of camouflaging their vehicles.

Within this region of France, the SS soldiers noticed that the local population was less hostile to their presence. Before the Allied invasion, most farmers and villagers in Normandy lived in a state of peaceful co-existence with the Germans. When British and American bombers, artillery batteries, warships and armoured units tore apart the countryside and destroyed houses, barns and livestock, these residents often became upset and resentful toward their would-be liberators. In contrast, relations with the Germans were sometimes very friendly.

In one incident, members of *Das Reich*'s Artillery Regiment displayed an extraordinary amount of goodwill towards a Norman farmer. When a truck failed to arrive and pick them up from a location that was about to be over-run by enemy forces, Anton Fehlau and his comrades had to confiscate a wagon and a team of horses to remove wounded soldiers and heavy equipment from danger. As he left the area,

Fehlau noticed that the farmer was sad to see his animals leave and promised to return them when the Germans had finished using them.

After transporting their equipment and wounded comrades behind friendly lines, Fehlau and a few of his colleagues received permission to return the horses. Although they were aware that they would be travelling through dangerous territory, the soldiers pressed forward. En route to their destination, they surprised a small group of drunken partisans sitting at a table inside an isolated farmhouse. Instead of shooting these men as subversives, the SS soldiers merely chided them for their carelessness. Speaking French, a signaller from Alsace asked, 'How could

Below: The interior of the church at Oradour-sur-Glane after the fire. The remains of the altar are clearly visible on the left. About 400 women and children perished here, their menfolk in houses and stables in the village.

Above: Sylvester Stadler (seen here in March 1943), commander of the *Der Führer* Regiment in June 1944, initiated court martial proceedings against Dickmann when he heard what had happened at Oradour.

you sit around and not put up a sentry?' He also noted, 'Tomorrow the war will have passed this place. Do you really want to die on the last day?'

Leaving these nervous partisans unharmed in their sanctuary, the SS troops continued their journey. As they moved closer to their destination, Fehlau recalled, 'shell explosions which grew louder and louder showed that we were on the right road. Then the shells began to land very close to us'. Eventually, 'the barrage was almost continuous and the animals were trembling with fear'. Ten minutes later, after passing through this bombarded area, 'bathed in sweat and with trembling knees we took a short rest'.

As they approached the farm, the horses sensed that they were going home and began to gallop.

When the SS gunners reached the stables, Fehlau noted that the farmer and his wife were as surprised as they were elated. 'They thanked us so warmly that any doubts that we might have had whether it was worth taking the risk to return their horses was quickly answered. Yes it had been.' During the course of the evening, the farmer allowed the Germans to sleep in his barn and kept watch over his guests. The following morning, the hosts provided Fehlau and his comrades with food and escorted them part of the way back to their regiment.

UNDERSTRENGTH DIVISION

Shortly after the *Das Reich* Division moved into Normandy, *SS-Sturmbannführer* Otto Weidinger replaced Stadler as commander of the *Der Führer* Regiment. Stadler had received a promotion and assumed command of the 9th SS-Panzer-Division *Hohenstaufen*. Because some of Lammerding's infantry battalions were still in the area around Toulouse and had only recently left south-west France, *Das Reich* was not yet a full-size division. Thus, the commanders of the 7th Army divided the organization into separate units and attached them to different *Wehrmacht* formations at areas along the front lines.

As they had done so many times before in the Soviet Union, the regiments and battalions of *Das Reich* were serving as 'fire brigades' for the German war effort, being sent to hot spots within the battlefield in order to extinguish enemy attacks. At Normandy, the 7th Army dispatched a divisional artillery battalion and a panzer battalion to a sector near Torigny-sur-Virien, where the SS units were to aid II *Fallschirmjäger* Corps. Meanwhile, a battle group comprised of 1st Battalion, *Der Führer* Regiment and 1st Battalion, *Deutschland* Regiment went to the 2nd (Army) Panzer Division at an area between Caen and Villers-Bocage.

Within this sector, the SS battle group immediately saw action while trying to close a gap between the 2nd Division and the 12th SS-Panzer-Division *Hitlerjugend*. After the battalions sustained a massive artillery bombardment, the *Deutschland* unit checked a group of British infantrymen that were attacking

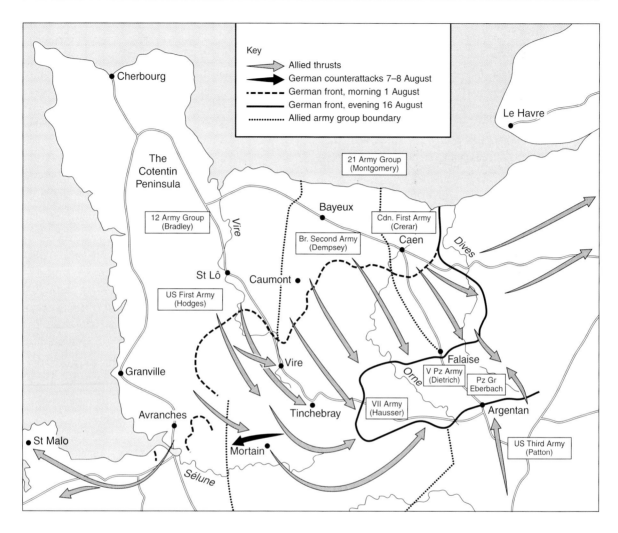

Key
⟶ Allied thrusts
⟶ German counterattacks 7–8 August
– – – German front, morning 1 August
⟶ German front, evening 16 August
·········· Allied army group boundary

Cherbourg

Le Havre

The
Cotentin
Peninsula

21 Army Group
(Montgomery)

Bayeux

12 Army Group
(Bradley)

Vire

Cdn. First Army
(Crerar)

Br. Second Army
(Dempsey)

Caen

Dives

St Lô

Caumont

US First Army
(Hodges)

Granville

Vire

Falaise

Orne

V Pz Army
(Dietrich)

Pz Gr
Eberbach

Avranches

Tinchebray

VII Army
(Hausser)

Argentan

St Malo

Mortain

US Third Army
(Patton)

Sélune

German positions. Meanwhile, the Allies began Operation 'Epsom', an action aimed at isolating Caen and forcing the Germans forces within the area to withdraw in order to avoid being entrapped in an encirclement. If the offensive went well, the Allies hoped to achieve a breakthrough to the River Orne. Using three divisions and several brigades, British VIII Corps launched this operation in late June.

In reaction, the Germans initiated a counter-attack that was intended to spoil the British offensive. Specifically, II SS Panzer Corps was to lunge into the right flank of VIII Corps as the British divisions moved between Villers-Bocage and Caen. During this

Above: After the failure of the attack at Mortain, *Das Reich* and other German units were squeezed into a pocket near Falaise. Pounded constantly by Allied guns and fighter-bombers, the division barely escaped.

action, the *Der Führer-Deutschland* Battle Group was transferred to the 9th SS Division. On 29 June, the German counter-attack began. Fighting in close quarters among hedges and other tall obstructions that restricted all of the combatants' vision, the SS units temporarily stalled the British advance.

To break this stalemate, the British exploited their air supremacy. Observation planes flew over the countryside and provided artillery batteries and offshore warships with the coordinates that were necessary to shell German positions. Pummelled relentlessly by this bombardment, the II SS Panzer Corps counter-attack stopped in its tracks. Meanwhile, a squadron of Sherman tanks rolled across the *Das Reich* Battle Group and almost penetrated its tactical headquarters. When two companies in the SS unit knocked out four tanks with flame-throwers and anti-tank weapons, the British squadron retreated.

Losing Effectiveness

By the end of June, the SS battle group had lost 846 of its men and was becoming ineffective as a fighting unit. However, its soldiers did their job well and helped prevent the British VIII Corps from rupturing the German defences and breaking through to the Orne. On 2 July, after repelling a British infantry attack, the two battalions left the front line and returned to their division. For the rest of the month, *Das Reich* served under LXXXIV Corps at an area near Saint Lo. When Allied troops seemed to be breaching the lines, the corps commander frequently dispatched under-strength battalions from the division into troubled areas. During these 'fire brigade' actions, the manpower in the SS units dwindled steadily.

On 4 July, the division received orders to form more battle groups. Commanded by Otto Weidinger, the first battle group included a panzer and an artillery unit and was attached to the 353rd Division. The second group joined the 17th SS Division at Sainteny and contained 2nd Battalion, Panzer Regiment and 4th Battalion, Artillery Regiment, as well as the Nebelwerfer and Flak battalions. *SS-Obersturmbannführer* Gunther Eberhardt Wisliceny led a third battle group comprised of two battalions from *Deutschland* and the Pioneer Battalion. This group was also attached to the 17th SS Division. Finally, a small attack group that included elements of *Der Führer* served as a reserve force for II *Fallschirmjäger* Corps.

During the month of July, the armoured formations within these battle groups wreaked havoc upon Allied forces. North-east of Sainteny, Panther tanks

from No. 4 Panzer Company repelled an attack launched by units from the American 3rd Armored Division. On 13 July, another American armoured formation struck, only to lose three Shermans before withdrawing from the field. The man responsible for destroying these vehicles was *SS-Unterscharführer* Ernst Barkmann, one of the greatest tank aces of World War II.

A day later, Barkmann led a rescue operation aimed at retrieving four tank crews trapped behind enemy lines. After accomplishing this mission, he liberated several wounded SS soldiers who had been captured by the Americans. Later in the month, he fought a battle at a road junction in the village of Le Lorey that would turn him into a legend among the soldiers of the *Waffen-SS*.

At this village, Barkmann spotted 14 American Shermans that were escorting several fuel and transport trucks west from Saint Lo. After moving his Panther next to a large oak tree at the crossroads, he fired the 75mm (2.95in) gun on his turret, hitting the first two tanks in the column. When the trucks stopped behind the burning Shermans, he destroyed these vehicles with little difficulty. Two more tanks pushed past the wreckage and headed straight for his Panther. The German panzer was hit with two shells but smashed these two Shermans as well.

To remove this Panther that was blocking an entire armoured column, the Americans summoned air support. Although the enemy fighter-bombers inflicted considerable damage upon Barkmann's vehicle, he demolished more Shermans that were charging at him. Low on ammunition, he directed his driver to vacate the area, leaving nine wrecked American tanks smouldering at the crossroads. The following day, his Panther smashed two more Shermans.

In an area between Periers and Saint Lo, the Weidinger and Wislicency battle groups launched small-scale counter-attacks against American forces

Right: A heavily camouflaged PzKpfw IV from *Das Reich* moves through the Normandy hedgerows. Such precautions were vital to avoid detection by the roving bands of Allied fighter-bombers flying over the region.

that were punching large holes in the German line. Although the SS troops executed their tasks with their usual amount of discipline and diligence, they and other German forces were hopelessly outnumbered and undersupplied. Within this sector, LXXXIV Corps had only seven divisions to block the advance of the American 1st Army and its 14 divisions. The Americans also enjoyed overwhelming superiority in armoured formations.

On 25 July, General Omar Bradley, the commander of the 1st Army, unleashed Operation 'Cobra', an offensive aimed at capturing Saint Lo. At the time, the *Das Reich* Division was under the temporary command of *SS-Obersturmbannführer* Christian Tychsen, as Lammerding had suffered serious injuries during an inspection. The American assault began in the morning, with squadrons of B-17 heavy bombers tearing into German positions with several tonnes of explosives. These sorties were supposed to tear large gaps into the enemy defences, enabling American infantrymen to pour through and achieve a breakthrough.

At first, these bombing missions seemed as if they were fulfilling this objective. General Fritz Bayerlein, the commander of the *Panzer Lehr* Division, recalled how 'carpets of bombs wiped out artillery positions, overturned and buried panzers, flattened infantry positions and destroyed all roads'. Although these air raids ripped large holes into the German lines, the destruction inflicted upon the landscape actually slowed down the American advance. Massive craters and piles of debris prevented Shermans and other vehicles from pushing forward at an effective speed.

Moreover, the Norman countryside created conditions that favoured the Germans. Tall hedges, clusters of trees, and the lack of roads frustrated American armoured units seeking to destroy enemy tanks in open areas. Aided by this terrain, the SS troops in *Das Reich* held their sector along the front line near Saint Lo, repulsing 13 infantry and armoured assaults during the course of the day. Encouraged by this success, the *Der Führer* Regiment launched a counter-attack. Bereft of panzer support, the assault fizzled

out as enemy artillery shells tore into the ranks of the advancing regiment.

While *Das Reich* and other units along the front line contained the American attack, its commanders received confusing retreat orders from LXXXIV Corps during the course of the day. When the SS soldiers executed their withdrawal, the Americans struck hard. While tank units plowed through the German lines, the 1st Army swept down the Cotenin Peninsula, heading toward Avranches. This movement threatened to encircle LXXXIV Corps.

SAVAGE AIR ATTACKS

To prevent this, the Germans pulled back to a line running along the Coutances–Saint Gilles Road. Moving to this new area in broad daylight, *Das Reich* withstood relentless air attacks, only to find that enemy forces were already occupying its objective. Thus, the SS infantrymen had to dislodge these Americans before establishing their own defences. By this time, combat units had become too depleted to man the trenches effectively, requiring the division to send clerks, cooks and other support personnel to help maintain the front.

Meanwhile, Bradley's divisions continued to press forward, gradually surrounding LXXXIV Corps. To break out of this noose, General Erich Marcks, the corps commander, formed *Das Reich* and the 17th SS Division into a battle group and sent this makeshift force to Percy, where they were to launch a breakout assault. Hammered relentlessly by Allied air- and armoured attacks, the battle group was thrown back with heavy losses. During this débâcle, 1st Battalion, Artillery Regiment, *Das Reich* Division had been completely decimated.

At the end of the month, the American offensive intensified, forcing Marcks to pull back his divisions to the south-east. Despite this precaution, Allied pressure intensified as Bradley's armoured forces swept in from Brittany and threatened the southern flank of the German forces fighting in Normandy. In an effort to prevent an encirclement of its forces, OKW devised Operation 'Liege', a plan to enable the German armies to escape entrapment and retreat towards Belgium.

Above: A soldier from *Das Reich* tightens the wristband of one of his colleague's camouflage smocks during a lull in the battle. Some smocks were reversible, with darker hues of green and brown for use in spring and autumn.

Essentially, the operation was a spoiling attack launched upon Avranches by roughly 120 armoured vehicles under the command of XLVII Corps. The intent of this manoeuvre was to knock the Allies off balance for long enough to permit the Germans to withdraw from Normandy. During this action, *Das Reich* was attached to this corps, as were the *Leibstandarte* and the 17th SS Division. Elements of these divisions constituted the spearhead of the assault.

In preparation for Operation 'Liege', which began in early August, *Das Reich* assembled three battle groups. On the right, a unit comprised of *Der Führer* and an SP battalion was to seize high ground north-west of Mortain and link up with the *Leibstandarte* group. Meanwhile, the 17th SS Panzer Division constituted the centre battle group and had the task of capturing a ridge known as Point 317. On the left, *Deutschland* and the *Das Reich* Reconnaissance Battalion acted as the third battle group and were to sweep into an area situated between Milly and Fontenay.

When the attack began, the SS units immediately ran into trouble. At the right wing of the German advance, the American 30th Infantry Division called in an effective artillery- and mortar bombardment that knocked out several SPs. Pinned down for several hours by enemy fighter-bombers, *Der Führer*

Regiment was not able to attack the American lines until the afternoon and was thrown back with heavy losses. In the centre, the attempt by the 17th SS Division to take Point 317 also failed.

To the left, the *Deutschland* Regiment had better luck against the Americans. Driving rapidly to the west, its 3rd Battalion seized Mortain by mid-morning. However, enemy resistance became stronger as the regiment pressed forward and the SS commanders quickly realized that Operation 'Liege' stood little chance of success. On 10 August, Marcks ordered *Das Reich* to pull back from Mortain and abandon the offensive, thus bringing the unsuccessful operation to an end.

FALAISE POCKET

Meanwhile, the Allied gauntlet around the German 7th Army and the 5th Panzer Army tightened. To the left of these formations, armoured divisions under the command of General George S. Patton pushed to the River Seine and turned north. On the right flank of the Germans, Allied forces advanced from the coast in the direction of Falaise. To avoid encirclement, the Germans began heading east and towards the town in a fighting retreat.

During these manoeuvres, *Das Reich* participated in ferocious counter-attacks against Allied units that were pushing through the German lines. As they had done many times before in the Eastern Front, the SS soldiers often engaged in brutal, hand-to-hand combat against the enemy. In these contests, a veteran of *Deutschland*'s pioneer company noted that some of the American soldiers 'pretended to be dead but we could pick them out quite easily because they all lay face downward with their head to one side and with their eyes closed'.

When the Germans moved towards Falaise, *Deutschland* received the task of holding Le-Bourg-Saint-Leonard, a town located east of Argentan. However, when the regiment reached the area on 15 August, Le-Bourg-Saint-Leonard was already occupied by American troops. In a desperate attack upon the town, the SS soldiers failed to seize their objective and were dispersed by armoured units. On

the following day, several Shermans tore into 2nd Battalion and almost captured its tactical head-quarters before the Germans blunted the assault and destroyed the tanks.

After this engagement, *Das Reich* received an order to join II SS Panzer Corps and proceed to Vimoutiers, a town that was located several miles to the east and outside the Falaise Pocket. The division was to help maintain a strong presence in this area in order to ensure that the German armies had an escape route. On 18 August, the division arrived at its destination just before the Allies closed Falaise Pocket and initiated a punishing offensive against the 15 German divisions still trapped in the area. The closure of the pocket meant that the SS corps would have to force

open a passage to provide these divisions with an escape route.

ALL-OUT ATTACK

Near Vimoutiers, a Canadian unit seized the village of Trun, thereby consolidating the Allied gauntlet around Falaise. In response, Field Marshal Walther Model, the overall commander of German forces in Western Europe, ordered an attack to be launched by divisions inside the encirclement, as well as the SS units positioned on the outside. By assailing the sector around Trun from both sides, Model hoped to establish an opening in the pocket. As a participant in this operation, *Das Reich* was to capture several strategic areas, including a steep ridge known as Mount Ormel.

Above: A StuG III Ausf G in action against approaching US targets in Normandy. The tight Normandy hedgerows were tailor-made for the German defenders, restricting rapid movement and providing large amounts of cover.

At the time, the Allied garrison on Mount Ormel consisted of the Polish 1st and 2nd armoured brigades, in addition to a group of motorized light infantry formations. Collectively, this force included 1500 men and 80 Shermans occupying a very favourable defensive position. However, the Poles were also isolated and had a limited amount of ammunition to defend this ridge, which they called the 'Mace'.

The Nazi attack on the Falaise Pocket began on 20 August. While the 9th SS Division comprised the right wing of the assault, *Das Reich* advanced on the left and carried out the main burden of the operation. The units involved in this offensive were to press forward until they made contact with their beleaguered comrades inside the encirclement. Fortunately for the SS divisions, Allied warplanes were busy carrying out missions over other sectors within the pocket and thus did not participate in the defence of the Mace or other locations targeted by them.

THE MACE

Situated at the right flank of *Das Reich*, the *Der Führer* Regiment received the task of dislodging the Polish divisions from Mount Ormel. At the front of the attack, 3rd Battalion struggled up the steep slopes of the ridge, while the Poles fired bullets and artillery shells into the assailants. After several determined attempts, the attack faltered and the SS battalion soon had to fend off a massive counter-offensive. At a sector west of Champosoult, the rest of the regiment had better luck and opened a passage for the Germans trapped in the pocket. As a result, thousands of soldiers and several high-ranking officers were able to escape Falaise and reach safety. The *Leibstandarte* furnished ambulances to evacuate the wounded.

Meanwhile, the Reconnaissance and SP Battalions served as the centre battle group of *Das Reich* during the attack on the Falaise Pocket. North-west of Trun, they struck a British armoured formation, quickly destroyed six tanks, and repelled a counter-attack. On 21 August, the Germans clashed with elements of the 1st Polish Armoured Division. According to the commander of the SS battalions, 'no other unit which we had met since the invasion fought so well as these Polish formations'. Nevertheless, his battalions repelled enemy attacks and forced an opening at Chambois. While the centre battle group held open this passage, thousands of refugees poured out of this breach in the

Falaise Pocket. One of them was *SS-Obergruppenführer* Paul Hausser, who quickly received medical attention for the wounds that he had sustained.

GREAT ESCAPE

To the left of the Reconnaissance Battalion, the *Deutschland* Regiment also enjoyed success as it

Right: Remnants of an army: US artillery moves past the wreckage of a German column near Falaise in August 1944. The original US caption states 'They tried to stop us here and we blasted them right off the road'.

advanced on Saint-Pierre-la-Riviere. After demolishing several Shermans from the 1st Polish Armoured Division at close range, the soldiers of the *Deutschland* Regiment punched through the walls of the pocket and helped several Army and *Waffen-SS* comrades in their escape from the pocket. Thanks to the combined efforts of the 2nd and 9th SS Divisions, 20,000 out of 50,000 servicemen were able to slip out of the Allied encirclement. With this mission completed, the *Das Reich* Division and other German military units in the Western Front retreated across north-eastern France and Belgium and prepared to defend their homeland against the victorious Allied armies.

CHAPTER NINE

BULGE

Badly hurt after the disaster at Falaise, the division retreated to Germany to lick its wounds. The tide of the war was clearly flowing against the Germans, but Hitler had one last throw of the dice to make in the West, and *Das Reich* would again be at the forefront.

During the late summer and autumn of 1944, the badly mauled German armies in the west pulled out of France and retreated through Belgium. After reaching the Westwall (Siegfried Line), they prepared for the defence of their own soil against the Allied powers. In late August, the 2nd SS Panzer Division *Das Reich* participated in this withdrawal when it crossed the River Seine at Elboeuf. For several days, the division moved east at a steady pace, fending off pursuing enemy forces as it went.

As they travelled across Belgium, the SS soldiers had to watch out for local partisans ambushing isolated units. By 9 September, *Das Reich* was in the wooded plateau of the Ardennes region. Two days later, the division reached the Westwall and occupied a 16km (10 mile) wide sector situated between Brandscheid and Leidenborn. To help the depleted units of *Das Reich* maintain this area, a battalion from the 12th SS Panzer Division *Hitlerjugend* arrived and took a position between the Reconnaissance Battalion on the left and the *Deutschland* Regiment on the right.

Left: SS soldiers shelter in the lee of a knocked-out US half-track during the Ardennes offensive of December 1944. The offensive was a desperate attempt to cut off part of the Allied armies and repeat the victory of 1940.

By this time, the Third Reich was in desperate need of manpower and thus pressed other branches of the armed forces into service along the Siegfried Line. Because the Luftwaffe had lost most of its aircraft to bombings and aerial combat, it possessed many more fliers than warplanes. As a result, the organization relinquished some of its squadrons, which now became infantry units. They were ordered to help the *Wehrmacht* and the *Waffen-SS* at the Belgian border and, not surprisingly, many of the pilots were unhappy with this new assignment.

RUSSIAN ASSISTANCE

In addition, the *Das Reich* Division received assistance from a battalion of Russians fighting on the side of the Axis powers. Assigned to 2nd Battalion, *Der Führer* Regiment, these expatriates did not impress Otto Weidinger. Shortly after moving into their positions, the Russians 'abandoned some bunkers', according to the regimental commander, taking 'both their weapons and their NCOs with them. It is inexplicable that a battalion of such men should have been used on the German side'.

Although the Siegfried Line appeared to be an impressive network of fortifications, it had significant problems. Most noticeably, the gun slits in the bunkers had been designed for 1939 firearms and

Above: An MG 42 machine gun position somewhere west of the Westwall or Siegfried Line, in the autumn of 1944. German resistance stiffened appreciably once the Allies reached German soil.

had not been enlarged for 1944 weapons. Moreover, the lack of troops available to man the Westwall meant that many points along it were vulnerable. Nevertheless, Hitler issued an order proclaiming that his armies were to hold this area to the last man if – or when – the Allies should attack.

In mid-October, *Das Reich* received an order to retire from the line. Relieved by another division, the SS units went to Saürlach to train replacements and acquire new equipment. After about a month of rest, the division returned to the Western Front to participate in another offensive. On this occasion, the attack was to take place in the Ardennes Forest and would be known to the Germans as Operation '*Wacht am Rhein*' ('Watch on the Rhine').

Developed personally by Hitler, Operation 'Watch on the Rhine' called for three armies to push through the wooded plateau and capture Antwerp within a week. Presumably, this would drive a large wedge between British forces in the north and the Americans in the south. With the Allied armies thus divided, the Germans could destroy one half first and the other at a later time. Not surprisingly, the Führer assigned to his *Waffen-SS* formations the task of spearheading the offensive.

Under the command of SS-*Oberstgruppenführer* Josef 'Sepp' Dietrich, the recently established 6th SS

Panzer Army contained I and II SS Panzer Corps. Attached to II Corps, the *Das Reich* Division finished crossing the Rhine on 24 November and, along with the 9th SS Panzer Division *Hohenstaufen*, took up positions south of I Corps near Losheim. I Corps consisted of the 1st and 12th SS Panzer divisions, along with three army formations. In addition, Dietrich commanded LXVII Corps, which was comprised of two more *Wehrmacht* divisions.

PREPARATIONS FOR THE OFFENSIVE

The 15th Army was to the north of Dietrich's divisions, while the 5th Panzer Army and 7th Army moved into their starting places south of the SS units near Bitburg. Meanwhile, OKW kept the 9th and 167th *Volksgrenadier* divisions and the 3rd Panzergrenadier Division held back as reserve forces that would eventually join the offensive. At the start of the operation, the armoured units within SS divisions

had been brought up to full strength, collectively possessing 640 Panther and PzKpfw IV battle tanks. However, General Hasso Freiherr von Manteuffel and the divisions in his 5th Panzer Army had only 320 of these vehicles.

By the end of 1944, the German armed forces seemed as if they might not even be strong enough to maintain the Westwall, let alone mount an offensive on the scale that Hitler envisioned. Spurning advice from his generals to reconsider launching the operation, the Führer believed that 'Watch on the Rhine' could succeed as long as fog and clouds covered the sky, preventing enemy warplanes from striking German ground troops. He also anticipated that his

Below: The German offensive depended on a rapid advance capturing large quantities of Allied fuel, which was stored in dumps on the roadside. If the Germans did not capture sufficient fuel, the attack would fail.

divisions would overcome the problem of chronic fuel shortages by seizing Allied supply areas as they pushed forwards.

Far-Fetched Scheme

Not surprisingly, observers at the time and many years after the war considered Operation 'Watch on the Rhine' to be a far-fetched scheme at best. In his detailed and comprehensive narrative on the 2nd SS Panzer Division, James Lucas noted that 'any enterprise predicated upon bad weather and upon capturing enemy fuel supplies to maintain its advance, stands on brittle glass'. Along with rampant petrol shortages, he cited chronic manpower deficiencies that kept *Das Reich* and other divisions well below their established strength.

Ardent Nazi ideologues might have been willing to support any plan devised by their beloved party leader. However, less fanatical German officials harboured justifiable reservations regarding the upcoming offensive in the Ardennes. 'It was a nonsensical operation,' Field Marshal Karl Rudolf Gerd von Runstedt conceded during a post-war interrogation, 'and the most stupid part of it was the setting of Antwerp as the target. If we reached the Meuse we should have got down on our knees and thanked God – let alone try to reach Antwerp.' Even Sepp Dietrich attempted to dissuade his Führer from ordering the offensive. Despite these and other efforts on the part of senior military officers, Hitler remained committed to his scheme to save the Third Reich and thus ordered his armies to launch the operation on schedule.

During preparations for the offensive, the commander of II SS Corps, Willi Bittrich, temporarily detached units from *Das Reich* and formed them into battle groups that were to guard the flanks of the corps during the advance. On 16 December, the Ardennes Offensive began with an assault across a sector in the front line that was about 135km (84 miles) wide and guarded by four American divisions. However, II Corps waited two days before joining the advance, following the spearhead established by SS-*Gruppenführer* Hermann Preiss and his I Corps divisions.

Problems bedevilled *Das Reich* and other divisions, even in the early stages of the offensive. Rushing into the battle zone, the SS units quickly became bogged down in traffic jams induced by petrol shortages. To reach Antwerp, the Germans needed to refuel their vehicles at least five times. However, Hitler provided his forces with enough petrol for only two refuellings. To maintain the secrecy of the operation, he had forbidden the establishment of fuel dumps close to the front line.

Along with fuel, the Germans also lacked adequate amounts of artillery- and tank ammunition. While drivers in transportation and armoured units abandoned their immobile vehicles, infantrymen had to

Above: A still from a propaganda film captured by US troops after the offensive, showing SS troops armed to the teeth. Heavy cloud cover meant that the much-feared Allied fighter-bombers were grounded.

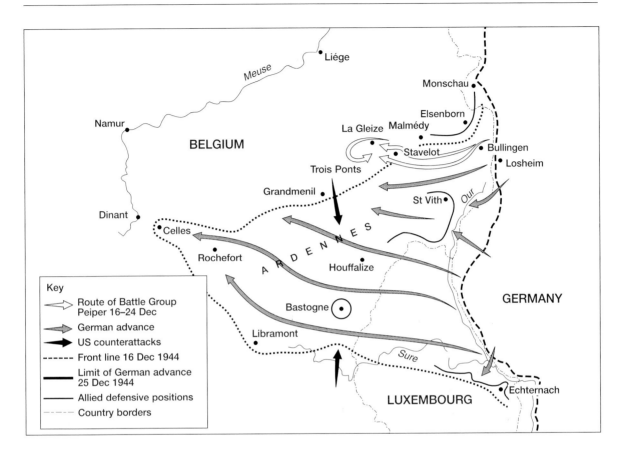

Key

→ Route of Battle Group Peiper 16–24 Dec

⟹ German advance

⟹ US counterattacks

----- Front line 16 Dec 1944

▬ Limit of German advance 25 Dec 1944

── Allied defensive positions

─·─ Country borders

march across the snow-covered ground in the dead of winter without suitable boots or clothing. Not surprisingly, this problem led to many cases of frostbite. The rugged terrain of the Ardennes plateau also inhibited rapid movement across Belgium.

On 20 December, Bittrich directed *Das Reich* to relieve the 560th *Volksgrenadier* Division, which was attempting to capture the Baraque de Faiture crossroads. After accomplishing this task, the SS division was to push north-west through Manhay and establish a bridgehead across the River Ourthe at Bomal. By this time, Heinz Lammerding had resumed command of *Das Reich*.

Before Lammerding's units could begin their operation, they had to wait for two days until petrol trucks arrived to refuel their stranded vehicles. Unfortunately for the Germans, Hitler's prediction regarding the seizure of enemy fuel dumps turned

Above: A map of the Ardennes offensive showing the main thrusts of the German attack, the besieged positions at Bastogne and St Vith, and the US counterattacks. The offensive fell short of its objective, the port of Antwerp.

out to be a fanciful chimera. As a result of this delay, the Americans at Baraque de Faiture were able to consolidate their control over the area and bring reinforcements to help blunt the German attack. Specifically, paratroopers from the 82nd Airborne Division and tank regiments from the 3rd and 7th Armored Divisions stepped forward to guard the crossroads and nearby sections.

On 23 December, the *Der Führer* Regiment began the attack on Baraque de Faiture. While 2nd Battalion launched a frontal assault with assistance from a group of PzKpfw IV tanks and a Flak company, 3rd Battalion and a group of SPs rushed in from the west. During the course of an intense battle, the SS units demolished 17 Shermans and 34 half-tracks, while losing four Panzer IVs. After overcoming this stubborn resistance and capturing the crossroads, the *Der Führer* Regiment pursued the retreating Americans north-west to Malempre before settling at another road junction near Belle Haye.

ATTACK ON ODEIGNE

Later in the day, the *Deutschland* Regiment launched an attack on Odeigne. At first, the SS troops experienced a great deal of difficulty because of the divisional batteries' lack of ammunition. During the attack, an infantry officer named Freihoffer observed in his combat journal that 'when our artillery does open fire then the Americans respond with a hurricane from hundreds of medium and heavy guns'. Although the first assault fell apart in the face of determined resistance, a second charge with support from tanks, Flak vehicles and a pioneer company succeeded, and the Germans occupied the village by nightfall.

After this objective had been fulfilled, Freihoffer looked up to the sky and noted that many of his people back home were about to undergo an unpleasant experience for the Christmas holiday. 'High above our heads there is a monotonous droning as heavy bombers fly eastward to drop bombs on German cities. Peace on earth, goodwill to all men?????' Fortunately for him and his comrades, heavy cloud cover prevented Allied fighter-bombers from strafing or bombing the *Deutschland* Regiment in the Ardennes. Meanwhile, the regiment received an order to press forward and capture a road running between the towns of Manhay and Grandmenil. On the night of Christmas Eve, 3rd Battalion and a pioneer company initiated this action.

Unfortunately for the SS battalion, a preliminary barrage launched by the *Das Reich* Artillery Regiment failed to inflict any significant damage upon the Americans. Incredibly, the dwindling supply of shells forced the batteries to conserve ammunition. Thus, 3rd Battalion and its pioneer attachment suffered heavy casualties as they carried out their task. During this attack, the commander in the pioneer company

noted the danger of 'moving over open ground and without the protection of white camouflage clothing. The men could be seen as dark spots and were soon under fire'.

On Christmas Day, 3rd Battalion and the rest of the *Deutschland* Regiment continued moving west and, although the SS troops had to avoid enemy fighter-bombers and artillery-spotting aircraft, had little difficulty with enemy ground forces. Protected by a barrage of artillery fire, the Americans retired to Manhay and Grandmenil. As the regiment advanced, many of its soldiers dropped out of the operation because of frostbite. The lack of adequate winter boots led to many instances of this affliction. After sunset, the Germans drove the Americans out of Manhay and Grandmenil and used houses within these villages as billets for the night.

Happy to sleep in warm quarters for a change, Freihoffer lamented the difficulty that his division was enduring in the offensive. 'Three years ago we would probably have stormed forward during the night in order not to allow the enemy any time to recover. But now after nearly five years of savage fighting things move much more slowly.' In his view, 'the men are all right but tanks and guns need fuel and shells and it does not matter how much fighting spirit there is, without those two things nothing much can be achieved'.

Despite these hardships, Freihoffer and other soldiers in the *Deutschland* Regiment remained determined to fight for their Fatherland: 'What still gives us hope for a successful outcome of the war are the secret weapons and the determination not to let our country fall into the hands of the Reds.' Alluding to the development of V-1 and V-2 rockets and jet-propelled warplanes, he perceived the possibility of 'the inventive genius of our scientists' saving Germany from conquest. Although *Das Reich* was currently fighting in the Western Front, he and other soldiers serving in the division seemed more concerned about the Communist menace from the East: 'We do not want our country to be under the heel of the Soviets. We have seen the "Soviet Paradise".'

The following morning, the SS soldiers were preparing to mount an assault upon Mormont when

Above: A PzKpfw VI Tiger tank of *Das Reich*'s Heavy Panzer Battalion seen in the Ardennes in late December 1944. The Tiger, although well armed and well armoured, was more suited to a defensive role.

an American armoured formation counterattacked. Although this pre-emptive strike spoiled the German advance, the ensuing battle led to the destruction of several Shermans. During a house-to-house battle in Grandmenil, the soldiers of the *Deutschland* Regiment soon realized that they were outnumbered and over-extended from the rest of their division. An armoured relief column tried to reach the village and aid the grenadiers, but was halted by fallen trees blocking its route and an enemy artillery barrage that forced the German tank crews to withdraw.

As casualties within Grandmenil mounted, medical orderlies became so busy that they had to leave many wounded soldiers unattended. However,

Freihoffer noted that his troops were willing to provide adequate medical treatment for a wounded American tank officer in their captivity. Interrogated while under the influence of morphine that had been administered to relieve the pain of a shattered knee-cap, the prisoner informed his captors that *Waffen-SS* soldiers were known within the United States for their cruelty towards captured enemies. 'Now he is astounded that he receives the same treatment as one of our own men and hands out his Chesterfield cigarettes.'

AMERICAN SUPERIORITY

Using their substantial numerical superiority, as well as their massive air power, the Americans recaptured Manhay and began to encircle the Germans at Grandmenil. Before this action could be completed, the SS regiment retreated south through an opening in the American lines. 'Silently we filtered through the gap,' the commander of a pioneer company recalled, 'marched across meadowland, over a small stream and reached at last a large wooded area. It was there we gained touch with our own forces.'

Meanwhile, Friehoffer led 60 men from various regimental units through enemy-held territory to reach friendly forces. As his small band of refugees approached the front lines, he came across a group of soldiers of an unknown nationality blocking his path to safety. According to his account, 'I go a few more paces and suddenly meet a Captain. I can think of nothing else to say but "Are you American?". "Yeah," is the stupid answer to my stupid question.'

Freihoffer believed that the Americans could have obliterated his tiny SS group with little effort. However, his would-be enemies 'seemed to be paralyzed despite their superior numbers. "You want to fight?" I ask the Captain. Once again I could think of nothing better to ask. "No, we don't," and I finish the session with a short "OK" and with a casual salute walk back to my men.' The Germans then melted back into the woods and eventually reached the 560th *Volksgrenadier* Division early the following morning. After this and other units in *Deutschland* completed their withdrawal from Grandmenil, the regiment retired to Odeigne.

During this fight for Manhay and Grandmenil, SS-*Oberscharführer* Ernst Barkmann waged another destructive battle against American armoured units. On Christmas Eve, he led No. 4 Company, 1st Panzer Battalion on a raid into enemy territory. Momentarily halted at Belle Haye by an artillery bombardment that knocked out two tanks, he pressed forward and almost collided with a Sherman,

which he destroyed after reversing his Panther to a safe distance.

After demolishing two more American tanks, Barkmann took his Panther down a winding country road. En route to Manhay, he spotted nine Shermans lined up in a field. To nullify their overwhelming numerical advantage, he manoeuvred his vehicle so that it faced the American tanks in a single file, thus permitting only the lead tank to fire at him. Before he could initiate hostilities, the enemy crewmen climbed out of their tanks and ran into the countryside. Because ammunition was so scarce, he chose not to fire his 75mm (2.95in) gun into these abandoned vehicles, simply leaving them behind for the company to destroy.

As he moved closer to Manhay, Barkmann travelled through crowds of retreating American soldiers who did not notice in their panic that his tank was a German Panther. Eventually, a detachment from the US 2nd Armored Division spotted the tank and fell upon him. Using a smoke-screen device, he prevented the Shermans from drawing a bead on him and ran over a jeep to escape. After a collision with an enemy tank that locked the two vehicles together, the engine in the Panther expired. However, Barkmann's driver soon managed to re-start it and pulled away without exchanging insurance information. While fleeing the scene of the accident, Barkmann demolished a pursuing Sherman and eventually returned to his battalion, which was involved in the capture of Grandmenil.

In the last days of the month, the Americans continued to apply pressure upon the retreating Germans. By this time, the 5th Panzer Army had replaced the 6th SS Panzer Army on the front line. As a result, Dietrich ordered the *Das Reich* Division to occupy an area south of the Ourthe, next to the 2nd (Army) Division and the 560th *Volkgrenadier* Division. In addition, Lammerding's units were again detached to serve with other organizations. The Panzer Reconnaissance Battalion, an artillery battalion and two infantry companies went to the 12th SS Panzer Division *Hitlerjugend*, while 3rd Battalion, *Der Führer* served with the 9th SS Panzer Division *Hohenstaufen*.

The rest of the regiment was attached to the 560th *Volkgrenadier* Division.

SMALL-SCALE OPERATIONS

As the year drew to a close, the soldiers of *Das Reich* spent most of their time engaged in patrolling and other small-scale actions. Although some high-ranking SS officials still harboured grand ideas for another aggressive operation, the divisions within their command – as well as those in other sectors throughout the Ardennes – were clearly in no condition to fulfill such visions. Instead, the Germans could do little more than hold their ground and try to beat back Allied counter-attacks.

In early January 1945, after a brief hiatus in the fighting, enemy forces struck elements of the *Der Führer* Regiment at a wooded area north of Magoster.

Above: The long retreat begins again, as SS troops pass a PzKpfw V Panther tank which may well have been abandoned due to the chronic shortage of fuel, which resulted in much German equipment being lost.

Supported by several Sherman tanks, American infantrymen pushed No. 5 and No. 7 Companies out of the area, forcing No. 5 Company to take up new positions in the eastern part of the village. At this new location, the Americans hammered the Germans with mortar and phosphorous shells and sent more armoured and infantry units into the area. Despite this pressure, the SS troops held their ground.

While the *Der Führer* units were thus engaged, No. 9 Company from the *Deutschland* Regiment fought the Americans in the northern part of Magoster. During the course of the morning, the Americans wore down

the Germans and gradually conquered much of the village. When the commander of the *Deutschland* company perished from a gunshot through the head, SS-*Obersturmführer* Georg Vilzmann, the commander of No. 5 Company, assumed overall control and attempted to coordinate an effective defence.

Later in the day, Vilzmann recalled in his battle report that 'we were now under fire from all sides and I decided to hold the remaining five houses and the chapel until the last'. By this time, he noted, 'we were then involved in house-to-house fighting of an intensity which I had not met before in all my front-line service'. In the early afternoon, the Americans seized his tactical headquarters and more buildings. Now confined to two ruined houses, Vilzmann and his ragtag band of soldiers refused to capitulate and were determined to force the enemy to earn every square inch of ground taken from them.

Above: SS soldiers in a SdKfz 251 on the Luxembourg–Belgium border on 4 January 1945. By now the once-proud *Das Reich* Division was severely depleted, but still they kept trying to hold the Allies back.

Although the Germans were willing to suffer high casualties in their fruitless effort to remain in Magoster, they realized that they were doomed when they ran out of bullets. After incinerating important maps, messages and other documents, Vilzmann sent a final signal to his battalion commander: 'Ammunition used up. Documents destroyed. Situation hopeless. No escape possible.' By this time, only 15 of his men were still alive and 'the enemy was now in the front room of the last ruined house'.

Just when Vilzmann and his surviving troops seemed as if they were about to perish, a Nebelwerfer unit from the *Der Führer* Regiment opened fire on the village. While the shells tore into the attacking Americans, Vilzmann exploited the smoke cover created by the bombardment to lead his men out of danger. As the SS soldiers crept out of the village and headed down a road to Beffe, 'two enemy spotter planes flying about 15 metres above our heads tried to stop our retreat by firing at us. Some of my men who had not been able to follow us that far lay out in the open until dark, pretending to be dead'.

SEVERE CASUALTIES

During the course of the afternoon and evening, Vilzmann and other surviving members of the Magoster garrison trickled into battalion headquarters. Although the walking wounded had enough strength to traverse hostile territory and reach friendly forces, Vilzmann was forced to leave behind those who were too severely injured to flee the village. Reassembled at battalion headquarters, No. 5 Company possessed a total strength of one officer, three non-commissioned officers and eight grenadiers.

On 4 January, Bittrich ordered *Das Reich* to leave the battle zone and serve as a reserve unit. However, the division's regiments and battalions that had been dispersed to other organizations at various sectors throughout the Ardennes initially did not hear about this order and remained at the front lines. As a result, some of them suffered more losses when the Americans opened a major offensive five days later.

Directed to withdraw to Dochamps, 1st and 2nd Battalions, *Der Führer* Regiment retired from the front under the protection of a heavy artillery barrage. Because the companies in these battalions were so debilitated, they could not even form rearguards to cover their slow-paced retreat. Continuously harassed during their withdrawal, the SS troops formed defensive positions in the day and moved towards their objective at night until they linked up with their division.

In mid-January, the *Deutschland* Regiment returned to the Westwall. By this time, Operation 'Watch on the Rhine' effectively came to an end as *Das Reich* and other German divisions headed toward the Rhine, and Allied armies steadily shrank the Ardennes

salient. Within a month, all German units were on the east bank of the river preparing for an inevitable invasion of their homeland. Like other costly battles launched by Hitler and OKW, the Ardennes Offensive had produced several heroes. More than 60 soldiers received the Knight's Cross of the Iron Cross for bravery or skilled leadership. Recipients included 11 *Waffen-SS* veterans and seven of these men were members of the *Das Reich* Division.

The Ardennes Offensive, or what the Allies called 'The Battle of the Bulge', was a costly engagement for both sides. German losses included almost 82,000 casualties, 324 demolished battle tanks and 320 aircraft shot out of the sky or obliterated on the ground. Many armoured vehicles had been destroyed by their occupants to prevent them from falling into enemy hands after running out of fuel. In contrast, the Allies suffered almost 77,000 casualties and lost 733 tanks and 592 warplanes. However, the British and the Americans were able to replace men and equipment with little difficulty, while the German armed forces gradually bled to death.

As the last major offensive launched by the Third Reich on the Western Front, Operation 'Watch on the Rhine' was an unqualified failure. For the men of the *Waffen-SS*, the Ardennes Offensive was a significant turning point in the war. For the first time since the outbreak of hostilities, their divisions were unable to fulfill their role as Hitler's 'fire brigades', stepping into battlefields to plug gaps in the lines and launch bold counter-attacks that blunted enemy assaults. At this stage in the war, the *Waffen-SS* was as depleted as the other branches of the German armed forces, and was unable to continue performing such miracles.

While the mauled units of *Das Reich* licked their wounds back in Germany, rumours circulated among the ranks about their next assignment. Even before the Ardennes Offensive had come to an end, the division received instructions to return to Eastern Europe and participate in a desperate battle to save Austria and Hungary from the Red Army. As the Third Reich slipped into its death throes, the soldiers of the *Waffen-SS* prepared to make a final stand on behalf of their country.

CHAPTER TEN

FINAL BATTLES

If the situation in the West was desperate, it was even worse on the Eastern Front. Ever since the failure of Operation 'Citadel' the Red Army had been pushing ever closer to Germany. Now the remnants of *Das Reich* were called upon to perform one last service for the Führer.

In early December 1944, the Red Army invaded Hungary and reached a point along the River Danube 30km (18.6 miles) south of Budapest. Before the bulk of the Communist forces could cross the river, German formations arrived in time to stall the advance and establish the 'Margarethe Positions', a series of defensive lines arrayed from the Plattensee (Lake Balaton) to the Hungarian capital. In response, Stavka redirected the Soviet offensive and concentrated its forces at a bend in the Danube north of Budapest.

Later in the month, the 2nd and 3rd Ukrainian fronts launched an attack on the city. After four days of combat, the Russian 18th Tank Corps blocked the main road running between Budapest and Vienna. To the south, two Soviet armies seized Gran (or Esztergom) and established a bridgehead near the town. However, a German infantry division recaptured Esztergom in early January and repulsed efforts to re-take the town. Despite this setback, the Red Army retained their bridgehead.

At Budapest, the Germans launched several unsuccessful attacks at various sectors along the line in an

Left: Werner Ostendorff, commander of the *Das Reich* Division for Operation 'Spring Awakening', seen here in the Soviet Union in September 1941. He died from wounds sustained in Hungary on 5 May 1945.

effort to raise the siege of the city. After crushing these actions, the Red Army took the capital on 12 February. With this task accomplished, the Soviets were now able to commit most of their forces to an invasion of the oil-refining region of southern Hungary. If this area were to fall into Russian hands, the Third Reich would forfeit its primary source of fuel and thus be unable to continue the war. The loss of Hungary would also deprive the Germans of a vital grain-producing area.

FIRE BRIGADES

To prevent such a catastrophe from befalling Germany, Hitler pulled his *Waffen-SS* divisions from the Western Front and dispatched them to the 'Margarethe Positions'. In fact, the 6th SS Panzer Army had received orders to that effect even before the fall of Budapest. For the last time in the war, the *Das Reich* Division and other SS formations were to participate in a desperate counter-offensive that stood little chance of success against powerful and determined adversaries.

Hitler called his new plan of attack against the Soviets Operation 'Spring Awakening'. The German organizations involved in the offensive were Army Group South and Army Group South-East, which were supposed to destroy the 3rd Ukrainian Front

and other formations occupying an area situated within the River Drau, the Danube and Lake Balaton. Attached to Army Group, South, the 6th SS Panzer Army, the German 6th and 8th Armies, and the Hungarian 3rd Army were to drive to the south, while the armies of Army Group, South-East struck eastward. Thus creating a pincer formation, the two army groups were to crush enemy forces trapped within the area.

No Surprise

Unfortunately for the Germans, the Red Army would not be surprised by Operation 'Spring Awakening'. When intelligence reports indicated the presence of *Das Reich* and other SS divisions within the area, Stavka advised its field commanders to expect an attack that would be launched sometime between late February and early March. Moreover, the Soviet High

Above: Seen here in 1943 is Sepp Dietrich (left, leaning) the overall commander of the 6th SS Panzer Army in Hungary, of which *Das Reich* was a part. Although a supporter of Hitler, he refused to waste men's lives.

Command correctly anticipated that the offensive would take place near Lake Balaton. Thus, Marshal F.I. Tolbukhin, the commander of the 3rd Ukrainian Front, covered his sector with anti-tank trenches, minefields and concentrated units armed with anti-tank weapons.

As a member of Army Group, South, the 6th SS Panzer Army was to advance along the Sarviz Canal and sever enemy communications across the Danube. I SS Panzer Corps comprised the centre of the formation, while II SS Panzer Corps served as the left wing and I Cavalry Corps occupied the right. Still attached to II Corps, the 2nd SS Panzer Division 'Das Reich' was now under the command of SS-Gruppenführer Werner Ostendorff. After punching through enemy lines, the SS divisions were to press forwards until they reached Dunaföldvar along the Danube, then turn north and assail Budapest.

EARLY THAW

Although 'Spring Awakening' was supposed to begin on 8 March, Sepp Dietrich and other high-ranking SS officers feared that unfavourable weather conditions might prevent their troops from arriving by the start date of the offensive. An early spring thaw had melted the snow that covered the Hungarian countryside, saturating the land with water and creating large swamps and mud-pits through which the soldiers had to march. Moreover, the moist terrain prevented trucks and even tanks from moving forwards, unless they remained on roads that were strong enough to support convoys of military vehicles. Few such facilities existed within this part of Hungary.

After the war, Dietrich reflected on the difficulties that his army faced even before the opening shots were fired in the offensive: 'The marshy terrain, impassable for panzer units, held 132 of our vehicles fast in the mud and 15 Royal Tigers sank up to their turrets.' Frustrated by this transportation problem, he and other field commanders pleaded with OKW to postpone the operation to a date that would enable armoured units to reach their starting points on time. However, their requests fell on deaf ears.

Although the two infantry regiments in the Das Reich Division had received replacements, the new recruits were not able to receive adequate training in time for the offensive. Moreover, this new transfusion of manpower was insufficient and the division was not up to full strength at the start of Operation 'Spring Awakening'. In fact, 2nd Battalion, Deutschland Regiment could not participate in the opening stages of the attack because it was still too weak. By 1945, Germany and its allies seemed as if they were running out of men to die for the Axis cause.

On 2 March, the division moved to its concentration area. The lack of roads and continuing snowfall

ensured that the journey to the front would be both miserable and time-consuming. For the last 20km (12 miles) of their trip, the SS soldiers had to march through the mud to their destination because OKH did not want to risk giving away the element of surprise by moving groups of transport vehicles so close to the front. Since the Soviets already suspected an upcoming offensive near Budapest, this precaution was clearly unnecessary.

As he watched his troops struggling through the swampy terrain, Willi Bittrich, the commander of II SS Panzer Corps, suspected that they could not possibly reach their concentration areas by the start time of the attack, which was scheduled for the morning of 6 March. Nevertheless, his superiors balked at his request to postpone the date of the offensive. On that day, recalled a soldier in the Das Reich Division's Artillery Regiment, 'we fired a heavy barrage behind which our grenadiers should have attacked. They did not because they could not and the barrage only served to warn the enemy'.

The infantry units arrived several hours later, and charged the enemy the next morning after a much shorter bombardment. Their task was to reach the Danube and establish a bridgehead between Dunaföldvar and Dunapentele. Because of the soft terrain, the grenadiers had to attack without aid from the divisional armoured units. Despite this deprivation, the SS battalions over-ran several lines of trenches and captured useful high ground.

But as the German grenadiers pressed forward, the Red Army threw more reinforcements in their way, and the advance gradually slowed down and stalled. During the attack, SS field officers informed their divisional and corps commanders that they did not have enough men to carry on Operation 'Spring Awakening'. Bittrich and other high-ranking officers passed this information along to OKH and OKW, only to receive a laconic demand that the SS divisions should continue assailing enemy forces.

Meanwhile, Das Reich received a new divisional commander when Ostendorff was mortally wounded near Stuhlweissenburg in early March. His replacement was SS-Standartenführer Rudolf Lehmann, who led the organization until mid-April. From that point in time until the end of the war, SS-*Standartenführer* Karl Kreutz assumed control of the *Das Reich* Division, serving as its last commander.

Although the SS infantry units continued to press forward into the Red Army, senior officers in Army Group South eventually realized that the offensive did not stand any realistic chance of success. By mid-March, aerial reconnaissance reports indicated that the Soviets were planning to launch a powerful

Below: SS panzergrenadiers from the 6th SS Panzer Army hitch a ride on a PzKpfw IV tank in early 1945. By this stage of the war supplies of food, clothing and equipment were scarce.

counter-attack. Near the town of Stuhlweissenburg, the Red Army moved about 3000 vehicles to the line in preparation for a strike toward the Plattensee in an effort to isolate the SS divisions.

On 16 March, the Soviet attack began as predicted. It effectively brought Operation 'Spring Awakening' to an inglorious end. Suddenly, the soldiers of the *Das Reich* Division found themselves fighting enemies that were attacking from three directions. After pushing back the 6th *(Wehrmacht)* Army, Soviet armoured forces drove around Szekesfehervar and practically encircled the 6th SS Panzer Army.

Between Stuhlweissenburg and Varpalota, the *Das Reich* Division fought tenaciously to maintain a narrow corridor that enabled the army to escape. After the SS

divisions slipped through the closing pocket, they retreated to positions south-east of the River Raab. By this time, 2nd Battalion, Regiment *Deutschland* was at full strength and had arrived to prepare the German defences and keep the Red Army at bay for a short time.

LACK OF SUPPORT

While trying to halt the Soviet juggernaut, some SS soldiers noticed that the Hungarian divisions seemed as if they were dropping out of the war. Instead of taking up positions with the Germans along the front line, their allies were moving back and forth to different locations, avoiding combat with the Red Army. Moreover, many Hungarian units even lacked weapons for their soldiers but had abundant amounts of food in their field kitchens and ration trains.

Above: StuG III assault guns move up to the front line in Hungary. One of the reasons for launching Operation 'Spring Awakening' was to secure the Hungarian oil fields as a precious source of fuel for the Third Reich.

During a brief hiatus in the fighting, some German soldiers extracted rations from their war-weary allies. One transport driver from the *Das Reich* Division recalled stopping his truck in front of a Hungarian field kitchen and lining up with his comrades to indulge in the local cuisine: 'The cook filled our mess tins with potatoes, cabbage, meat [all rare commodities for the Germans at this stage of the war] and a fiery red sauce. It was made of paprika and pepperoni and burned like fire.' After consuming this goulash with a cup of wine, he 'spent the next three days drinking water wherever I found it. Not until the end of the third day could I breathe properly again.'

Meanwhile, Army Group South retreated to the west in the face of the Red Army's overwhelming numerical superiority. The withdrawal proceeded in an orderly manner until a Hungarian cavalry division abruptly bolted the area, creating a gap that exposed the left flank of II SS Panzer Corps. As Soviet troops poured into this hole in the German lines, the *Deutschland* Regiment fought a costly battle to keep the enemy from achieving a breakthrough. By this time, more replacements had arrived to add more strength to the worn-out SS units, but many of these men were sailors who lacked experience in land-based fighting.

HITLER UNHAPPY

Meanwhile, soldiers within the SS divisions heard that their beloved Führer was displeased with their performance in Hungary. In fact, Hitler was even planning to order the men in the *Waffen-SS* to cut off their cuff titles as a gesture of contempt for their failure to stop the Soviet war machine. Although Dietrich's troops had already removed these articles from their uniforms as a security precaution, they appreciated the symbolism behind this order. Some SS soldiers retained their faith in Hitler and assumed that he had been misinformed about the situation in Hungary, while others became disillusioned. Dietrich's Chief of Staff urged his immediate superior to ask Berlin if the Führer also wanted the cuff titles of those killed and maimed in battle.

By the end of the month, the Soviets had pushed into the Vertes Mountains and decimated several German units in their path. Using large tank formations and squadrons of fighter-bombers, the Red Army punched large holes into the lines held by Army Group South. At Stuhlweissenburg, the *Das Reich* Assault Company and other SS battle groups tried to hinder the Russian drive across Hungary, only to be shoved aside with terrible losses.

Initially containing 250 men, the *Das Reich* Assault Company confronted an enemy force that included 40 T-34 battle tanks. One of the surviving members of

the SS battle group noted in his account that the Soviets 'bombarded us from every direction. Waves of Russian soldiers came storming towards us, advancing through their own barrage which increased in intensity'. During the course of the day, the battle group struggled with their small infantry weapons against Red Army tanks. By the time it was pulled from the lines, the unit had only 15 survivors.

With these SS units crushed, the Russians easily captured Stuhlweissenburg. From this area, the Red Army moved across the River Raab and into Körmend and Steinamanger, near the Austrian province of Burgenland. Within this region, the 6th SS Panzer Corps occupied new positions east of the Neusiedlersee, a large lake located south-east of Vienna. After slowing the Soviet advance into Austria, *Das Reich* and other SS divisions pulled back to an area closer to the city.

In early April the 3rd Ukrainian Front descended upon Vienna. After surrounding the city on three sides, Tolbukin developed a plan of attack. While I Guards Motorized Corps assailed Vienna from the south-east, V Tank Guards Corps and IX Guards Motorized Corps were to strike from the south-west. To keep the Germans contained within the city, Tolbukin dispatched a blocking force to a hilly area west of the city. Meanwhile, the 46th Army, 2nd Ukrainian Front approached Vienna from the north-east.

Within Vienna, Dietrich assigned *Das Reich* Division the task of guarding a collection of bridges situated across the Danube. At the same time, the *Der Führer* Regiment occupied an area near the eastern suburb of Leopoldsdorf. For nine days, the soldiers in the division fought in brutal, house-to-house battles as the Soviets used their substantial numerical superiority in manpower to push back the Germans and take one bridge after another. Beneath the streets, German and Soviet detachments battling for control of the sewers torched each other with flame-throwers.

After launching several waves of frontal assaults, the 2nd Ukrainian Front opened a large gap between *Der Führer* and *Deutschland*. To close this opening, an independent detachment known as Battle Group *Hauser* arrived and took up positions between the two

infantry regiments at Münchedorf. When the battle group reached the village, it attacked three T-34s that were crossing a bridge, destroying one tank and chasing away the other two.

With this task accomplished, the battle group consolidated its control over Münchedorf. Meanwhile, a messenger arrived from *Das Reich* Division's headquarters, notifying Hans Hauser that his troops were to retain the village for at least three days until the division re-established a solid front behind the battle group. Fortunately for the unit, Hauser and his troops were fighting enemy forces led by officers with little imagination or initiative. In his account of the fight for Münchedorf, he noted that 'the Russians had not

Above: Weary SS panzergrenadiers prepare to launch another assault against the Red Army. The men of 6th SS Panzer Army could only hope to delay the inevitable, as halting the Soviet advance was utterly beyond them.

carried out proper reconnaissance in our sector'. Otherwise, 'it would have been easy for them to have bypassed the village on both sides and to have cut us off. Instead, they persisted in making frontal assaults'.

After four days of combat, these costly human-wave attacks took their toll on Battle Group *Hauser*, forcing it to pull back and relinquish part of the village. However, the detachment had fulfilled its mission by this time and thus received permission to withdraw and link up with the *Der Führer* Regiment. Otto Weidinger, the regimental commander, praised Hauser and his troops for their discipline and courage. In his report, Weidinger wrote, 'thanks to Hauser's inspired leadership and his tireless personal example the Russian attacks failed'. As a result, Hauser assumed command of Weidinger's 1st Battalion, whose commanding officer had been killed. The *Der Führer* Regiment's commander also suggested to his superiors that Hauser be awarded the Knight's Cross.

Despite this momentary triumph, conditions worsened for *Das Reich* and other German divisions as the Red Army continued to penetrate their lines. On 5 April, the SS troops withdrew to a perimeter surrounding the inner city of Vienna. Although a full-scale battle was now spreading throughout the city,

local residents actually continued with their daily routines, commuting to work, operating cafes and taverns, and shopping in the markets. Amid this surreal atmosphere, anti-Nazi Austrian partisans sniped at the beleaguered SS units. Meanwhile, Soviet armoured units pressed into these new positions from two directions, forcing the Germans to retire to the Danube Canal.

In his account of this retreat, a soldier in the *Das Reich* Division Artillery Regiment recalled marching 'with the rest of the Division through the "eye of the needle" corridor which the assault guns of

Below: The last months of the war were days of constant struggle for the men of the *Das Reich* Division, but they maintained their fighting spirit despite the enormous losses that the division had suffered over the last year.

"*Grossdeutschland*" [Panzer Division] were holding open'. Not surprisingly, travelling through this thin passage was a harrowing experience for the soldiers of the SS regiments and battalions, who had to move past enemy artillery-, armoured- and infantry units firing bullets and shells into them. Although the division reached the canal, it could not remain there for very long. Soviet troops pushed across the water-way at an area held by the 4th Panzer Division, forcing the *Das Reich* Division to pull back to the Florisdorf Bridge to avoid being encircled.

On 9 April, the division concentrated at the bridge and a large piece of territory covering both banks of the Danube. By this time, its two infantry regiments had sustained such heavy losses that they were now roughly the size of battalions. Despite these debilitating casualty rates, the SS troops were still motivated to fight. A junior officer within the division noted that 'the most shameful thing was to

Above: Former allies now fighting for the Red Army: Bulgarian troops advance during an attack on a village in March 1945. Support for the Nazi cause in Eastern Europe had all but disappeared, even in Austria.

leave one's comrades in the lurch. In war there was the risk of being killed'. However, 'traitors and cowards were certain to die. The Division had spent weeks in battle but not one man thought of running away. In battle one has many chances of surviving – but no one escaped the execution squads'.

Within their new perimeter, the SS soldiers excavated trenches in parks and sports facilities and converted houses into fortified positions. For two days, they held their ground and repelled several attacks, although they were also suffering high rates of casualties from artillery and sniper fire. 'We fought the Russians on the ground, below ground in the sewers and above ground against the Red Air Force,' recalled a veteran field officer of the division, 'whose planes swarmed like flies over the city, striking everything indiscriminately'.

Gradually, the 3rd Ukrainian Front pushed into the divisional perimeter and forced the SS troops into a bridgehead that was only a few hundred meters in circumference. Within this area, the Soviets hammered the Germans mercilessly with frequent artillery and mortar bombardments. Meanwhile, the few Panthers and other armoured vehicles that were still intact drove continuously back and forth, protecting sectors that seemed in danger of being over-run. On 11 April, an entire panzer company had to leave the area to aid the 4th Panzer Division, which had lost every one of its tanks in combat.

The following day, SS-*Standartenführer* Lehmann determined that his division could not hold the Florisdorf Bridge much longer and thus began preparations for an evacuation to new positions up river at Melk and Saint Pölten. By this time, the Soviet conquest of Vienna was only a matter of time. To ensure a relatively safe withdrawal, he ordered an armoured detachment to cross the severely damaged bridge to the southern bank of the Danube and reinforce that side of the bridgehead.

Once on the other side, the German Panthers soon confronted enemy tanks and anti-tank units. Karl Heinz Boske, the commander of No. 6 Company, Panzer Regiment, described the intensity of the ensuing battle. 'A hit in the hull on the driver's side set my vehicle alight and mortally wounded both the driver and the radio operator,' he recalled, 'but we others leapt clear. I fell badly and shattered my right heel. Our Panther burned for several hours.' After enduring this ordeal, he and his crew went back across the bridge on foot, while the other Panthers withdrew from the area.

Later in the day, the *Das Reich* Division and other German formations began pulling out of Vienna and headed west towards Melk and Saint Pölten. By 13 April, the city was in the hands of the Soviets. During this retreat across rutted paths filled with mud, Red Army troops harassed the divisional rearguard with infantry and artillery strikes. As the rearguard passed through the village of Bisamberg, the Soviet attacks intensified. Eventually, some of the Germans fell into Russian captivity.

At Melk, the soldiers of the *Das Reich* Division were able to take a short break from the fighting and receive new replacements. Many of these recruits were fire-fighters from Dresden. During this hiatus, Lehmann received an order directing the main part of his division to proceed to that city. Meanwhile, most of the *Deutschland* Regiment was to go to the border town of Passau and help repel an American offensive in that area. When these orders had reached the division, the *Der Führer* Regiment was in southern Czechoslovakia and never rejoined the rest of the division at Dresden. Thus, for the rest of the war, the 2nd SS Panzer Division *Das Reich* was divided into various groups and would never again fight as a unified organization.

TANK WRECKING

As the bulk of the division withdrew to Germany, the Panzer Regiment performed rearguard action near Saint Pölten. At the time, the armoured unit still possessed 22 Panthers, five recovery vehicles, and one Tiger II. When the *Das Reich* Division reached Dresden, the Panzer Regiment prepared to disband and destroy its tanks so that they would not fall into the hands of the Red Army. While preparing for this action, the commander of No. 2 Company noted that 'the day was absolutely quiet and my thoughts returned to the events of the past years'.

Before wrecking the tanks, his company staged a final pay parade. During this ceremony, the commander recalled, 'after my favourite marching song had been sung I made a short speech thanking my comrades for their efforts on behalf of our people and for the nation. They were now,' he declared, 'released from military discipline as well as from the oath of allegiance which they had sworn. We sang the national anthem and then I went along the ranks shaking each man by the hand.' Some of his troops were residents of Vienna who received orders to leave promptly so that they could look after their endangered families. Then he directed the rest of his

command to board a truck that would take them to an area under American occupation.

After disbanding his company, the officer remained with a small detachment to destroy the tanks. For the soldiers carrying out this duty, he noted, the demolition of their armoured vehicles was a profound moment of sadness: 'With a lump in our throats we fired at and destroyed our panzers one after the other. The feeling which this aroused in us cannot be described in words. The Tiger II would not die and we had to fire several rounds into it before it caught alight.'

Above: Czech partisans search their SS prisoner for hidden weapons or valuable goods worth looting. SS prisoners were lucky if they were handed over to the Allies, even the Soviets: many were never seen again.

As if staying by the side of dying comrades during their last moments of life, the panzer detachment watched as the tanks burned and exploded. The company commander noted that 'the wall of flames was split by one mighty detonation after another as the ammunition inside the panzers exploded. The death-throes of the vehicles which had become part of

Left: An SS officer signals to his men while a building burns behind him. By April 1945 the *Das Reich* Division had been split into several battlegroups and was no longer functioning as a coherent unit.

Stationed at an airport situated roughly 5km (3 miles) east of the Czech capital, this *Deutschland* battle group contained 1300 men distributed into eight companies. Some members were green recruits, while others were battle-hardened veterans responsible for holding the formation together. Because of obvious supply shortages that afflicted the German armed forces at this stage in the war, many members of this detachment did not even have proper uniforms, and were armed with old carbines and only 30 rounds of ammunition.

RENEGADE ATTACK

At the end of April, the SS-*Sturmbannführer* commanding the *Deutschland* battle group received a message indicating that a pro-Nazi Russian division with 18,000 men had just switched sides and was now heading toward Prague in an effort to restore the city to Czech control. A few days later, he received an order directing him to block the renegade division while protecting the airport from local insurgents. By early May, the Russians had arrived and a pitched battle for the airport ensued. Hopelessly outnumbered, the SS troops held their ground as well as they could when a Luftwaffe officer informed their commander that OKW had just issued a directive proclaiming the unconditional surrender of all German armed forces to the Allies.

Like other German servicemen, the soldiers of the *Deutschland* battle group did not wish to fall into Soviet captivity and thus sought to capitulate to the Americans. Surrounded by Russian troops and Czech partisans at the airport, the detachment broke out of its perimeter on 8 May and headed west toward the town of Saaz. To ensure a successful drive through enemy lines, a rearguard unit comprised of 120 men kept the Russians preoccupied. En route to their destination, the SS troops were supposed to board Luftwaffe transport vehicles at a designated area.

ourselves, seemed to be a symbol of our defeat.' With this task accomplished, the detachment boarded a truck and headed towards the American zone of occupation in the former Third Reich.

Meanwhile, the main part of the *Deutschland* Regiment spent the rest of the war fighting minor skirmishes with American units at Saint Pölten. During this period, German forces throughout the area received the news that Hitler was dead. On 8 May, after 6th SS Panzer Army headquarters ordered the regiment to surrender, the officers of the *Deutschland* Regiment held a final parade, distributed medals and then capitulated to the Americans. However, a battalion-size detachment from the regiment was still in operation against the Red Army near Prague.

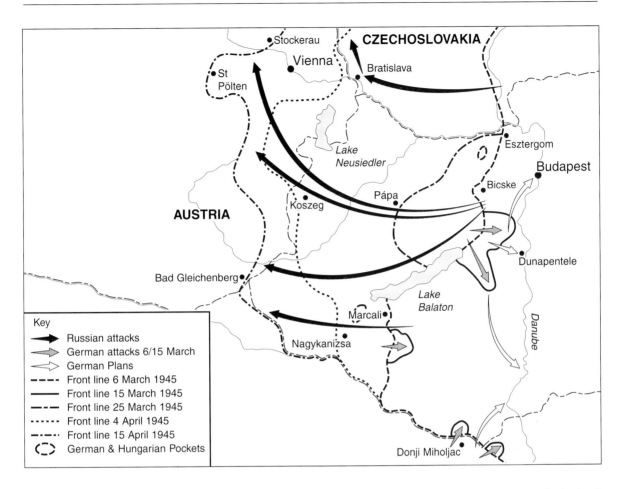

Above: A map showing Operation 'Spring Awakening' and the subsequent closing moves of the war in Hungary, Austria and Czechslovakia. Although the *Waffen-SS* fought well, they could not hold the Red Army back.

However, the airmen failed to appear. The battle group pressed forward with its wounded personnel on its own SPs and trucks.

As the SS troops moved closer to Saaz, they learned that Russian armoured units were blocking all roads leading into the town. Thus, the Germans would have to disperse into company-size units and travel through the countryside on foot to have the slightest chance of reaching the Americans. Moving through wooded areas under the cover of darkness, some members of the battle group managed to cross the American lines at Pilsen. However, most of them were either killed or captured by Russian troops or Czech partisans.

Meanwhile, the *Der Führer* Regiment received an order dispatching it to Prague in order to carry out a rescue operation. As the Red Army pushed deeper into the country, the *Allgemeine-SS* administration that had been governing the city developed a plan to evacuate local German residents before they suffered reprisals from the Russians or Czech partisans. In early May, Otto Weidinger led his regiment towards Prague to perform this operation. After almost six years of participating in a vicious war of aggression on behalf of the Nazi regime, the *Der Führer* Regiment was to spend the last days of its existence carrying out a mission of mercy.

As the regiment approached Prague after a three-day journey, the SS soldiers noticed the erosion of German authority while passing through the suburbs of the capital. Czech national flags flew on top of houses and buildings, while disarmed German soldiers filed out the city after turning their weapons into partisans. In one suburb, Czech insurrectionists had constructed a large barricade from cobblestones that had been torn up from the streets. For several hours, *Der Führer* Regiment troops were busy dismantling the obstruction while enemy snipers fired at them. By nightfall, the Germans had cleared an opening large enough for the vehicles to pass through and the column moved forward.

Later that night, the regiment stopped in front of a bridge. It was occupied by partisans, who fired their rifles and machine guns at the approaching SS soldiers. For several hours, until the following morning, Weidinger kept his men in defensive positions. During a street battle that ensued, a German and a Czech Army officer approached the regimental commander and offered to serve as intermediaries between the two belligerents. While waiting for these two emissaries to return with a truce allowing them to enter the city, the SS soldiers gathered fuel, rations and ammunition from nearby supply areas. The regiment also received German soldiers and airmen who flocked to the SS perimeter and joined the rescue mission.

ARMISTICE

By mid-afternoon, Weidinger grew impatient and was just about to order an artillery bombardment against the partisans when the officers returned, informing him that the German garrison in Prague and the Czech rebels had agreed to an armistice. Thus able to cross the bridge and drive into the city, the *Der Führer* Regiment linked up with the German military and SS governors at the Hradschin Palace. By this time, a rescue committee directed by Her Highness Ingeborg Alix, Princess Stephanie of Schaumburg-Lippe, had already moved about 500 German women and children from Prague to safety in Bavaria. Within the city, the Princess worked on the staff of the local SS

bureaucracy, which was responsible for administering Nazi policies in Czechoslovakia.

In May 1945, Princess Stephanie noted that 'absolute chaos reigned in Prague and we were at its centre'. Although a truce between the Germans and the Czech partisans was supposed to be in effect, snipers continued to shoot into the palace from adjacent buildings. 'Outside on the pavements lay dead and wounded people,' she observed, 'including several women. I myself witnessed how one woman with a shopping basket, walking along a relatively quiet street during a pause in the fighting, was shot dead.' In her opinion, 'the bullet which killed her certainly did not come from a German weapon'.

As the soldiers of the *Der Führer* Regiment gathered the German residents of the city into a truck convoy, Weidinger and other officers determined that they would not leave behind a single refugee. With many of their trucks overloaded, the SS troops prepared for their trip to Pilsen. To facilitate their departure, the Czechs removed roadblocks and left signs directing the convoy out of the city. Collectively, the Germans used about 1000 vehicles. Around this time, Weidinger and his men learned that the new Führer of the Third Reich, Grand Admiral Karl Dönitz, had agreed to the unconditional surrender of Germany to the Allied powers.

Before the convoy left Prague, the SS soldiers heard about a trainload of German troops who had been abandoned in the city railway station. After the regiment had spent more time collecting these men and squeezing them onto the trucks, a group of female SS signallers arrived and joined the procession out of the capital. Apparently safe from vengeful Czech partisans and Red Army forces, the long column headed for the American zone.

On the morning of 9 May, a German general and a Czech colonel stopped the convoy and ordered the SS troops to surrender their firearms. After directing his men to spike their weapons, Weidinger complied with the demand and thus received permission to continue to Pilsen. Before resuming the journey, he staged a final pay parade and distributed rations to his troops. Later in the day, the SS soldiers reached the American zone, unloaded their passengers from their vehicles, and drove to Rokiczany. At this Bohemian town, the *Der Führer* Regiment surrendered to the 2nd US Infantry Division. Meanwhile, the rest of the division capitulated in areas around Dresden.

Scattered into separate battle groups, the 2nd 'SS-Panzer-Division *Das Reich* thus disbanded, along with all the other *Waffen-SS* formations. Many of the soldiers who were fortunate enough to elude Soviet captivity were able to return home after a brief period of internment. Others had to answer for atrocities committed at Tulle, Oradour-sur-Glane and other places. Those who fell into the hands of the

Red Army were either executed right away or sent east to perform hard labour for several years.

After almost six years of ferocious combat throughout Europe, the soldiers of *Das Reich* and other *Waffen-SS* divisions developed a reputation for discipline, bravery and cold-blooded ruthlessness rarely seen in the history of warfare. 'There was agreement in this point,' Paul Hausser asserted in his post-war memoirs, 'that a warrior spirit was to be found in the *Waffen-SS* which was never equalled or ever surpassed by any other formation.' In his history of the 2nd SS Panzer Division, James Lucas concurred, pronouncing this assertion 'no exaggeration but rather a sober appraisal of the fighting ability of that formation and the men who were part of it'. During the course of the war, the men of *Das Reich* Division left their mark upon battlefields from Bordeaux to Moscow.

Below: SS troops in Prague at the end of the war. The last task for the *Der Führer* Regiment in May 1945 was a mercy mission, rescuing German refugees from the advancing Red Army and Czech partisans.

CHAPTER ELEVEN

KEY FIGURES

The history of the *Waffen-SS* is littered with names that have
become famous for their deeds, whether on the field of combat or for
the crimes and atrocities that they committed, and the history of the
Das Reich Division is no exception to that rule.

During the course of its existence under various
names, the 2nd SS Panzer Division *Das Reich* had
several different commanders. Some, such as Paul
Hausser, Georg Keppler, Walter Krüger and Heinz
Lammerding, led the division for several months.
Others commanded it for only a few weeks. Along with
these high-ranking officers, the division also had many
soldiers who distinguished themselves in battle and
helped create a mystique for the *Waffen-SS* as a
formidable and destructive force in World War II.

ERNST BARKMANN

Born in 1919 near Bad Segeberg, Holstein, Ernst
Barkmann was making a living as a farmer on his
father's land when he received a draft notice in April
1939. Instead of serving in the *Wehrmacht*, he joined
the *Germania* Regiment, one of the original
Verfügungstruppen that comprised the nucleus of the
Waffen-SS divisions. After serving in Poland and
Russia, where he was wounded, Barkmann rose to the
rank of SS-*Oberscharführer* and became an instructor
for European SS volunteers in the Netherlands. In

Left: *SS-Hauptsturmführer* Fritz Klingenberg, seen here in
1941 after he was personally awarded the Knight's Cross
of the Iron Cross by Hitler for his part in the capture of
Budapest. He died in March 1945.

1942, he went back into action, serving in No. 2
Company, 2nd SS Panzer Regiment, *Das Reich*
Division on the Eastern Front.

In 1944, Barkmann became a legendary hero in
the *Waffen-SS* when he and his crew destroyed as many
as 50 enemy tanks during the Normandy campaign.
Before the end of the war, he won several awards,
including the Knight's Cross of the Iron Cross, for his
bravery and skilled leadership. After seeing action in
the Ardennes Offensive and in the final battles in
Austria and Hungary, Barkmann surrendered to
British troops.

OTTO BAUM

A native of Swabia, Otto Baum was born in 1911 and
was an early volunteer who served in the SS-
Verfügungstruppen. During the war he fought in
Poland, France and Russia. During the invasion of
the Soviet Union, he was a battalion commander in
the 3rd *Totenkopf* Infantry Regiment and won the
Knight's Cross for his performance at Demjansk. In
1943, he recovered from severe battle injuries,
earned the Oak Leaves medal, and became a
regimental commander. Eventually promoted to the
rank of SS-*Oberführer*, he assumed command of the
Das Reich Division in July 1944 and oversaw
operations in the Falaise Pocket.

WILLI BITTRICH

Born in the Harz Mountains, Willi Bittrich was a decorated army officer and pilot in World War I. After serving in the armed forces of the Weimar government, he joined the SS-*Verfügungstruppen* in 1934 and later commanded the *Deutschland* Regiment in Poland and France. On the Eastern Front he won the Knight's Cross and later assumed command of the *Das Reich* Division, which he led until the end of 1941. As the chief officer of II SS Panzer Corps, he distinguished himself in Normandy and received the Oak Leaves. By the end of the war, he had risen to the rank of SS-*Obergruppenführer und General der Waffen-SS.*

KURT BRASACK

The commander of the divisional Artillery Regiment in the spring of 1943, SS-*Oberführer* Kurt Brasack assumed temporary command of the *Das Reich* Division when Herbert Ernst Vahl was wounded in combat. After running the division for a little more than two weeks, Brasack relinquished command to Walter Krüger. During the war, Brasack won the German Cross in Gold.

OTTO DICKMANN

A veteran of some of the greatest battles fought on the Eastern Front, Otto Dickmann eventually achieved the rank of SS-*Sturmbannführer* and commanded 1st Battalion, *Der Führer* Regiment while the *Das Reich* Division was in France during the spring and summer of 1944. A dedicated servant of the *Waffen-SS* and its ideological doctrines, he enthusiastically carried out anti-partisan operations within the country, executing civilians in retaliation for Resistance activity. In June 1944, while the division was moving north from Montauban in order to help repel the Allied landings in Normandy, a local insurgent group kidnapped, and later killed, his colleague and good friend, SS-*Sturmbannführer* Helmut Kampfe.

During a fruitless search for Kampfe, Dickmann led his No. 3 Company into Oradour-sur-Glane. After his troops failed to locate Kampfe within the town, Dickmann ordered them to shoot its male residents and lock the women and children inside a church,

which was then torched. Killing 642 people, the company returned to the regiment and resumed the journey to Normandy. Although Dickmann was tried for his actions, the court-martial failed to reach a verdict and he remained in command of his battalion. On 30 June, during the Normandy campaign, he stepped out of his bunker without wearing his helmet and quickly died from a shell splinter that hit him in the head.

Almost eight years after the war, a French court convicted several of Dickmann's German and Alsatian soldiers for carrying out the atrocity at Oradour. Two of them received death sentences and another 18 went to prison for terms ranging from 8 to 12 years. Both death sentences were later commuted and most of the others received pardons or were released for time served. Another 42 German soldiers received death sentences *in absentia* but were never extradited.

Above: Wilhelm or 'Willi' Bittrich (left, gesturing), seen in September 1943 when commander of the *Hohenstaufen* Division. Bittrich is perhaps best known in the West for his victory at Arnhem as commander of II SS Panzer Corps.

PAUL HAUSSER

Perhaps the most important officer in the history of the *Waffen-SS*, Paul Hausser was a decorated army officer during World War I. After retiring in 1932 as a

Major-General, he became involved in veterans' organizations before joining the SS-*Verfügungstruppen* two years later. Within this organization, Hausser began a second military career as an officer responsible for bringing proper organization, training and discipline to this armed branch of the *Schutzstaffel*. As the inspector of the original regiments of the future *Waffen-SS*, he developed close ties to his troops, who referred to him as 'Papa' Hausser.

After the conquest of Poland, Hausser organized the *Deutschland, Germania,* and *Der Führer* regiments into a unified division, which would eventually be known as the 2nd SS Panzer Division *Das Reich*. While leading this division during Operation 'Barbarossa', he was severely wounded, losing an eye. As a result, Willi Bittrich assumed command of the division, while Hausser received the Knight's Cross, one of many medals that he earned during the course of the war.

The following year, Hausser became commander of the SS Panzer Corps and continued to distinguish himself on the Eastern Front. In early 1943, he defied Hitler and pulled his divisions out of Kharkov when the Red Army threatened to encircle them inside the city, then recaptured Kharkov in a brilliant counterattack, earning the Oak Leaves as a result. A year later, he distinguished himself by directing the successful breakout through the Falaise Pocket in France. By the end of the war, he had achieved the rank of SS-*Oberstgruppenführer und Generaloberst der Waffen-SS*.

GEORG KEPPLER

A native of Mainz, Georg Keppler had won the Iron Cross and other medals for his actions during World War I. For 15 years, he pursued a career as a police official before joining the SS-*Verfügungstruppen* in 1935. After becoming a battalion commander in the *Deutschland* Regiment, Keppler raised and organized the *Der Führer* Regiment.

In 1940, he received the Knight's Cross for his leadership in the invasion of Holland. Two years later, Keppler took charge of the *Das Reich* Division, leading that organization for almost a year before becoming a corps commander in the *Waffen-SS*. Like Bittrich, he finished his military career holding the rank of

SS-*Oberguppenführer und General der Waffen-SS* at the end of the war.

MATTHIAS KLEINHEISTERKAMP

A distinguished veteran of World War I, Matthias Kleinheisterkamp hailed from the Rhineland. Before the Nazi seizure of power, he had served in the *Freikorps* and the *Reichswehr* (the German Army of the Weimar Era). In 1938, Kleinheisterkamp became an officer in the *Deutschland* Regiment and saw action in France two years later. After serving in the *Totenkopf* Division, he assumed command of *Das Reich* in January 1942, earning the Knight's Cross during his tenure. Later in the war, Kleinheisterkamp became a corps commander and achieved the rank of SS-*Obergruppenführer und General der Waffen-SS* before committing suicide on 8 May 1945.

FRITZ KLINGENBERG

Born in 1912, Fritz Klingenberg joined the SS-*Verfügungstruppen* shortly after its creation and later attended the cadet school at Bad Tölz. At first a company officer in the *Deutschland* Regiment, he later became the commander of the *Das Reich* Motorcycle Battalion. During the Balkans Campaign of 1941, Klingenberg became a national celebrity and earned the Knight's Cross when he captured the city of Belgrade with only a handful of men. Eventually promoted to the rank of SS-*Obersturmführer*, he later commanded the 17th SS-*Panzergrenadier*-Division *Götz von Berlichingen* and was killed in action in March 1945.

WALTER KRÜGER

A native of Alsace, Walter Krüger was a decorated army officer during World War I. Like Kleinheisterkamp, he also spent time during the interwar period serving in the *Freikorps* and the *Reichswehr*. In 1935, Krüger joined the SS-*Verfügungstruppen* and served in the *Germania* Regiment before becoming an instructor at the cadet school at Bad Tölz. After commanding the SS Panzergrenadier Division *Polizei* and reaching the rank of SS-*Obergruppenführer*, he took over *Das Reich* in March 1943 and led the division until the end of the

year, earning the Oak Leaves during his time of service. In May 1945, he died under mysterious circumstances after Germany's surrender.

OTTO KUMM

Born in 1909, Otto Kumm distinguished himself in combat during the conquest of France, earning two Iron Cross medals and a promotion to battalion, and later regimental, commander. On the Eastern Front, he won the Knight's Cross and the Oak Leaves as

Above: Matthias Kleinheisterkamp, seen here as commander of the *Nord* Division in May 1943, served only briefly as commander of *Das Reich* from 1 January 1942 until April of that year. He committed suicide on 8 May 1945.

leader of the *Der Führer* Regiment. Later in the war, Kumm commanded the 7th SS-*Freiwilligen-Gebirgs*-Division *Prinz Eugen* in Yugoslavia. Eventually, he won the Oak Leaves with Swords and attained the rank of SS-*Brigadeführer und Generalmajor der Waffen-SS*.

HEINZ BERNARD LAMMERDING

An engineering officer in the SS-*Verfügungstruppen* before the war, Heinz Lammerding served in the *Totenkopf* Division during the 1940 invasion of France. A year later, he went with his division to fight in the Soviet Union. On two occasions, Lammerding commanded *Das Reich*. In the spring and summer of 1944, his division was training new recruits in southern France, where they were stationed when the Allied invasion of Normandy began on 6 June.

For several days, Lammerding and his subordinate officers struggled to move their regiments and battalions north to help repel enemy forces in France. However, transportation problems and sabotage activities on the part of the French Resistance hindered *Das Reich* in its efforts to reach Normandy. Eventually, guerilla attacks against the division provoked a battalion in the *Der Führer* Regiment into massacring most of the inhabitants of Oradour-sur-Glane. Although Lammerding was convicted and sentenced to death *in absentia* by a French court after the war, the German Government refused to extradite him, and he lived a prosperous existence until dying of cancer in 1971.

WERNER OSTENDORFF

Born in the city of Königsberg in 1903, Werner Ostendorff was an officer and skilled pilot in the *Reichswehr* before joining the SS-*Verfügungstruppen* in 1935. During the war he saw action in Poland, France and the Soviet Union, receiving several medals for his bravery. As an officer in the *Das Reich* Division, Ostendorff participated in the attack on Moscow and the battles at Yelnya and Kharkov.

In 1944, he assumed command of the 17th SS Panzergrenadier Division. Severely wounded during the Normandy campaign, Ostendorff eventually recovered and took charge of *Das Reich* on 4 February 1945, at a time when the severely depleted unit was trying to stop the Red Army in Hungary. Wounded again near Stuhlweissenburg, he died of his injuries in a hospital in Austria and was posthumously awarded the Oak Leaves.

SYLVESTER STADLER

A native of Austria, Sylvester Stadler distinguished himself in combat in Poland, France and the Soviet Union. During the course of the war, he won the Iron Cross, the Knight's Cross, the Oak Leaves, the Oak Leaves with Swords, and other decorations. In southern France, Stadler was serving as commander of the *Der Führer* Regiment when he heard that Otto Dickmann, one of his battalion commanders, had ordered the massacre of the population of Oradour-sur-Glane. Although Stadler initiated court martial proceedings against Dickmann, the battalion

commander perished in Normandy before any verdict could be reached. Meanwhile, Stadler received a promotion to SS-*Brigadeführer* and assumed command of the 9th SS Panzer Division. Like most other SS divisional officers, he served in Hungary and Austria when the war came to an end.

FELIX STEINER

Born in East Prussia, Felix Steiner was one of the most important officers in the history of the *Waffen-SS*. In World War I, he had seen a great deal of combat and won the Iron Cross and other medals. During the interwar period, Steiner served in the *Freikorps* and the *Reichswehr*. About two years after the Nazi seizure of power, he joined the SS-*Verfügungstruppen* and participated in the development of the *Deutschland* Regiment and an SS training camp in Dachau. Before the war, Steiner established a model training regimen that stressed the importance of physical fitness and light infantry tactics.

As commander of the *Deutschland* Regiment in the early years of the war, Steiner led his troops in Poland, France and the Ukraine. Earning several decorations for his leadership, he later assumed command of the *Wiking* Division. In 1943, Steiner formed III SS Panzer Corps, an organization that included non-German volunteers from all over Europe. Like other senior German military officers, he sought to prevent his troops from falling into Soviet captivity when the Third Reich was in its death throes. Steiner and his troops spent the last days of the war fighting past the Red Army in order to surrender to the Western Allies.

CHRISTIAN TYCHSEN

Born in 1910 in Schleswig-Holstein, Christian Tychsen joined the SS-*Verfügungstruppen* just before reaching the age of 24. During Operation 'Barbarossa', he commanded a motorcycle company in *Das Reich*. In 1943, Tychsen was in charge of a panzer unit at Kharkov, earning the Knight's Cross for his performance in combat. After distinguishing himself in action along the River Dnieper, he won the Oak Leaves and was promoted to the rank of SS-*Obersturmbannführer*.

Wounded several times during the course of the war, Tychsen assumed command of the *Das Reich* Division on 26 July 1944. Two days later, an American tank attacked him while he was riding in his staff car during the struggle for Normandy. Severely wounded from the encounter, Tychsen eventually died from his wounds while receiving medical treatment, and was buried in an unmarked grave.

Left: (left to right) Karl Kreutz (later the final commander of *Das Reich*), Heinz Harmel, commander of the *Deutschland* Regiment, Paul Hausser, corps commander, and Heinz Lammerding, twice divisional commander.

HERBERT ERNST VAHL

An experienced Prussian military officer and decorated veteran of World War I, Herbert Ernst Vahl commanded a *Wehrmacht* panzer unit during the Polish invasion. On 1 August 1942, he transferred to the *Waffen-SS* and took charge of the *Das Reich* Panzer Regiment. Within this organization, Vahl earned the Knight's Cross for distinguished service on the Eastern Front.

For little over a month, he temporarily assumed command of the *Das Reich* Division in 1943 before being replaced by Kurt Brasack. After this assignment, Vahl became inspector general for all SS panzer formations. In July 1944, he took charge of the SS Division *Polizei* and oversaw anti-partisan operations in northern Greece. Nine days after beginning this assignment, Vahl died in a car accident.

FRITZ VOGT

A native of Munich, Fritz Vogt was born in 1913. A member of the SS-*Verfügungstruppen* since 1935, he served in the SS-*Verfügungs* Division Reconnaissance Detachment during the invasion of Holland and France. After wrecking a section of fortified bunkers along the Meuse-Waal Canal and capturing an entire French battalion near Lys, Vogt earned the Knight's Cross. During the invasion of the Soviet Union, he fought in other SS divisions and eventually was killed in Czechoslovakia in April 1945.

OTTO WEIDINGER

The son of a post-office worker, Otto Weidinger was born in 1914. After being rejected by the Army and the police, he enlisted in the SS-*Verfügungstruppen* in 1934. A year later, he graduated from the SS cadet school in Brünswick and served in a reconnaissance unit attached to the *Deutschland* Regiment. After seeing action in Poland, France, Yugoslavia and the Soviet Union, he returned to his school as an instructor. From June 1944 until the end of the war, Weidinger commanded the *Der Führer* Regiment, distinguishing himself in France and later Hungary. His last operation in the *Waffen-SS* was the evacuation of German residents from Prague as the Red Army approached the city.

HEINZ WERNER

Born in 1917, Heinz Werner served in Holland, France and the Soviet Union, earning two Iron Crosses and the German Cross in Gold during the campaigns within these areas. Eventually promoted to SS-*Sturmbannführer*, he assumed command of 3rd (Armoured) Battalion, *Der Führer* Regiment. On the Western Front, Werner received the Knight's Cross. Shortly before the German surrender in May 1945, he won the Oak Leaves.

GÜNTHER EBERHARD WISLICENY

A native of East Prussia, Günther Eberhard Wisliceny came from an aristocratic family that had forfeited its

Left: Herbert Ernst Vahl was temporary commander of the *Das Reich* Division for approximately five weeks before being replaced by Kurt Brasack, who was replaced himself by Walter Krüger at the end of March 1943.

wealth to the Polish Government after World War I. For three years he worked as a coal-miner before serving in the Army. A member of the *Allgemeine-SS* since 1933, he transferred to the *Leibstandarte-SS Adolf Hitler* in the early years of the war.

Later transferred to *Das Reich*, he became a battalion commander in the *Deutschland* Regiment. At Kursk and other areas in the Soviet Union, he earned the Gold Wound Badge, the Knight's Cross and other decorations. During the last year of the war, he also distinguished himself in Normandy, the Falaise Pocket and the Ardennes. After Wisliceny surrendered to the Americans at the end of the war, the French imprisoned him until 1951.

FRITZ WITT

Born in 1908, Fritz Witt began his career in the *Waffen-SS* as a member of the *Leibstandarte* before transferring to the *Deutschland* Regiment. A company commander during the Polish campaign, he won two Iron Crosses and later distinguished himself in Holland. After showing more talented leadership at La Bassee Canal and the Plateau of Langres, Witt earned the Knight's Cross. In October 1940, he returned to the *Leibstandarte* and received more medals for his actions in the Balkans and the Soviet Union. Commanding the 12th SS Panzer Division *Hitlerjugend* during the Normandy campaign, Witt perished amid an Allied naval barrage.

HEINRICH WULF

The son of a waitress, Heinrich Wulf grew up in a single-parent household after his father had been killed fighting in World War I. After dropping out of school at the age of 16, he unsuccessfully attempted to enlist in the *Reichswehr*. In 1934, he gained entrance into the SS-*Verfügungstruppen* and became an officer within four years. After serving in Poland and France, Wulf became an instructor at the SS cadet school in Bad Tölz, then in October 1943 assumed command of the *Das Reich* Reconnaissance Battalion. He led this formation until the Normandy campaign, when an artillery shell crippled his left leg and thus took him out of the war permanently.

Above: Günther Eberhard Wisliceny won the Knight's Cross of the Iron Cross with Swords for his distinguished conduct in combat in the last months of the war, the 151st recipient of the award.

During the march from Montauban to the front in Normandy, SS-*Sturmbannführer* Wulf led his battalion into the village of Tulle and chased a group of Resistance partisans out of the area. Before leaving the village, he ordered the execution of almost 100 residents by hanging in retaliation for German soldiers who had been killed by the insurgents. After the war, a French court sentenced Wulf to a prison term of 10 years. Meanwhile, the hangman at Tulle, Otto Hoff, received a life sentence and the battalion interpreter, Paulette Geissler, a three-year term. Ultimately, the three defendants went free in 1952 after sitting in jail for only a few months. Wulf, Hoff and Geissler were the only members of the *Das Reich* Reconnaissance Battalion to be tried for these executions.

LINEAGE

SS *Verfügungstruppe*

SS Division *Verfügungstruppe*

SS Division *Deutschland*

SS Division *Reich* (mot)

Kampfgruppe SS Division *Reich*

SS Division *Das Reich*

SS Panzergrenadier Division *Das Reich*

Kampfgruppe SS Division *Das Reich*

2nd SS Panzer Division *Das Reich*

ORDER OF BATTLE: JUNE 1944

Many of the men who fought in Normandy with the *Das Reich* division were not grizzled veterans of the Eastern Front. Waffen-SS divisions suffered high casualties due to the length of time they served on the front line. The division lost 11,000 men in 1941/2, and only approximately 2500 men were left when the division moved to France in April 1944. These men formed the core of the new division which rapidly grew to a strength of over 15,000 men.

3rd SS Panzergrenadier Regiment *Deutschland*

3242 men

527 vehicles

88 motorcycles

24 flame-throwers

12 x 120mm (4.7in) mortars

12 x 105mm (4.1in) howitzers

6 x 150mm (5.9in) howitzers

4th SS Panzergrenadier Regiment *Der Führer*

As the *Deutschland* Regiment

2nd SS Panzer Regiment

2401 men

313 vehicles

64 PzKpfw IV tanks

62 PzKpfw V Panther tanks

53 motorcycles

8 x 37mm (1.47in) Flak cannon

6 x 20mm (0.79in) Flak cannon

2nd SS Artillery Regiment

2167 men

534 vehicles

40 motorcycles

12 x 170mm (6.9in) howitzers

12 x 150mm (5.9in) howitzers

12 x 105mm (4.1in) howitzers

12 x 105mm (4.1in) SP guns

6 x 150mm (5.9in) SP guns

2nd SS Pioneer Battalion

984 men

212 vehicles

52 motorcycles

20 flamethrowers

6 x 20mm (0.79in) Pak cannon

2nd SS Aufklärungsabteilung (Reconnaissance) Battalion

942 men

193 vehicles

35 x 20mm (0.79in) Pak cannon

22 motorcycles

13 x 75mm (2.95in) SP guns

6 flamethrowers

2nd SS Nachrichtensturmbann (Signals) Battalion

515 men

114 vehicles

14 motorcycles

2nd SS Panzerjäger Battalion

513 men

135 vehicles

31 x 75mm (2.95in) SP guns

17 motorcycles

12 Pak guns

2nd SS-Nebelwerfer Battalion

473 men

107 vehicles

18 Nebelwerfer weapons

8 motorcycles

2nd SS Sturmgeschütz Battalion

344 men

100 vehicles

30 Sturmgeschütz III and IV SP guns

11 motorcycles

Division Headquarters

141 men

32 vehicles

8 motorcycles

ORGANIZATION

SS Verfüngs Division

I,II,III/SS.VT-Standarte *Der Führer*

I,II,III/SS.VT-Standarte *Deutschland*

I,II,III/SS.VT-Standarte *Germania*

I,II,III/SS.VT-Artillerie-Standarte

IV,V/SS.VT-Artillerie-Standarte

SS.VT-Aufklarung-Abteilung

SS.VT-Panzerjäger Battalion (formed 10.6.39)

SS.VT-Flak-Abteilung (formed 10.6.39)

SS.VT-Pioneer-Abteilung

SS.VT-Nachrichten-Abteilung

SS.VT-Panzerabwehr-Abteilung

SS.VT-Flak-Abteilung

SS-Ersatz-Abteilung

SS-Regiment *Germania*, plus other divisional elements, detached on 1.12.40 to form nucleus of SS Division *Wiking*. SS Regiment 11, formerly SS-*Totenkopf*-Standarte 11, replaced it. The division was designated SS-Division *Reich* (mot.) on 28.1.41

SS-Division *Reich* (mot.)

SS-Regiment *Deutschland*

SS-Regiment *Der Führer*

11.SS-Infanterie-Regiment

SS-Artillerie-Regiment *Reich*

SS-Panzerjäger-Abteilung *Reich*

SS-Pioneer-Abteilung *Reich*

SS-Flak-Abteilung *Reich*

SS-Nachrichten-Abteilung

Reich Divisional Support Troops

June 1941

SS-Regiment *Der Führer*

SS-Regiment *Deutschland*

SS-Regiment 11

SS-Kradschutzen-Abteilung

SS-Artillerie-Regiment

SS-Aufklarung-Abteilung

SS-Panzerjäger-Abteilung

SS-Flak-Abteilung

SS-Pioneer-Abteilung

SS-Sturmgeschutz-Batterie

General Composition

Stab der Division

SS-Standarte *Germania* (removed from division 11.40)

3rd SS-Panzergrenadier-Regiment *Deutschland*

4th SS-Panzergrenadier-Regiment *Der Führer*

SS-Infanterie-Regiment *Langemarck* (removed summer 43)

SS-Infanterie-Regiment 11 (disbanded 11.40)

2nd SS-Panzer-Regiment

2nd SS-Panzerjäger-Abteilung

2nd SS-Sturmgeschutz-Abteilung

2nd .SS-Panzer-Artillerie-Regiment

2nd SS-Flak-Abteilung

2nd SS-Werfer-Abteilung

2nd SS-Panzer-Nachrichten-Abteilung

2nd SS-Panzer-Aufklarungs-Abteilung

2nd SS-Panzer-Pioneer-Batallion

2nd SS-Kradschutzen-Batallion

2nd SS-Dina

2nd SS-Feldlazarett

2nd SS-Kriegsberichter-Zug

2nd SS-Feldgendarmerie-Trupp

2nd SS-Feldersatz-Batillon

COMMANDERS

19.10.39 – 14.10.41 Oberstgruppenführer **Paul Hausser**

14.10.41 – 31.12.41 Obergruppenführer **Wilhelm Bittrich**

31.12.41 – 19.4.42 Obergruppenführer **Matthias Kleinheisterkamp**

19.4.42 – 10.2.43 Obergruppenführer **George Keppler**

10.2.43 – 18.3.43 Brigadeführer **Herbert-Ernst Vahl**

18.3.43 – 29.3.43 Oberführer **Kurt Brasack**

29.3.43 – 23.10.43 Obergruppenführer **Walter Krüger**

23.10.43 – 24.7.44 Gruppenführer **Heinz Lammerding**

24.7.44 – 28.7.44 Standartenführer **Christian Tychsen**

28.7.44 – 23.10.44 Brigadeführer **Otto Baum**

23.10.44 – 20.1.45 Gruppenführer **Heinz Lammerding**

20.1.45 – 29.1.45 Standartenführer **Karl Kreutz**

29.1.45 – 9.3.45 Gruppenführer **Werner Ostendorff**

9.3.45 – 13.4.45 Standartenführer **Rudolf Lehmann**

13.4.45 – 8.5.45 Standartenführer **Karl Kreutz**

WAR SERVICE

Date	Corps	Army	Army Group	Area
1.41 – 3.41	XXXXI	1st Army	D	France
4.41	XXXXI	12th Army	-	Yugoslavia
5.41 – 6.41	refitting	BdE	-	Wehrkreis XVII
7.41 – 9.41	XXXXVI	2nd Panzer Group	Centre	Smolensk, Kiev
10.41	LXVII	4th Panzer Group	Centre	Vyasma
11.41 – 12.41	XXXX	4th Panzer Group	Centre	Moscow
1.42	XXXXVI	4th Pz. Army	Centre	Moshaisk
2.42	VI	9th Army	Centre	Rzhev
3.42 – 4.42	XXXXVI	9th Army	Centre	Rzhev
5.42	XXVII	9th Army	Centre	Rzhev
6.42	Reserve	9th Army	Centre	Rzhev
9.42 – 11.42	SS Panzer Corps	15th Army	D	Rennes
12.42 – 1.43	Reserve	-	D	Rennes
2.43	Reserve	OKH	B	South Russia
3.43	SS Panzer Corps	4th Pz. Army	South	Kharkov
4.43	Reserve	Kempf	South	Kharkov
5.43 – 6.43	refitting	-	South	Kharkov
7.43	II SS	Kharkov	South	Belgorod
8.43	Reserve OKH	4th Pz. Army	South	Stalino
9.43	III	8th Army	South	Poltava
10.43	XXIV	8th Army	South	Dniepr
11.43	XXXXVIII	4th Pz. Army	South	Kiev, Fastow
12.43	XXXXII	4th Pz. Army	South	Zhitomir
1.44*	XXXXVIII	4th Pz. Army	South	Vinnitsa
2.44 – 3.44*	LXXXVI	1st Army	D	Toulouse
4.44	I SS	refitting	D	Toulouse
5.44 – 6.44	Reserve	7th Army	D	Toulouse
7.44	LXXXIV	5th Pz. Army	B	Normandy
8.44	II SS	7th Army	B	Normandy
9.44	I SS	7th Army	B	Eifel
10.44	LXVI	6th Pz. Army	B	Eifel
11.44	refitting BdE	6th Pz. Army	-	Paderborn
12.44	Reserve	6th Pz. Army	OB West	Ardennes
1.45	II SS	4th Pz. Army	B	Ardennes
2.45 – 3.45	refitting/Reserve	BdE	South	Hungary
4.45	II SS	-	South	Hungary
5.45	-	-	Centre	Bohemia

A battle group (kampfgruppe) remained in the Soviet Union from 2.44 – 3.44:

2.44	XXXXVIII	4th Pz. Army	South	Vinnitsa
3.44	LIX	1st Pz. Army	South	Hube pocket

II SS PANZER CORPS CASUALTIES, 5–20 JULY 1943

	Leibstandarte				Das Reich				Totenkopf				Corps Troops			
	KIA	WIA	MIA	Total	KIA	WIA	MIA	Total	KIA	WIA	MIA	Total	KIA	WIA	MIA	Total
5 July	89	496	17	602	67	223	0	290	31	119	2	152	0	3	0	3
6 July	84	384	19	487	43	180	2	225	53	234	0	287	0	5	0	5
7 July	41	164	2	207	18	103	1	122	39	117	1	157	1	2	0	3
8 July	32	99	6	137	50	186	0	236	26	89	0	115	2	36	0	38
9 July	12	34	2	48	22	127	2	151	19	69	5	93	1	1	0	2
10 July	18	34	3	55	16	94	2	112	77	292	5	374	0	0	0	0
11 July	37	286	0	323	29	181	1	211	75	355	0	430	0	1	0	1
12 July	39	235	5	279	41	190	12	243	69	231	16	316	0	4	0	4
13 July	64	259	2	325	17	44	0	61	24	136	0	160	0	1	0	1
14 July	12	75	13	100	58	229	0	287	20	154	1	175	0	2	0	2
15 July	23	94	3	120	26	88	0	114	19	46	0	65	0	0	0	0
16 July	16	84	3	103	58	166	0	224	17	70	2	89	0	4	0	4
17 July	5	34	2	41	10	23	3	36	5	46	3	54	1	3	0	4
18 July	2	2	0	4	1	8	0	9	21	97	3	121	0	2	0	2
19 July	0	2	0	2	0	2	0	2	17	63	0	80	0	0	0	0
20 July	21	19	23	63	0	5	0	5	19	110	5	134	0	0	0	0
Total	495	2301	100	2896	456	1849	23	2328	531	2228	43	2802	5	64	0	69

Note: Losses are given as Killed in action (KIA), Wounded in action (WIA), Missing in action (MIA).

BIBILIOGRAPHY

Ailsby, Christopher, *SS: Roll of Infamy*, Osceola, W.I., Motorbooks International, 1997

Ailsby, Christopher, *SS: Hell on the Eastern Front*, Staplehurst, Spellmount, 1998

Barker, A. J., *Waffen SS At War*, London, Ian Allan Publishing, 1982

Butler, Rupert, *SS-Leibstandarte: The History of the First SS Division 1933–45*, Staplehurst, Spellmount, 2001

Davis, Brian L., *Badges and Insignia of the Third Reich, 1933–1945*, London, Blandford Books, 1999

Forty, George, *German Tanks of World War II*, London, Blandford Books, 1999

Hastings, Max, *Das Reich: The March of the 2nd SS Panzer Division through France*, New York, Berkley Publishing Group, 1984

Höhne, Heinz, *The Order of the Death's Head: The Story of Hitler's SS*, New York, Ballantine Books, 1971

Lucas, James, *Das Reich: The Military Role of the 2nd SS Panzer Division*, London, Cassell Military Paperbacks, 1999

Mann, Chris, *SS-Totenkopf: The History of the 'Death's Head' Division 1940–45*, Staplehurst, Spellmount, 2001

Williamson, Gordon, *SS: The Blood-Soaked Soil*, Leicester, UK, Blitz Editions, 1999

Young, Brigadier Peter, *et al.*, *Illustrated World War II Encyclopedia*, Westport, C.T., H.S. Stuttman, 1972

Zetterling, Niklas and Frankson, Anders, *Kursk 1943: A Statistical Analysis*, London, Frank Cass, 2000

INDEX